The Scientific Education of Girls
Education Beyond Reproach?

*Work carried out by the French Commission for UNESCO
under the supervision of Renée Clair*

Jessica Kingsley Publishers / UNESCO Publishing

First published in the United Kingdom in 1995 by
Jessica Kingsley Publishers Ltd
116 Pentonville Road
London N1 9JB, England
and
1900 Frost Road, Suite 101
Bristol, PA 19007, U S A
and
the United Nations Educational,
Scientific and Cultural Organization
7 Place de Fontenoy
75732 PARIS 07-SP, France

Copyright © 1995 UNESCO/FNCU

Translation into English by Sandy Schopbach

The designations employed and the presentation of material throughout this publication do not imply the expression of any opinion whatsoever on the part of UNESCO concerning the legal status of any country, territory, city, or area or its authorities, or concerning the delimitation of its frontiers or boundaries.

Library of Congress Cataloging in Publication Data
A CIP catalogue record for this book is available from
the Library of Congress

British Library Cataloguing in Publication Data
A CIP catalogue record for this book is available from the British Library

Jessica Kingsley Publishers ISBN 1-85302-346-9

UNESCO ISBN 92-3103168-6

Printed and Bound in Great Britain by
Biddles Ltd., Guildford and King's Lynn

Contents

Which Strategies for Change?

Foreword
Jean Sirinelli
Chairman, French Commission for Unesco

Preface
Marianne Grunberg-Manago
President of the Academy of Sciences

Presentation
Renée Clair
University degree as Senior Teacher.
Professor of physical sciences.
Technical Advisor for Science at
the French Commission for UNESCO

Authors
Véréna Aebisher, Huguette Bergeron, Gloria Bonder,
Yvette Cagan, Josée Desmet-Goetals, Marie Duru-Bellat,
Yiping Huo, Josette Loubet-Verdier, Mary R. Masson,
Graciela Morgade, Nicole Mosconi, Claude Musnil,
Nadine Plateau, Anne-Garance Primel, Sue V. Rosser,
Claire Terlon, Catherine Valabrègue,
the Division of Statistics of UNESCO

This book was published with the help and support of:

Jean Sirinelli, Chairman of the French National Commission for UNESCO;

Marianne Grunberg-Manago, President of the Academy of Sciences, France.

The definition of the theme, the finalities and objectives of the book, along with the coordination of the work of the editing staff was supervised by:

Renée Clair, University degree as Senior Teacher. Professor of physical sciences. Technical Advisor for Science at the French National Commission for UNESCO.

The articles were written by:

Véréna Aebischer, Lecturer in social psychology and member of the 'Social Representations and Ideological Processes' research staff at the University of Paris X, Nanterre, France. Has published several books and articles on language and women, identity processes, and girls' attitudes toward mathematics. This last topic was the focus of international cooperation on an Equal Opportunity Program organized by the Commission of the European Communities.

Huguette Bergeron University degree as Senior Teacher. General Inspector in economics for the French Ministry of Education. Principal Private Secretary of the Junior Minister in charge of Women's Affairs (1988–89).

Gloria Bonder Degree in psychology. Research on 'gender and education'. Director of doctoral studies on women at the University of Buenos Aires. General Coordinator of the National Program to Promote Equal Opportunities for Women, launched by the Ministry of Culture and Education of Argentina.

Yvette Cagan Studies Officer at ONISEP (Office of Information on Education and Professions).

Josée Desmet-Goethals, Ph.D From 1989 to 1991, worked on education issues for Belgium's Junior Ministry in charge of Social Emancipation. Coordinator of the 'Diversification' Project of Flemish Belgium.

Marie Duru-Bellat Professor of Educational Sciences at the University of Bourgogne and researcher with IREDU (Education Economics Research Institute). Has published several books and articles on the mechanisms of orientation in secondary and higher education, the functioning of lower secondary schools, and scholastic inequalities between boys and girls. Led a study on theoretical reflection and methodology in the assessment of education systems.

Yiping Huo Professor at the Institute of Pedagogical Administration at the East China Teacher's College in Shanghai. Specialized in the history of Chinese education. Member of the editorial staff of one volume of the *Great Encyclopedia of Education* in China published by Education Editions in Shanghai. Has worked on research comparing the history of French and Chinese education systems in conjunction with France's INRP (National Institute of Pedagogical Research).

Josette Loudet-Verdier Master's degree in educational sciences. Junior High school teacher, associate member of CREF (Center of Research in Education and Training), France.

Mary R. Masson CChem FRSC. Chemistry professor at the University of Aberdeen, Scotland. In addition to her scientific work, has published several reports on the role of girls studying science.

Graciela Morgade Degree in educational sciences, Master's Degree in social sciences and education. Research on 'gender and education'. Operational Coordinator of the National Program to Promote Equal Opportunities for Women, launched by the Ministry of Culture and Education of Argentina.

Nicole Mosconi University degree as Senior Teacher of philosophy. Ph.D in education. Professor of Educational Sciences at the University of Paris X Nanterre, France. Member of CREF (Center of Research in Education and Training). Has published several books on coeducation in secondary schools and in technical and vocational education.

Claude Musnil Advisor in school and university administration. Mission Officer with the Ministry of National Education. Expert on equal opportunity for girls and boys for the European Community and the French National Commission for UNESCO.

Nadine Plateau Teacher and member of the Women's University of Belgium.

Anne-Garance Primel Research Fellow in Sinology and the sociology of education in contemporary China. Wrote her doctoral thesis on girls in vocational and technical secondary schools in the People's Republic of China.

Sue V. Rosser Ph.D in zoology. Director of Women's Studies at the University of South Carolina at Columbia and Professor at its Medical School. Author of numerous books and articles on science and health from a feminist perspective.

Claire Terlon University degree as Senior Teacher. Ph.D. Professor at the University of Paris II, Panthéon-Assas, in physical sciences.

Catherine Valabrègue Author. Journalist. Founding president of the 'Association for Non-sexist Education'. Coordinator of research action to incite girls to opt for sciences and technology, as part of the Equal Opportunity Programs of Commission of the European Communities.

Foreword

At the fourth World Conference on Women scheduled to be held in Beijing in September 1995, UNESCO has been invited to take part in the discussion in its field of specialization. Within this field, the French National Commission for UNESCO has chosen to concentrate its efforts on a theme it feels corresponds to a worldwide concern.

This theme is the access young women are allowed to education and research in the field of the exact sciences, with particular emphasis on mathematics. It cannot be denied that major progress has been made in this area. In times past, the arms seen holding test tubes in the illustrations of physics and chemistry manuals always disappeared up particularly masculine sleeves, thus affirming the predominance of men in the laboratory. That is no longer true. Nevertheless, experience has shown that, even if their capabilities equal those of boys, many girls choose to turn away from the sciences for numerous conscious and unconscious reasons which it could prove interesting to study.

It is this observation that led to the present project. The French Commission offered to lead an in-depth debate grouping teachers, sociologists and psychologists with specialists in educational sciences in order to attempt to analyze the causes underlying this situation and to study how it can be remedied.

This volume focuses on assessing situations and diagnosing causes. It also gives a few examples of national 'strategies' designed to fight this insidious trend. Subsequent volumes will focus more on remedies. They will concentrate on providing teachers with a clearer, more concrete, day-to-day vision of the problem and arming them to fight that problem.

We also hope future volumes will feature contributions by an even wider international group of researchers, thereby guaranteeing success and universality. The ambition of the Commission, as we stand on the threshold of a much-discussed millennium, is to inaugurate yet another worksite, so as to ensure equal opportunity on a more concrete level, one where the adage 'practice what you preach' will be more than just words.

Jean Sirinelli
Chairman of the French Commission for UNESCO

Preface
A Woman in Science

Marianne Grunberg-Manago

It is not without significance that, at the very moment I write these few lines intended to encourage the scientific education of young women (April 1995), the ashes of Pierre and Marie Curie are being transferred to France's Pantheon. This initiative on the part of the President of the Republic makes Marie Curie the first woman to have been elevated to the ranks of 'great men' by the grateful Nation, an honor justified by her scientific career and merit. It is obviously a great joy for me and for all my colleagues to see the country recognize the outstanding nature of the accomplishments of such an exceptional woman, the winner of two Nobel Prizes. Yet it is sad that it took nearly a century to do so.

When I began my doctoral thesis at the Institut de Biologie Physico-Chimique in 1943, the street on which the Institute was located was named after Pierre Curie. It was only in 1967, on the centennial of Marie's birth, that someone felt it would be fitting to add her name alongside that of her husband. And yet, at the turn of the century, France was one of the pioneers, all things considered, in allowing women access to scientific knowledge. Many European countries authorized women to complete studies in upper secondary schools, but barred them from university studies. A woman had to be exceptionally gifted, motivated and courageous to overcome such obstacles and continue her education. This situation explains why two of the first three women in France to receive a Ph.D were not French. One of the two was Marie Curie. Later on, between the two World Wars and even some time after World War II, women's access to scientific studies remained more open in France than elsewhere. At one time, five of the seven research teams at the Institut de Biologie Physico-Chimique were headed by women. What is the situation today? If we compare our era with that of Marie Curie, the ground covered and progress made is easy to perceive. And yet, I believe France is no longer a pioneer in this field, compared to countries such as the United Kingdom, Sweden, Russia and the United States. At present, less than 10% of university professors in scientific departments, or Class I Research Directors at the CNRS (National Center for Scientific Research), are women. At the Academy of Science, there are only four women among the 130 members, and this institution is more open than its four sister academies within the Institute of France, which only counts two women. At what level does the discrimination occur, and is there any reason to hope it will disappear? In the upper secondary schools of the Fifties and Sixties, few coeducational classes existed. In upper secondary schools for girls, there were far more literary classes than scientific ones, and when the selection between Science and the Arts was made two years before graduation, girls were usually oriented toward literary classes, which had to be filled. Today, most upper secondary schools are coed, and orientation occurs one year later. True coeducation, with no sex discrimination, has not yet been achieved. Considerable progress remains to be made, and the merit of the present book is to try to help mentalities evolve in this direction. To my mind, these changes represent an immense progress toward equal opportunity, and their effects are already being felt. In a field I know well, the Life Sciences, almost half the young scientists recruited by national research organizations are now women. What's more, equal opportunity should soon be reflected by equal opportunity in careers, as half the members of the commissions handing down promotions are often women.

Thirty years ago, I was the first woman to teach at Harvard, but now a large percentage of the professors at this university are women. The French Academy of Science, which blackballed Marie Curie and Irène Joliot-Curie, both Nobel Prize winners, appointed me as its head. I have also served as Chairperson of the Commission of Molecular Biology and of the General Research Delegation, as well as President of the International Union of Biochemistry and Chairperson of one of the CNRS commissions. I have never encountered any difficulties as a woman either in my scientific career (Life Sciences), or even earlier in my secondary school studies. But I know that my situation probably seems envious to many women who carry out research in other scientific areas or work in other parts of the world. Perhaps I was born at the right time, and the fact of being a woman paradoxically was an advantage in an era when few of us chose this career. I was chosen to teach at Harvard because I *was* a woman, and that may also have been a consideration in choosing me to chair some of the other organizations.

I should also say that my career was facilitated by the profession of my husband, who was an artist and worked at home. It was easy for the whole family, children and all, to move to suit my various missions. The presence of my family made me stronger and more serene.

Today I see all around me women in key jobs, for example as Chairperson of CNRS commissions. There is no longer any administrative obstacle on their upwardly mobile career path. My personal case, and that of a growing number of women in high positions, is proof that the sociological obstacles are regressing, at least in most countries.

I'd like to underline a third obstacle, a psychological one, an obstacle that may lie within women themselves. I'm talking about their dedicating themselves day after day to research instead of seeking managerial responsibilities. I understand their decision, because the joys research brings are immense, while heading a team requires considerable time and energy, especially when grants and funds have to be found, and the task is becoming increasingly demanding. Nevertheless, in France we are, to a large extent, judged by our ability to manage teams. (We might wonder whether this is entirely justified, a question which is hard to answer.)

After entering the scientific streams of education, then the research laboratories, in ever-growing numbers, women today are faced with a new challenge: stepping out of the shadows to take over leadership responsibilities, and *believe* in their future.

Introduction
Birth of a Project

Renée Clair

WORLD CONFERENCE ON WOMEN

1995 will be marked by the meeting in Beijing, the fourth World Conference on Women: Equality, Development and Peace. The first task of this important United Nations summit will be to assess the policies followed and actions taken to promote women since the Nairobi Conference in 1985, as well as to provide a new platform for actions in the years to come and to offer an opportunity to mobilize national communities – governments, economic decision-makers, women's associations, intellectuals – concerning the situation of women around the globe.

In preparation for this meeting, the member states, the agencies within the United Nations system, and the non-governmental organizations have organized consultations, carried out surveys and written up synthesis reports that underline the priorities to be implemented within the coming years.

This book was conceived in anticipation of the Beijing Conference. It is the French National Commission for UNESCO's contribution to the collective work carried out for many years in many countries. Its theme, the education of women in the sciences, was chosen in view of the international context and its evolution. This work is part of a greater story. To understand its intentions, its objectives and more importantly its dynamics, it must be viewed as part of an overall movement marked by a few key dates.

UNESCO

The World Conference on Women will coincide with the fiftieth anniversary of the founding of UNESCO.

On 16 November, 1945, some 40 states met in London to create the United Nations Educational, Scientific and Cultural Organization for a clearly defined mission. UNESCO is intended to 'contribute to peace and security by promoting collaboration between nations through education, science and culture in order to further universal respect for justice, for the rule of law, and for the human rights and fundamental freedoms which are affirmed for the peoples of the world, without distinctions of race, sex, language or religion'.

In the aftermath of the war, shortly after the revelation of the existence of concentration camps where millions of men, women and children were exterminated in violation of all society's underlying principles, the member states decided collectively that 'it is in the minds of men that the defences of peace must be constructed'. To fight murderous folly and dehumanization, the new organization used intelligence and morality, setting its main objective as the development of human potential.

STATUS OF WOMEN AROUND THE WORLD
Preserving peace by promoting knowledge means, first and foremost, the right to education for all children. In many regions of the world, most young people were denied access to basic instruction and couldn't read, write or count. Elsewhere, even though they attended schools under better circumstances, not all children were equal and, according to their social status, didn't set out to face life enjoying the same advantages. The problems to be solved were so urgent that the first step taken was to launch programs designed to promote 'education for all', regardless of sex.

It soon became obvious that there were considerable differences between the right to education enjoyed by girls and boys. Far fewer girls attended school than boys, and they had to drop their studies before the end of primary school far more often. As adults, they were often denied any additional schooling, and consequently any possibility of overcoming their handicap.

Excluded from intellectual institutions for economic and often cultural reasons, and being especially vulnerable to the hazards of life – family break-up, economic privation, political upheaval – they usually ended up the poorest of the poor, with no hope for change. The persistence of a huge number of inequalities between men and women, especially in the fields of education and training, led UNESCO to undertake specific actions in favor of women, taking into consideration their special needs and the many obstacles they had to overcome to enjoy the same rights and possibilities as men.

Many such obstacles still exist, and considerable work remains to be done. Today one out of three women is illiterate. Women are still often found on the bottom rungs of society, those with the least esteem and the greatest exploitation. And even if great progress has been made over the past century in certain countries, thanks to their continued effort in education, most women are still left to their fate, which is far from a happy one.

Given the scope of actions that must be taken to fight sexual discrimination, UNESCO has made the improvement of women's condition one of its three top priorities.

SCIENCE: A KEY FIELD FOR EQUALITY

While continuing its effort to help the least fortunate women get a basic education, UNESCO has encouraged activities to help them make inroads into bastions dominated by men. Among those bastions is the field of science and technology. Although the limited contribution of women to scientific and technical development has been underlined regularly at most international meetings, countries still haven't mobilized their forces with the determination needed to solve a problem of this scope.

The minutes of the major conferences have noted the limited participation of women in all sectors of scientific life – research, higher education, transfer of technology – especially at decision-making levels. Given the growing importance of scientific activities in economic development, they recommend that governments make a greater effort to remedy this situation. Certain countries have sometimes made major sacrifices to encourage women to enter these male bastions. And yet, on an international level, the question still wasn't given sufficient means to succeed.

THE RIO CONFERENCE

The United Nations Conference on Environment and Development (UNCED) marked a turning point in the perception of the part men and women play in world affairs. In Rio de Janeiro in 1992, the international community recognized that 'mankind is at a crucial point in its history' and that, faced with the perpetuation of inequalities between and within nations, with the aggravation of poverty, famine, disease and illiteracy, and with the continued deterioration of the ecosystems, it had become imperative to find a way to achieve 'sustainable development' within an international partnership. The danger of irreversible damage to the common resources, and the consequences such destruction would have on the lives of present and future generations, were clearly expressed.

In order to combat a danger of such magnitude, the Rio Conference adopted a program called 'Action 21' which attributed a greater role to science and its applications, not only as one of the driving forces in the economy but also as a means of understanding and controlling development.

The program emphatically underlined the fact that excluding women from essential public debates was one of the major causes of the problems observed. How could the rational use of land, the economic management of water, the protection of forests, the preservation of biodiversity be envisaged if the women who play a vital role in each of these sectors don't have sufficient schooling and information to understand what is at risk and how to adapt their behavior to new situations? How can sanitary conditions be improved, malnutrition be fought and new birth control policies instituted if most women are unable to master the new situations they must face?

Sustainable development would only become a reality if women were given an education that fit the needs of the moment. First of all, most women had to be taught the basics of scientific and technical culture which are necessary to take part in societal life. Secondly, women technicians, engineers and scientists had to be trained so they could play a part in the drafting of research and development policies or help put them into application. Finally, the women in these professions had to be given the same salary and entrusted with the same responsibilities as men, a fact that was far from reality, even in the industrialized countries.

By defending the principle that it was not conceivable to keep a vast part of mankind in ignorance, especially in ignorance of the knowledge indispensable to understanding the world, the Rio Conference gave the question of women's access to science and technology a new dimension. Demanding that men and women have an equal right to this type of knowledge was no longer just the duty of justice; it became part of the determination to save mankind.

INEQUALITY OBSERVED WORLDWIDE

How much has been accomplished between Rio and the Beijing Conference?

In spite of the major differences encountered, due to a lack of data – a situation that demonstrates clearly that this question is not sufficiently taken into consideration by governments and international organizations – recent studies have revealed a stagnation, and sometimes even a regression, compared with the figures for 1985. In all fields and in lower echelon positions, women's participation rarely exceeds 30%. For positions involving national and international responsibilities, this figure drops to 1–5%, and sometimes less in fields such as engineering.

One event stands out. The United Nations Commission on 'Science and Technology for Development' recently created a working group responsible for studying the effect science and technology have on the lives of men and women. It has just published its first report on interaction between science and society, viewed from the standpoint of differences between the sexes. The report makes two observations. Science and technology are developed mainly by men, better trained than women, progressing faster professionally and defining most policies on research. Scientific and technological development seems to benefit men more than women, especially given the depreciation of 'local knowledge' where women often play an important role.

The report concludes that no satisfactory development can be envisaged under these conditions. In a declaration of intentions, it asks governments to implement policies focusing on the education and training of young women.

As it was written up by the United Nations Commission in charge of scientific affairs, this document will probably influence the debates in Beijing, and subsequently affect the orientations of United Nations member states and organizations.

Given its specificity, UNESCO necessarily paid special attention to the evolution in progress. In the new edition of its *World Science Report*, one chapter is set aside for the situation of women in scientific activities. A group of activities centered on the topic of 'women, science and technology for development' is being created as part of its educational and scientific programs. Cooperation with the national commissions that work closely with the intellectual communities is now centering its efforts on this major question. Based on meetings and discussions with the various authorities within the Organization, the French National Commission, with UNESCO's backing, proposed a book that would be the concretization of international recommendations, as well as the trigger for subsequent actions to be taken with the other partners.

EDUCATION BEYOND REPROACH?

The book's subtitle is a question. A question aimed at those who don't generally think about that issue. For one very simple reason: it usually falls outside their interests. Is scientific instruction 'suspicious', that is to say 'capable of being questioned'? That is the crux of the book, crystallized in this question that is less concerned with national policies than with a practice that generally is not subjected to scrutiny. How can instruction, which could be called 'the illumination of the mind', be suspicious? Or in other words how could it be suspected of harboring an area of darkness?

One remark must be made here. The 'doubt' – if any such doubt exists – concerns the education and not the educator. No one's sincerity or capabilities are being doubted. This question is primarily aimed at teachers, and more specifically at science teachers, because of their aptitudes.

After having honed their sense of observation for many long years, after working with the most abstract concepts, applying precision in all instances and mastering the manipulation of methodical doubt, they are perhaps better equipped than anyone to question their own prac-tices. Having chosen to dedicate all or part of their lives to passing on to young people their love for research, along with the skills required to carry that research out, they are probably more able than many scientists to understand the human challenge of a possible change.

What is the question being asked? Or rather what questions?

Does the education girls receive have a role to play in girls' orientation toward scientific studies, or more generally speaking in their attraction to the sciences? Does the teaching of mathematics, physics, chemistry and biology (the so-called 'exact' sciences) – as it is usually provided – have an effect on the profession chosen by girls and boys, and conse-quently on their entire existence? Do teachers, involuntarily and un-knowingly, become the vector of the social conformity of which they may even disapprove?

Are they 'under the influence'?

While the main objective of the book is to raise questions, it also attempts to provide some answers. By presenting interesting experi-ments carried out in certain countries in order to change young women's approach to the sciences, the authors have sought to propose action plans rather than examples to be followed.

Subsequently a discussion should be instigated with the teachers, the representatives of secondary schools and universities, and people in research in order to support and initiate cooperation programs on this subject, especially in teacher training centers.

A BOOK TO CHANGE PERCEPTIONS AND BEHAVIORS

The book includes four parts. The first, 'Inequality Worldwide', focuses on the comparative study of the situation of girls in secondary schools and in universities, based on the international statistics available.

The second part, 'Better Understanding Helps Fight Inequality', groups the conclusions of recent theoretical research. The objective was not to be exhaustive. Nor to publish a collection of scientific theories aimed at experts, usually in the social and human sciences. But rather to 'communicate' a few of the most noteworthy conclusions to teachers concerned by the subject, but usually not familiar with these theories.

Part III, 'Which Strategies for Change', presents national and international experiments carried out to promote the scientific and vocational training of young women, along with some examples of action that can be taken in the classroom.

Finally, the book includes an international bibliography of a selection of recent works that can be consulted by those anxious to go into the questions covered in more depth.

Part I

Inequality Worldwide

Chapter 1

Grandeur and Penury of International Statistics

Claude Musnil

ABSTRACT: *The text addresses the difficulties one researcher encountered while trying to study the situation of young women in the scientific and technical streams of secondary and higher education, working from international statistical yearbooks. It reports on the data compiled using vague indicators that are impossible to compare, given their heterogeneous reference dates, and that are particularly inapplicable due to the lack of any breakdown by gender. The fact that such statistics are unavailable may well prove that the question of women's access to scientific careers, and to scientific culture in general, has not been raised as yet by international organizations.*

Studies and research on women's access to education highlight their meager presence in scientific and technological training. A similar observation arises from work on female participation in professions in the science and technology sector. Given the convergence of conclusions reached at all levels (regional, national, international), it is clear that this situation exists on all five continents. This reveals to the need to obtain figures throughout the planet in order to achieve a better understanding of the scope and extent of the problem.

How can this panoramic vision be obtained? By using international statistics to build a reliable image of the present situation and to measure any progress or regression in women's access to science and technology over the past few years.

The 1993 edition of the *UNESCO Annual Statistical Yearbook* gathered up data from some 200 countries and territories. That made it a prime source, and the best suited to our purposes. A careful study of the tables on secondary and higher education, as well as of the human potential in the scientific and vocational fields, reveals how extremely difficult it is to carry out the proposed task, due to obstacles such as:

- the way the data is presented,
- the disparity in the dates of the latest available data,

- the absence of a breakdown by gender in many responses.

(1) PRESENTATION OF DATA

Data on secondary education falls into three categories:

- general education,
- pedagogical education (preparation for the teaching profession),
- technical and vocational education (preparation for a profession or a job other than in teaching).

As no distinction is made between the scientific and non-scientific streams of general education, this information is not pertinent. The structural differences between the educational systems obviously explain this globalization. Nevertheless, it would be extremely wise to design new survey questionnaires that indicate the main subjects in the secondary school streams, as the choices made at this level affect the type of university studies elected.

Technical and vocational education obviously includes service sector training (mainly attended by girls), and training in the industrial sector where their presence is to be inventoried. Unfortunately this presentation doesn't reflect the diversity of the data gathered, which resulted in an excellent document (*cf infra*) drawn up by UNESCO's Division of Statistics as part of the preparation of the Fourth World Conference on Women.

The data contained in this document would be far easier to utilize if UNESCO, like all the major international organizations, didn't conform to the ISCED (International Standard Classification of Education), whose fields of activities should be rethought and adapted to follow the changes in the professional world. Some headings are surprising (religion and theology), some are old-fashioned (home economics) or far too vast (commerce and service trades; craft and industrial production), which is even more serious.

If we look at the statistics on higher education, we find that activities are grouped in ways that are not very compatible with our approach:

- The 'natural sciences' heading groups physics, chemistry, biology and geology.
- Mathematics and computer science are put together.
- Health studies are combined.

Finally, the 'crafts and industry' heading makes no distinction between traditionally feminine trades (chiefly clothing, furs and leather) and sectors where women are rarely present, if at all.

Only the 'engineering' heading offers information that can be used, as it is less liable to group dissimilar situations. That is why it was possible to carry out a study based on the figures it contains (*cf infra*) and to present a view of female participation in this field of study in certain countries.

Turning away from the area of education, let's look at 'scientific and technical manpower', the subject of a table that gives the following information for a given nation:

- either the total 'stock' of people with the required qualifications to be classified in one of two categories: 'scientists and engineers' or 'technicians';

- or the number of such people working or actively seeking employment in any branch of the economy at a given date.

Here again, the 'technicians' heading is just as vague as the education field, and gives no information on the sector of qualification.

The grouping of the truly active population with job-seekers is even more problematic. A comparison between men and women regarding this specific point would shed precious light on the chances both sexes have of obtaining a job in scientific and technological fields. It would also be good to have a broader choice of responses, as they concern only 69 countries, of which 22 provide information on the 'stock' of qualified staff and 47 indicate the number of actively employed and job-seekers.

Information of this type, even partial, would provide a preliminary vision that is of interest if only the reference dates were not so diverse as to make any overall view impossible.

(2) REFERENCE DATES
In spite of the rather unsatisfactory character of the headings used, as pointed out above, data on higher education could be used to give an approximate assessment of the female population involved in scientific and technological studies, if the reference dates didn't vary so much from one response to the next. 149 states or territories are included in the 'higher education' tables in the 1993 edition of the *Statistical Year-book*. Only 45 responses date from 1991, 41 from 1990, 28 from 1989 and the remaining 35 go back even further, including 10 prior to 1985. Obviously, any attempt to make a comparative assessment of female

movement would concern a very limited number of countries and be of no significance.

The possibilities of using the data on 'human manpower' are even worse. Out of 69 responses, 30 refer to the years 1980 through 1984, and there are only 17 entries for 1990 and 1991.

(3) ABSENCE OF BREAKDOWN BY GENDER

As we have seen, the inadequate, heterogeneous classification of data entry dates is a serious handicap in drawing up any coherent statistics on female participation in education and professions in the fields of science and technology. This is of less consequence, however, when the data, no matter how imperfect, makes a distinction according to gender. Some countries do not even follow UNESCO's recommendations on this subject; 28 of them quoted figures for the total student body for higher education in the surveys between 1985 and 1991. Nineteen responses to the questionnaires on 'human potential' adopted the same approach. In this specific case, 25% of the total data gathered cannot be used, due solely to the absence of any breakdown by gender.

Consequently, a credible statistical approach to the presence of women in the fields of science and technology is necessarily very limited. Only the years 1990 and 1991 can be used to measure an evolution in comparison with the five preceding years. Of the 86 entries on higher education corresponding to these dates, 14 give no information as to the female public. That leaves 72 usable responses, less than half of the 149 responses gathered (48%).

Charting any evolution in female workers from 1985 to 1990–91 would require using only 55 countries, due to the total absence of data for 1985 or to the lack of any gender breakdown. Instead of the desired panorama, all we would get is a partial view limited to 37% of the countries and territories having responded to the survey.

As for 'human potential', 1990 and 1991 are covered in only 17 responses out of 69, and five of those give global figures that cannot be used. Obviously, these low figures make any utilization impossible.

On the eve of the Fourth World Conference on Women, it seems somewhat surprising that there isn't sufficient material to give as exhaustive a vision as possible of women's access to science and technology. Inadequate international classification, heterogeneity in the reference dates and the incomplete responses provided by the countries are all obstacles to a conscientious study.

A major effort must be made regarding the conception and gathering of statistical data. The choice of indicators should be rethought in order to obtain classifications that are sufficiently precise to pinpoint what studies and professions in science and technology are chosen by women. With these improvements, the statistics would provide in-depth knowledge of the scholastic path girls and boys follow through schools and universities, and would make a major contribution to present reflection on education in the twenty-first century.

Chapter 2

International Statistics and National Statistics... An Indispensable Entente

Anne-Garance Primel

ABSTRACT: *The integration of national statistics in the international data gathering system must be rethought, especially as concerns gender breakdown, which has been somewhat overlooked in the past.*

Gathering statistical data is a complex process. As the survey grows in size and the authorities and levels of authority increase, this complexity is compounded. Will the solutions devised by international organizations in response to the problems of gathering international statistical data[1] suffice to solve the overall statistics problem? In this realm, it is hard to dismiss the interaction between the international and national levels.

What statistics database does each country use when responding to the questionnaires of international organizations? And even when the responses of each country to international data compilations *do* come from national statistics – as is often the case for statistics on education[2] – it isn't surprising to find serious shortcomings. How much do defective or imperfect national statistics affect international compilations?

By comparing national statistical yearbooks with international statistical yearbooks, we find that the problems observed with international statistics are duplicated at the national level (insufficient breakdown by gender, very broad headings, disparity in dates of latest statistical data according to region or province, etc.). To this can be

---

1   Concerning international statistics in particular, see the previous chapter by C. Musnil.
2   It is hard to imagine that each country would carry out statistical surveys merely to respond to a questionnaire from international organizations.

added specific shortcomings in the production procedure of national statistics sources.

Some figures (for the same year and the same heading) vary from one national source to the next, and sometimes even within the same statistical yearbook.

Educational systems are not identical in all countries. Some types of schools don't depend on the Education Ministries[3] and therefore are not included in the national statistical yearbooks on education. Data on some countries as included in the international compilation come only from the statistical indicators of yearbooks published by the Education Ministries; consequently a certain number of schools, streams, students and teachers are *left out* of the statistics!

How does the breakdown of the student body in the main fields of study defined by each country correspond to that of the international yearbooks, as the International Standard Classification of Education (ISCED) very often differs from the national classification? The variations between national statistics and international statistics linked with the classification problem are sometimes significant. Are certain international headings 'blown up', or on the contrary 'deflated'?

There is also the problem of reliability and the production procedure used for national statistical data. Official statistical data on education come largely from censuses and statistics drawn up by educational establishments and passed on by various local authorities. Given the relatively fluctuating nature of the material (specific to education), it is necessary to take into consideration the bias and errors inherent in any statistical headcount, accentuated by the many intermediaries and the local material shortcomings.

Thanks to new tools and more in-depth reflection, the production and publication of international and national statistics has made great progress overall in terms of number (quantity), reliability and uniformity. Lately certain statistics compilations have explained how they produce and compile data, thus warning the reader of any bias or

---

3   In several countries, certain schools don't depend on the Education Ministry, as do most, but rather on the Labor Ministry or another ministry. These administrations vary according to the country and the type of educational establishment. Regarding the problems linked to the multiplicity of the administrations, see the next chapter, *Secondary technical and vocational education: female enrolement in the various fields of study (1980 and 1992)* in this publication.

eventual problems. Nevertheless, many shortcomings remain. For instance, certain national yearbooks provide no statistics on gender breakdown per main field of study in the various types of education. Consequently we can see how difficult it is for international organizations to produce this type of statistics. If, as C. Musnil suggests, the question of the representation of girls in education and women in the sciences seems not to have been raised by the international organizations, it is raised even less at the national level by certain countries.

In order to respond to new international classifications – indispensable for comprehending certain problems – it may prove necessary to redefine and coordinate the gathering of statistical data on the national level and to promote the relations between countries and international organizations. A joint reflection by the two types of partner seems inevitable if progress is to be made in statistical competency, which is vital to all those striving to understand today's social phenomena.

Chapter 3

Secondary Technical and Vocational Education
Female Enrolment in the Various Fields of Study (1980 and 1992)

Division of Statistics of UNESCO

ABSTRACT: *In 1992 women accounted for nearly 44% of total enrolments in secondar technical and vocational education, all fields taken together. This figure covers very diverse situations, however, depending on the field of study. This document addresses the situation in some 90 countries and territories for which recent data are available. After having established the size, in enrolment terms, of each broad field of study, we have analysed the levels of female participation in each one. The pattern that emerges clearly is that the female students continue to form the majority (two-thirds of enrolment or more) in fields traditionally reserved for women such as commercial programmes, which have very high enrolment figures, health and home economics. Men are clearly in the majority (three-quarters or more) in the broad field of industry and engineering, and in agricultural courses. On the whole, the comparisons that can be made with 1980 data indicate that this general pattern has not undergone significant changes since that date; a slight increase can be noted, however, in the proportion of women studying technical subjects in a certain population of European countries and Arab States.*

Data on secondary technical and vocational education,[1] not broken down by field of study, are published annually in the *UNESCO Statistical Yearbook*. In 1992, the number of women worldwide was estimated at about 44% of total enrolment, as in 1980. This percentage covers very diverse situations depending on the field of study. The data given on total enrolments in each field of study in Section 1 and on the propor-

---

1 The expression *technical and vocational education* is used here to mean education provided in secondary schools that aim generally but not exclusively to prepare pupils directly for an occupation or profession other than teaching. In this type of education, part of the curriculum can be provided in firms. The short form *vocational education* is used in the text and in the headings of the tables.

tion of women in each field in Section 2 give a more detailed analysis of female participation in this type of education.

LIMITATIONS OF THE DATA

The field of technical and vocational education is particularly difficult to study because the lines that separate it from general education on the one hand and out-of-school vocational training on the other are not very clearly drawn.

Within vocational education itself, the figures must be interpreted with care. Owing to the large number of both public and private authorities that could be responsible for this type of education, it is not always possible to ensure that all institutions are included in the annual surveys. As a result, for certain countries, programmes organized by authorities other than ministries of education, such as health or agricultural programmes, may thus appear erratically in educational statistics. In addition, this type of education may be provided in a variety of forms: apprenticeships, alternate education (firms and school), distance education and part-time education. It is therefore difficult to ascertain that education programmes delivered according to these different modalities are systematically included in annual surveys.

The reader must take these limitations into account when interpreting the data provided. As data are particularly meagre in certain regions (Africa in particular and, to a lesser extent, Asia), many countries, some with large populations and high enrolment figures, have been eliminated from the analysis. It must therefore be borne in mind that the results and conclusions offered below are based on a limited number of countries.

On the other hand, certain countries, including Canada and the United States, do not report on technical and vocational education as a *separate branch* of *formal* secondary education. Further information on the existence or absence of this type of education, secondary education structures in general, the proportion of technical to general education, etc., can be found in the *UNESCO Statistical Yearbook*.

(1) MAIN FIELDS OF STUDY

For countries for which data are available, Figures 1.1 to 1.5 give a global estimate of the size of enrolments (total and female) in each broad field for the two years.

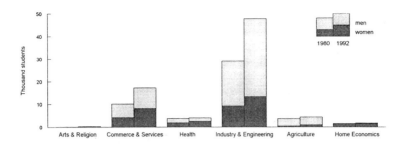

Figure 1a Africa, excluding Arab States (10 countries)

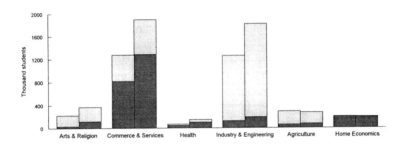

Figure 1b Asia, excluding Arab States, and Oceania (12 countries)

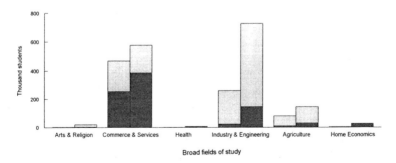

Figure 1c Arab States (14 countries)

Figure 1 Vocational education. Enrolment by broad field of study and by sex, 1980 and 1992

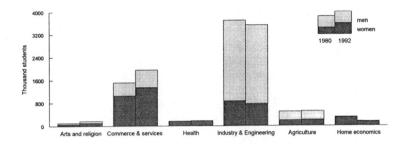

Figure 1d Europe (17 countries)

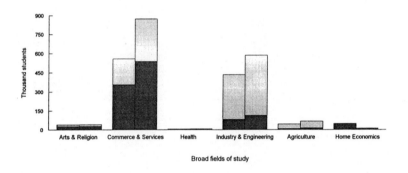

Broad fields of study

Figure 1e Latin America and the Caribbean (11 countries)

Figure 1 Vocational education. Enrolment by broad field of study and by sex, 1980 and 1992 (continued)

It shows that most enrolments are in two broad fields, namely, training for occupations in industrial production, the majority in Africa, the Arab States and Europe, and commercial programmes, predominant in the Latin America and Caribbean region. The two fields are practically on a par in the Asia and Oceania region.

A number of observations may be made for each region.

Africa, excluding the Arab States

- Training programmes for occupations in *industrial production* have by far the highest numbers of students: in one country in two, they account for 50% of enrolments or more. Enrolments increased considerably during the period covered (Fig 1.1).

- The second broad field is *commerce*, which accounts for more than half of enrolments in the Central African Republic, Chad, Mali and Togo. Available data seem to indicate that in certain countries (Botswana, Guinea Bissau and Malawi) commercial programmes were not offered until after 1980, since they do not feature in the 1980 statistics.

- Programmes relating to *health* and *agriculture* were reported on by half of the countries, with relatively high enrolments in health programmes in Angola (23% of the total), Botswana (16%) and Guinea (12%) and, for agriculture, Angola (17%), Guinea Bissau (10%) and Mozambique (10%). On the whole, the level of enrolments does not seem to have changed.

- *Home economics* programmes were offered in four countries only. The number of students does not exceed 5% of the total.

- There were few or no enrolments in programmes on the *arts and religion*, except for fine arts and applied arts programmes in the Seychelles (14% of the total).

Asia, excluding the Arab States, and Oceania

- In 1992, training for occupations in *industrial production* accounts for most of the vocational education provided in many countries. More than half of the total number of students are enrolled in training in this area in Bangladesh, Cyprus, French Polynesia, Iran and Malaysia.

- *Commercial* programmes constitute the main field in Indonesia, Japan and the Republic of Korea.

- On the whole, these two broad fields attracted the same number of students and progressed in equal proportions (Fig. 1.2).

- *Health* programmes were reported by a number of countries. They account for more than 10% of students in China, Iran and Laos.

- China, Laos and Japan also show more than 10% of total enrolment in *agriculture*.

- *Home economics* generally accounts for less than 10% of enrolment and does not feature in the statistics of certain major countries, such as China, Bangladesh, Iran, the Republic of Korea and Turkey.

- Courses on *the arts and religion*, which feature in certain countries of the region, account for a significant proportion of students in two countries only (Turkey and Kiribati), where the programmes relate to religion only.

Arab States

- In the 14 countries for which data are available for both years, *commercial* programmes, which came first in 1980, seem to have lost ground to training for work in *industry*, which, at the end of the period, attracted the majority of students (Fig. 1.3).

- Agricultural programmes account for a significant proportion of students in Egypt (12% of the total) and, to a lesser extent, in Syria and the United Arab Emirates (7%).

- The broad field of *arts and religion* accounts for a high number of enrolments in Kuwait (100% of pupils), Qatar (38%) and Sudan (27%). In these three countries, the data concern religious studies only. For Morocco and Lebanon, where enrolments are lower, the data for this broad field refer to art programmes and in Iraq they cover both the arts and religion.

- Programmes on *health* seem to have developed well in Oman (17% of enrolments) and Saudi Arabia (19%). In 1980, they did not feature at all in these countries' statistics.

- *Home economics* courses are dominant in Djibouti (55% of enrolments). In Syria, they account for a quarter to a third of enrolments. Mention may be made of the case of Tunisia, where these programmes, like all those that were provided for in the first stage of secondary education, now form part of general education.

Europe

- Programmes relating to *industrial production* took the lion's share (Fig. 1.4): in more than half the countries considered, they accounted for more than 50% of total enrolments. Enrolments remained stable in those countries for which data are available for both years.

- Enrolments in *commercial* programmes had progressed in 1992. These courses' share of total student numbers is close to or more than 50% only in Denmark (49%), Italy (49%) and Monaco (62%). In most of the other countries, the percentage of students enrolling for these courses is between 25 and 35%.

- *Agriculture* accounts for 5 to 10% of total enrolments, with generally higher percentages in Eastern European countries and in Albania (70%).

- *Health* programmes attract some 5% of enrolments, with more than 10 per cent in Finland, San Marino and Sweden.

- Courses on the *arts and religion* are offered in very limited proportions in all countries. The data given generally refer to the fine arts and applied arts. The only countries to report significant enrolments in religious studies are Greece, the former Yugoslav Republic of Macedonia, the former Yugoslavia and, to a lesser extent, Sweden and Norway, as well as Romania and Bulgaria at the end of the period.

Latin America and the Caribbean

- *Commerce* predominates in half of the countries and *industrial* programmes in the other half. In terms of total enrolments overall in the countries for which data are available for both years, however, *commercial* programmes attract a higher proportion of enrolments and the figures seem to have risen significantly during the period (Fig. 1.5).

- The next most important field, in terms of enrolment levels, is *agriculture*, which has progressed since 1980. Mention may be made of the particularly high level of participation in Costa Rica (33% of enrolments), Cuba (19%), Nicaragua (16%) and Venezuela (13%).

- Programmes on *health* and the *arts and religion* seem to carry little weight at this level of education.

- Home *economics* is taught in a few countries only, with significant numbers of students in Chile (22%) and Costa Rica (29%).

FEMALE PARTICIPATION IN EACH BROAD FIELD OF STUDY
Table 1 gives the percentage of women in each field of vocational education while Figures 1a to 1e give an overview of female enrolment in countries for which the data are complete.

In addition, Figures 2a to 2e permits a more detailed analysis of developments in female representation in the specifically technical field of *craft, industry* and *engineering*.[3] The percentages of female pupils would probably be lower if *engineering* only were taken into consideration. The data submitted to UNESCO do not permit a clear distinction, however, and so we prefer to group these areas together.

Women remain in the majority in the broad field of *commerce and service trades*, with very high enrolment figures; they predominate in *health* and *home economics* courses, but these two fields attract a limited number of pupils.

The following comments can be made on Table 1 and the charts:

Africa, excluding the Arab States

- Whereas the number of women in vocational education, all fields taken together, can exceed 30 and even 40% of enrolments, the analysis by field of study shows that women flock to traditionally 'female' fields such as *commerce*, in which they account for half of the total number of students, *health*, in which they constitute half to two-thirds and of course, when it is provided, home economics. The levels of female representation do not seem to have changed significantly between 1980 and recent years (Figure 1a).

- On the other hand, in the broad field of *industry*, which attracts the greatest number of enrolments, the data available for some countries for the two years show that women generally represent less than 20% of enrolments, except in Mauritius and Rwanda (Figure 2a). In the latter country, the data given under this heading concern 'integrated rural and crafts education' which comprises fields of study less specialized in the industrial production as such, and above all, the crafts.

---

3   The short form *industry* is sometimes used in the text and in the tables and charts.

Asia, excluding the Arab States, and Oceania

Levels of female representation and their progress since 1980 for the 12 countries of the region for which data are available can be seen in Figure 1b. Women form the majority (half of enrolments or more) in commercial courses, in which levels of enrolment are rather high and in courses on health and home economics. They form a very small proportion of enrolments in the other fields.

- In *commerce*, which constitutes the largest field, women account for close to or more than 80% in Israel, the Republic of Korea, Malaysia and Thailand. But in Bangladesh, Cyprus and Iran female enrolment is less than 20% and little more in Laos.

- In training for occupations in *industry* less than 15% of students are women in all countries except Turkey (28%). Where comparable data are available for the two years, the number of women has increased in countries where it was very low (less than 10%) in 1980 and fallen in countries where it was higher than 10% (see Figure 2b).

- Women are well represented in the broad field of the *arts and religion* with over 50% in Cyprus, Iran, Israel, Kiribati and Korea. The data concern courses in the fine arts and applied arts – with the exception of Kiribati and Turkey – and enrolments are generally rather small in absolute terms.

- *Home economics* courses are attended by women only except in Lao (59 per cent women).

- In *health*-related programmes, female participation in the countries of the region ranges from 45% in Indonesia to 100% in Japan.

Arab States

- Training for occupations in *industry* now leads the field, having increased markedly since 1980 (Figure 1c). The number of women, like total enrolments, has risen considerably in these countries. The increase in the number of female students was particularly marked in the Africa Arab States (Figure 2c). There are still no women, however, in this type of programme in a number of countries (Saudi Arabia, Jordan, Oman, Qatar, Sudan and United Arab Emirates)

- Female enrolments in *commercial* programmes constitute in most countries between half and two thirds of the total. In

Qatar, Saudi Arabia and United Arab Emirates, commercial courses are attended by men only.

- Female participation in courses on the *arts and religion* ranges from 20% in Kuwait to 45% in Syria. In Lebanon, where women account for 40% of the total, the data refer to art programmes only and in Iraq (26% women) the data cover courses on both the arts and religion.

- In *agriculture* there is generally a large majority of boys. The number of girls is nonetheless high in Algeria (39%) and, to a lesser extent, Egypt (23%).

- *Home economics* courses, when they exist, are attended almost exclusively by girls.

- In *health*-related programmes, women account for more than three quarters of total enrolments (very low in absolute terms). The 40% recorded in Saudi Arabia is exceptionally low for this traditionally 'female' field.

Europe

Figure 1d makes the situation most frequently found in the countries of the region quite clear: the broad field of training for occupations in *industry* is obviously in the lead with more or less the same total enrolment figures as in 1980, followed by *commercial* programmes which have expanded since 1980. In the former boys are in the majority, while there is a clear majority of women in the latter (between two thirds and three quarters of total enrolments).

- Figure 2d gives the percentage of women in the first broad field in 1980 and 1992 in the various countries. The percentage of female students increased in countries where it had been small (under 15%): Netherlands, Italy, Sweden, Switzerland and Denmark. Conversely, in most of the countries where women previously represented more than 15% of enrolments, as in the Eastern European countries, the percentage has tended to decline.

- Women account for 90% of enrolments in courses on *health*, which are provided in most countries.

- In the *arts and religion*, which includes arts programmes in most cases, women made up nearly two thirds of the pupils enrolled.

- Programmes relating to *agriculture* have changed little, with female students generally representing between 40 and 50% of total enrolments. Lower percentages are found in Bulgaria (18%) Ireland (25%), Malta (39%), Italy (24%) and Spain 22%).

- *Home economics*, in which enrolments have fallen sharply, records a high level of female participation. The only countries in which it is under 80% are Albania (61%), Bulgaria (59%) and Sweden (72%).

Latin America and the Caribbean

- In countries for which data are available for both years female representation in *commercial* programmes ranges from half of total enrolment, as in Paraguay, to three-quarters (Chile, Guadeloupe, Martinique, Nicaragua, Panama, Trinidad and Tobago, Uruguay and Venezuela). Enrolments rose sharply during the period under consideration (Figure 1e). The proportion of women remained much the same, although it dipped in some countries with high enrolment figures such as Argentina, Costa Rica, Panama, Uruguay and Venezuela.

- In the second broad field, *industry*, there has been a moderate increase in the number of students, with more or less the same proportion of women, close to 30% only in Costa Rica and exceeding 30% only in Martinique and Uruguay.

- In arts programmes, two students in three are women. This proportion has remained stable during the period.

- In the field of *health* there is a very large majority of women, but their impact on overall enrolment is negligible.

- Overall enrolment figures for *home economics*, almost 100% dominated by women, are negligible and lower than in 1980.

- The number of female students is particularly large in *agriculture* in Venezuela (one third of enrolments) and in Argentina and Chile (one quarter of enrolments)

Table 1. Vocational education: Percentage female enrolment in each broad field of study, 1980 and 1992

Country	Year	Total female enrolment	All fields	Arts & religion	Commerce & service trades	Health	Craft industry & engineering	Agriculture	Home economics
Africa, excluding Arab States									
Botswana	1979	697	33.1	•	•	45.0	–	18.8	–
	1991	1135	31.4	•	70.7	84.7	14.7	26.5	–
Burundi	1980	601	18.4	16.2	89.3	46.7	3.9	8.7	100.0
	1992	2692	39.2	16.1	80.0	78.7	3.1	20.7	73.7
Central African Rep.	1989	1468	41.8	•	58.2	–	2.3	–	100.0
Chad	1989	680	24.3	•	28.5	–	0.2	–	–
Comoros	1980	39	25.8	•	58.3	51.4	–	–	–
	1993	34	25.6	•	38.9	–	19.4	–	–
Eritrea	1992	58	10.8	•	•	–	10.8	–	–
Guinea	1985	1917	35.7	•	97.1	63.2	13.7	30.2	–
	1992	1977	25.6	•	61.6	38.8	2.8	7.2	–
Guinea Bissau	1981	11	6.0	•	•	–	6.0	–	–
	1988	56	8.6	•	–	–	8.1	32.8	–
Malawi	1980	–	–	•	•	•	•	•	•
	1989	67	8.7	•	68.4	–	–	–	–
Mali	1993	4049	34.1	•	40.2	–	11.4	5.9	–
Mauritius	1981	60	27.3	•	•	•	27.3	•	•
	1989	262	24.6	•	•	•	24.6	•	•
Mozambique	1981	2311	16.8	•	34.1	•	9.8	13.5	•
	1992	2485	25.4	•	49.6	•	12.6	14.9	•
Rwanda	1979	8500	60.6	•	49.4	52.3	62.3	25.5	•
	1989	16,749	43.5	7.2	47.3	65.9	40.9	29.0	92.0
Seychelles	1993	474	41.7	54.9	68.7	61.9	2.4	14.3	–
Togo	1979	2258	29.0	•	35.5	42.3	–	8.3	100.0
	1990	2161	25.8	•	32.0	•	2.5	•	100.0
Asia, excluding Arab States, and Oceania									
Bangladesh	1981	347	1.8	–	4.8	–	0.8	6.8	•
	1990	1970	7.6	3.4	14.3	•	6.7	•	•
Cyprus (1)	1980	823	14.2	–	56.3	•	9.1	•	•
(1)	1992	635	18.1	60.4	17.0	•	10.7	•	100.0
Indonesia	1980	166,872	27.3	•	54.9	–	2.3	–	98.0
	1989	573,331	42.5	•	67.7	44.8	2.3	44.0	96.6
Iran. Islamic Rep.	1982	17,671	13.9	34.5	15.0	58.0	0.1	–	89.4
	1992	57,646	20.6	56.9	14.0	70.8	10.3	–	•
Israel	1980	38,236	46.4	69.3	99.3	74.8	20.6	49.8	99.3
	1989	50,846	46.1	71.0	85.8	96.2	12.2	50.8	97.2

Table 1. Vocational education: Percentage female enrolment in each broad field of study, 1980 and 1992

Country		Year	Total female enrolment	All fields	Arts & religion	Commerce & service trades	Health	Craft industry & engineering	Agriculture	Home economics
						Percentage distribution				
Japan		1980	660,613	46.8	•	69.6	99.9	4.1	30.2	97.8
		1991	659,928	45.4	•	70.1	99.6	6.3	30.8	96.4
Kiribati		1988	127	36.3	51.6	•	•	•	•	•
Korea Rep		1981	352,852	43.4	87.4	69.3	•	12.2	4.1	•
		1990	437,639	53.1	87.7	78.9	•	6.4	11.6	•
Lao P D R		1983	1650	24.4	12.5	18.8	29.3	19.6	0.8	•
		1992	2602	31.0	20.8	21.7	58.2	7.9	18.1	58.7
Malaysia		1983	5384	29.4	•	87.6	•	11.9	19.0	100.0
		1991	8324	25.8	48.4	80.1	•	7.0	43.6	98.5
New Caledonia		1981	1636	48.3	•	60.7	•	1.2	•	99.0
		1991	3158	45.0	•	68.4	90.9	12.0	18.5	•
New Zealand		1981	2013	81.4	25.0	94.7	•	17.6	•	•
		1992	8234	45.4	•	68.5	83.7	12.6	29.4	81.8
Thailand		1990	190,494	42.9	28.4	83.3	•	2.6	24.3	97.9
Turkey		1981	149,899	29.1	13.4	39.0	93.8	36.3	–	99.7
		1991	342,473	35.1	29.8	50.3	74.9	28.2	–	100.0
Arab States										
Algeria		1981	3855	23.6	•	48.1	•	11.3	•	•
		1992	16,042	32.1	•	48.6	•	25.7	38.9	•
Bahrain		1980	988	35.2	•	55.2	•	–	•	•
		1993	1728	25.5	•	51.8	•	3.8	–	•
Djibouti		1993	962	63.2	•	62.5	•	–	•	92.2
Egypt		1980	242,974	38.3	•	54.2	•	11.5	12.4	•
		1991	479,103	43.2	•	69.9	•	25.1	22.5	•
Iraq		1980	16,678	29.3	•	78.9	•	6.3	16.8	•
		1992	33,694	25.9	26.2	76.4	•	3.8	–	•
Jordan	(2)	1980	4189	29.9	•	45.1	99.5	–	–	100.0
	(2)	1992	9894	36.1	•	57.2	83.6	–	–	100.0
Kuwait		1980	–	–	•	•	•	•	•	•
		1992	216	19.6	19.6	•	•	•	•	•
Lebanon		1981	15,775	40.4	44.8	60.5	94.8	5.9	•	84.6
		1991	14,400	38.5	40.0	55.9	95.4	5.7	•	93.5
Mauritania		1992	194	16.6	•	59.8	•	5.2	•	•
Morocco	(3)	1980	2321	23.0	•	32.1	•	3.7	•	•
		1990	6317	37.5	29.4	57.7	•	10.1	–	•
Oman		1980	–	–	•	–	•	–	–	•
		1992	392	13.9	•	7.7	76.3	–	–	–
Qatar		1980	–	–	–	–	•	–	•	•
		1993	–	–	–	–	•	–	•	•

Table 1. Vocational education: Percentage female enrolment in each broad field of study, 1980 and 1992

Country	Year	Total female enrolment	All fields	Arts & religion	Commerce & service trades	Health	Craft industry & engineering	Agriculture	Home economics
					Percentage distribution				
Saudi Arabia	1980	–	–	•	–	•	–	–	•
	1992	3632	14.0	•	–	40.2	–	–	100.0
Sudan	1980	3291	21.2	–	36.3	–	–	–	100.0
	1991	5068	17.5	–	41.1	–	--	–	100.0
Syria	1980	7506	28.7	38.2	52.7	–	5.6	–	100.0
	1992	30,121	42.2	45.1	51.5	–	3.7	11.3	100.0
Tunisia	1980	24,024	30.0	•	77.8	•	2.2	–	99.5
(4)	1993	5904	36.8	•	58.4	•	35.0	•	•
United Arab Emirates	1981	–	–	•	–	•	–	–	•
	1991	–	–	•	–	•	–	–	•
Palestine									
West Bank	1991	86	8.2	•	85.1	•	–	–	•
Europe									
Albania	1979	52,434	41.6	41.7	72.6	93.5	32.5	43.9	•
	1990	53,051	39.0	36.9	67.8	63.5	24.3	43.7	60.8
Austria (5)	1980	78,594	52.1	•	63.3	•	13.5	41.1	99.8
(5)	1992	82,653	51.9	68.7	63.4	86.5	13.2	42.5	96.1
Bulgaria	1980	88,856	39.9	53.4	89.9	84.3	35.0	18.2	76.6
	1992	83,351	37.6	50.9	80.1	•	34.3	18.4	59.1
Croatia	1992	69,929	47.3	65.4	74.0	86.1	25.3	71.0	•
Former Czech-oslovakia	1982	135,290	59.4	59.6	89.9	98.1	34.1	46.8	•
	1991	149,467	40.7	39.1	82.4	97.4	25.6	40.5	•
Czech Republic	1992	96,596	39.4	59.0	78.4	94.9	20.4	50.9	•
Denmark	1980	51,464	40.8	40.9	66.4	95.0	12.4	23.1	99.3
	1991	65,164	44.8	•	62.4	95.7	20.9	38.7	90.3
Estonia	1992	12,216	42.6	89.4	82.3	95.4	23.7	32.8	99.0
Finland	1981	51,267	47.1	87.5	75.8	93.2	16.7	22.0	99.7
	1992	75,672	54.3	70.5	69.4	91.8	16.5	41.9	97.9
Germany	1992	993,353	43.6	67.1	66.6	98.2	13.0	49.5	87.3
Former G D R	1985	162,203	42.8	72.7	90.1	80.3	28.5	44.9	•
	1989	129,846	41.3	72.8	88.2	73.6	26.0	41.6	•
Germany Fed. Rep (6)	1981	350,139	52.8	64.6	61.7	93.8	13.9	55.6	93.9
(6)	1990	910,112	45.1	66.7	68.2	98.5	13.5	47.1	89.1
Hungary	1981	113,607	41.0	62.5	80.0	98.4	20.7	23.3	•
	1991	169,587	42.7	61.4	75.1	96.6	23.4	36.0	•
Ireland (7)	1981	10,518	71.9	•	99.2	•	54.1	29.3	100.0
	1990	15,653	64.0	•	80.1	•	53.2	25.3	•
Italy	1981	665,123	41.4	65.0	62.9	•	7.4	21.8	93.2
	1992	828,911	43.5	69.9	61.3	•	11.7	23.8	90.4

Table 1. Vocational education: Percentage female enrolment in each broad field of study, 1980 and 1992

Country	Year	Total female enrolment	All fields	Arts & religion	Commerce & service trades	Health	Craft industry & engineering	Agriculture	Home economics
					Percentage distribution				
Latvia	1992	53,204	43.9	72.2	84.2	94.0	29.3	38.0	•
Malta	1980	896	21.7	•	•	•	22.2	–	•
	1990	1450	21.8	•	77.0	•	20.6	2.9	•
Monaco	1991	171	36.0	•	42.9	•	17.0	•	•
Netherlands	1981	234,226	40.6	•	49.3	•	5.6	21.9	96.7
(8)	1992	221,130	44.1	•	53.0	93.9	10.5	30.7	86.9
Norway	1980	38,050	46.9	81.5	67.3	93.2	16.4	25.5	99.2
	1992	55,368	41.8	72.9	59.1	95.1	10.7	36.4	84.7
Poland	1981	554,723	44.3	59.2	94.6	99.5	25.4	56.7	•
	1992	615,723	41.8	63.1	87.4	98.1	21.9	56.9	•
Romania (9)	1980	365,599	37.9	55.3	–	89.5	38.1	9.1	•
	1992	318,198	41.0	43.7	75.6	91.0	32.5	41.2	–
San Marino	1992	50	31.6	•	78.6	84.2	6.6	•	•
Slovenia	1992	31,461	43.6	66.0	72.4	84.8	22.8	55.4	•
Slovakia	1992	237,298	47.5	49.6	79.5	93.2	30.7	41.3	100.0
Spain	1991	591,890	51.2	62.1	68.3	83.6	8.9	22.4	98.6
Sweden	1980	85,253	52.2	65.2	65.8	91.5	8.3	28.6	88.2
	1992	96,952	43.8	66.9	56.6	88.5	14.5	43.4	72.4
Switzerland	1980	87,325	38.9	58.0	66.3	91.7	9.6	20.4	90.2
	1992	82,572	41.2	60.0	65.0	90.4	13.1	29.3	90.8
F.Y.R of Macedonia	1992	23,243	44.1	37.6	69.6	82.5	30.0	43.0	•
Former Yugoslavia	1990	347,145	44.5	57.5	71.4	83.8	29.9	40.2	•
Red. Rep. of Yugoslavia	1992	124,268	44.7	57.8	73.6	84.4	27.8	56.1	•

Latin America and the Caribbean

Country	Year	Total female enrolment	All fields	Arts & religion	Commerce & service trades	Health	Craft industry & engineering	Agriculture	Home economics
Argentina	1981	389,967	46.5	69.4	61.3	83.9	23.1	21.9	•
	1988	504,676	43.4	69.4	57.1	74.7	20.7	24.0	•
Chile	1980	79,982	47.3	•	71.9	•	3.7	25.9	98.3
	1990	121,923	47.7	•	75.9	•	5.0	25.6	•
Costa Rica	1980	15,428	50.4	58.6	74.7	•	30.2	19.6	100.0
	1992	16,166	48.2	59.8	67.8	•	29.4	1.8	99.8
El Salvador	1980	21,933	48.4	20.6	55.5	76.1	5.0	3.2	•
	1992	40,701	54.2	36.5	62.6	83.5	5.0	4.5	•
Guadeloupe	1979	5193	51.6	•	74.1	88.7	4.3	–	•
	1991	6692	45.8	•	72.9	87.8	21.4	16.7	•
Martinique	1979	5502	55.8	•	79.6	90.4	19.2	•	•
	1992	6705	51.5	•	76.6	60.3	35.4	•	•

Table 1. Vocational education: Percentage female enrolment in each broad field of study, 1980 and 1992

Country	Year	Total female enrolment	All fields	Arts & religion	Commerce & service trades	Health	Craft industry & engineering	Agriculture	Home economicsr
					Percentage distribution				
Nicaragua	1980	9301	55.8	•	66.7	•	16.2	15.4	•
	1990	8299	54.1	•	77.9	65.0	16.4	20.8	•
Panama	1981	23,101	53.5	23.5	77.3	•	4.9	13.8	91.4
	1990	25,214	50.8	•	73.4	•	4.2	8.9	93.8
Paraquay	1991	5148	44.1	•	51.2	•	14.4	•	•
Suriname	1988	3696	39.8	•	65.6	•	2.3	•	99.9
Trinidad (10)	1980	917	37.6	•	90.1	•	11.7	•	•
& Tobago (10)	1988	544	29.8	•	76.6	•	15.6	•	74.9
Uruguay (11)	1981	12,362	47.5	•	79.5	89.3	17.2	2.7	94.4
	1991	22,030	48.9	•	76.0	•	38.8	16.3	90.1
Venezuela	1979	19,652	48.8	•	81.8	•	14.9	20.0	•
	1992	28,820	54.6	65.7	74.9	96.6	18.8	34.3	100.0

The symbol – means *Magnitude nil*

The symbol • means *Category not applicable*

(1) Not including Turkish schools

(2) Data refer to the East Bank only

(3) Data do not include private professional schools

(4) Data for 1993 are not comparable with those for 1980 due to several changes in the structure of secondary education

(5) Not including apprenticeship training

(6) Territory of the Federal Republic of Germany prior to October 1990. Data for 1981 do not include technical education consisting of both on-the-job training and school-based education

(7) Craft, industry and engineering include health-related and service trades programmes

(8) Not including apprenticeship. Home economics includes part of health-related and service trades programmes

(9) Including enrolment in correspondence courses

(10) Data refer to craft courses in further education

(11) Public only

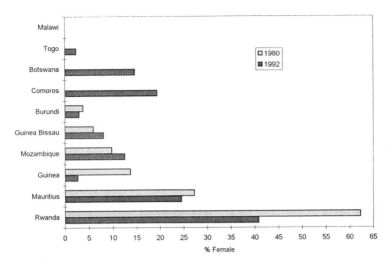

Figure 2a Africa, excluding Arab States

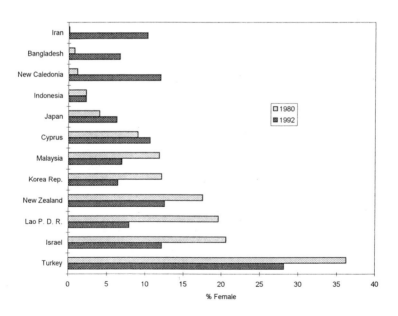

Figure 2b Asia, excluding Arab States, and Oceania

Figure 2 Percentage female in the broad field of study 'Craft, industry and engineering' 1980 and 1992 (in increasing order of 1980) (Source: Table 2)

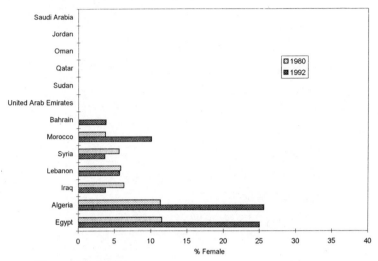

Figure 2c Arab States

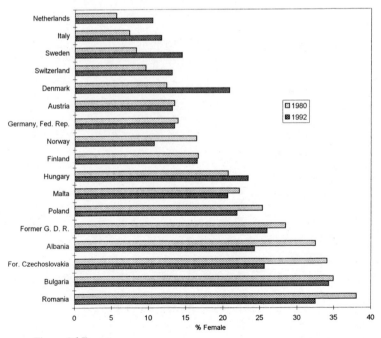

Figure 2d Europe

Figure 2 Percentage female in the broad field of study 'Craft, industry and engineering' 1980 and 1992 (in increasing order of 1980) (Source: Table 2) (continued)

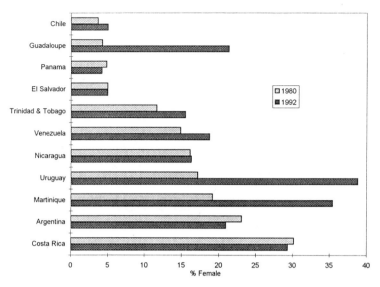

Figure 2e Latin America and the Caribbean

Figure 2 Percentage female in the broad field of study 'Craft, industry and engineering' 1980 and 1992 (in increasing order of 1980) (Source: Table 2) (continued)

ANNEX: COMPOSITION OF BROAD FIELDS OF STUDY IN
TECHNICAL AND VOCATIONAL EDUCATION AT THE
SECONDARY LEVEL

The International Standard Classification of Education (ISCED) defines 10
fields of study in secondary technical and vocational education. For the
purposes of presentation, in this document, these 10 fields have been grouped
together into the following six broad 'fields of study':

Broad fields of study[3]	ISCED fields of study
Arts and religion	Fine arts and applied arts; religion and theology
Commerce and services	Commercial education and service trades
Health	Health-related auxiliary programmes
Industry and engineering	Trade, craft and industrial programmes and assimilated activities; engineering sciences, transport and communications
Agriculture	Agriculture, forestry and fishery
Home economics	Home economics, nutrition and child care
Other programmes	Other programmes; unspecified field of study.

3   Shortened forms are sometimes used in the text and in the tables and
    graphs

Chapter 4

Did you say 'Future Engineers'?

Claude Musnil

ABSTRACT: *In spite of the difficulties encountered while researching, the author draws some conclusions from the study of the tables of statistics taken from the UNESCO Statistical Yearbook for the period 1985–91. It appears that female participation overall does not exceed 30% of the total student body.*

That's right! There are women training for a career in engineering, even if some languages, such as French, have no specific term for such a curious animal, thus perpetuating the traditionally masculine image of the profession.

But is she truly a rare animal? How many female students around the globe dare to venture into the reputedly masculine realm of engineering studies? Is this realm opening up to women as the years go by?

To try to answer these questions, let's open the 1993 edition of the *UNESCO Statistical Yearbook* and look at female population movements between 1985 and 1990–91, the most recent dates given. Due to the need for statistics that indicate gender for each of the years considered, 49 countries were chosen (see tables).

In spite of the partial nature of such a study, the results offer a comparative approach to the situation of men and women in engineering schools in terms of:

- a positive or negative change in each of the populations,
- the proportion of women within each of the totals.

(1) CHANGE IN POPULATIONS
Table 1 traces the respective evolution in the population for each sex, in number and in percentage of growth or regression.

With the exception of the African countries, where there is a drop of 15.3%, the male student body increased on all continents: +17.4% in America and +24.7% in Europe, with Oceania and Asia clocking in at

+22.4% and +23.4% respectively. For the continents as a whole, the change is an average +21.7%.

For the same period, the female population in these engineering programs also grew, but to a varying extent. In Africa, women progressed 1.8%, a very slight compensation for regression among males. In Asia and Europe, there was a considerable rise (+18.3% and 13.3% respectively), but it was of lesser amplitude than among boys. In the Americas, the number of women grew 48.7%, and in the two nations of Oceania the progression soared +160.2%. In total, the evolution among women was +22.1%, very slightly ahead of the +21.7% change recorded for boys.

These global results hide a vast diversity in the situation according to country, however, as is indicated in Tables 1a and 1b. While the two populations grew in most cases (increase among men in 33 countries and among women in 34 countries), there is also an inverse movement, with men regressing in 16 countries and women in 15.

The respective *growth* in percentage of each of the populations varied from 3.7% to 258.5% among men and from 5.7% to 434.8% among women. This can be broken down as follows:

	Male	*Female*
0–25%	13 countries	6 countries
25–50&	10 countries	6 countries
50–75%	3 countries	9 countries
75–100%	3 countries	3 countries
over 100%	4 countries	10 countries

(N.B.: In four of the ten countries where the female population increased more, the number of students in 1985 was under 100.)

The rate of *regression* also varied considerably in amplitude, ranging from 1.1% to 70.9% for men and 0.8% to 84.6% for women:

	Male	*Female*
0–25%	11 countries	8 countries
25–50&	3 countries	4 countries
50–75%	2 countries	1 country
75–100%	0 country	2 countries

Even if growth and regression have coefficients that vary as a function of gender, they evolve in the same direction in each country, with the following exceptions:

- increase among men and regression among women: Cyprus and Poland,

- increase among women and regression among men: Afghanistan, Canada, New Zealand.

This male regression can be explained by political events (cf. Afghanistan) or by new orientations chosen by male students. This is compensated for by a strong increase among women.

Table 1 Engineering sciences. Evolution in male and female student body. Absolute growth in each group

Country	1985		1990–91		Coefficient of variation (%)	
	Men	Women	Men	Women	Men	Women
AFRICA (6 countries)*	55,308	7547	46,422	7689	-15.3	+1.8
AMERICA (7 countries)*	301,972	45,266	354,694	67,341	+17.4	+48.7
ASIA (14 countries)*	385,994	38,006	476,319	44,989	+23.4	+18.3
EUROPE (20 countries)*	907,791	138,688	1,132,403	157,265	+24.7	+13.3
OCEANIA (2 countries)*	35,470	2087	43,450	5432	+22.4	+160.2
Total	1,686,535	231,594	2,053,288	282,816	+21.7	+ 22.1

* see Annex

Table 1a Rate of growth 1985–1990 of groups of each sex in engineering studies compared to the population of the same sex

Coefficient	Male	%	Female	%
0–25	Ex-Yugoslavia	3.7	Jordan	5.7
	Iceland	6.6	Malaysia	10.9
	Malaysia	7.3	Hungary	12.2
	Hungary	9.4	Nicaragua	15.2
	Netherlands	10.7	Turkey	17.1
	United Kingdom	14.1	Kuwait	18.4
	Poland	15.1		
	Denmark	18.0		
	Jordan	18.6		
	Tunisia	18.8		
	Finland	21.0		
	Trinidad	21.2		
	Cyprus	24.0		

Table 1a Rate of growth 1985–1990 of groups of each sex in engineering studies compared to the population of the same sex (continued)

Coefficient	Male	%	Female	%
25–50%	Turkey	27.1	Norway	25.9
	Rep of Korea	27.5	Ex-Yugoslavia	27.4
	Ireland	27.6	Switzerland	31.5
	Switzerland	28.5	Ireland	35.2
	Germany ex FRG	30.3	Canada	45.3
	France	32.6	Trinidad*	45.9
	Australia	33.6		
	Mexico	33.8		
	Nicaragua	38.9		
	Norway	42.1		
50–75%	Italy	57.7	Bulgaria	51.3
	Austria	65.8	Iceland	52.6
	Portugal	72.6	Arab Emirates*	53.8
			Germany ex-FRG	54.4
			France	56.6
			Finland	65.0
			Netherlands	72.9
			New Zealand	73.4
			Mexico	87.4
75–100%	Kuwait	82.0	Rep. of Korea	75.6
	Bahrain	91.8	Portugal	80.3
	Iran	95.6	United Kingdom	86.6
+100%	Bulgaria	103.8	Tunisia	128.0
	Ethiopia	110.0	Iran	145.2
	Arab Emirates	170.0	Austria	153.0
	Morocco	258.5	Denmark	170.0
			Australia	197.0
			Italy	200.5
			Afghanistan*	266.0
			Bahrain*	346.0
			Ethiopia	422.0
			Morocco*	434.8

NB: the sign * indicates a female presence of under 100 people in 1985

Table 1b Rate of regression 1985–1990 in presence of each sex in engineering studies compared to the population of the same sex

Coefficient	Male	%	Female	%
0–25%	Saudi Arabia	1.1	Syrian Arab Rep.	0.8
	Honduras	2.9	Egypt	11.0
	Canada*	3.7	Ex-Czech.	13.4
	New Zealand*	12.1	Poland*	14.4
	Israel	12.4	Israel	14.5
	El Salvador	13.4	Honduras	17.2
	Afghanistan*	16.8	El Salvador	17.8
	Mali	17.1	Albania	18.9
	Ex-Czechoslovakia	19.3		
	Albania	20.7		
	Egypt	21.3		
25–50%	Cuba	33.1	Madagascar	26.2
	Syrian Arab Rep.	34.5	Sweden	36.1
	Sweden	45.5	Cuba	36.4
			Cyprus*	42.0
50–75%	Madagascar	52.3	Mali	54.1
	Sri Lanka	70.9		
75–100%			Sri Lanka	83.9
			Saudi Arabia	84.6

NB: the sign * indicates a female presence of under 100 people in 1985

(2) PROPORTION OF WOMEN

In terms of the coefficient of growth or regression, as the populations of both sexes evolved at the same rate for the countries studied in general, the proportion of female students out of the total student body obviously remained unchanged. Table 2 evaluates this share at 12.1% in 1985 and in 1990–91. While progress was recorded in Africa (+2.2%), America (+2.9%) and Oceania (+4.7%), there was a relapse in Asia which affected a greater number of people (-0.3%) and in Europe (-1.1%).

Obviously, this average of 12.1% is the result of a broad range of situations (Tables 2a and 2b). In 1985, the share of women in 'engineering' varied from 1.7% to 46.9%, compared with 0.2% to 37.3% in 1990–91, broken down as follows:

	1985	1990–91
0–10%	16 countries	10 countries
10–20%	19 countries	23 countries
20–30%	8 countries	14 countries
30–40%	4 countries	2 countries
40–50%	2 countries	0 country

There is a shift in the lower and upper brackets toward an average position of 10% to 30%:

- In six countries, the female population exceeded the threshold of 10% and in five other cases exceeded 20%. On the other hand, the highest percentages went from the 20% to 50% brackets to lower rates in eight cases;

- Moreover, within the same bracket, certain female populations also slipped (seven cases).

As regards the scope of these changes, the evolution in the proportion of women can be summarized as follows (Table 2d):

	Increase	Decrease
0–5%	28 countries	10 countries
5–10%	3 countries	3 countries
10–15%	2 countries	1 country
over 15%	1 country	1 country

The 24.9% rise observed in Afghanistan is atypical, because it is the result of sharp growth in the female population (almost non-existent in 1985: 50 students) and a regression in the male student body. As for Cyprus, where the situation is the opposite, the female population decreased 42% between 1985 and 1990–91, dropping from 107 to 62, while the number of male students rose 24%.

With the exception of these two extreme situations, variations, both positive and negative, remained between 0.1% and 12.5%.

If we take the limited number of countries studied into consideration (49), what can we conclude from this data?

Yes, women remain present in engineering studies. Their number grew overall, but within limits comparable to the variations among the male population. This population represented between 54% and 98% of the total student body in 1985, and this huge majority persisted in 1990–91. Moreover, it would appear that the number of female students does not exceed the 30% threshold on a continuous basis; of the six countries that had a percentage of female students over this threshold

Table 2 Growth in % of the proportion of women studying engineering sciences compared to the student population of both sexes (Average by continent)

Country	1985			1990–91			Coef Of Change (%)		
	M + F	Fem.	%	M + F	Fem.	%	M + F	Fem.	%
Africa (6 countries)*	62,855	7547	12.0	54,111	7689	14.2	-8744	+142	+2.2
America (7 countries)*	347,238	45,266	13.0	422,035	67,341	15.9	+75,597	+22,075	+2.9
Asia (14 countries)*	424,000	38,006	8.9	521,308	44,989	8.6	+97,308	+6983	-0.3
Europe (20 countries)*	1,046,479	138,688	13.2	1,289,668	157,265	12.1	+243,189	+18,577	-1.1
Oceania (2 countries)*	32,557	2087	6.4	48,832	5432	11.1	+16,275	+3345	+4.7
Total	**1,913,219**	**231,594**	**12.1**	**2,335,954**	**282,716**	**12.1**	**+422,825**	**+51,122**	**none**

* See Annex,

in 1985, five had regressed sharply five years later. What's more, except in the above-mentioned case of Afghanistan, wherever the proportion of women progressed, it remained below this 30% threshold. This being the case, those responsible for education systems cannot proclaim there is equal access to engineering studies. They are forced to admit that the weight of tradition and social images is still maintaining the invisible barriers that limit the impact of legal measures more favorable to women. Consequently, extreme vigilance will be required in order for half of humanity to take its rightful place among the top-level technological professions.

Table 2a Proportion of women in engineering studies (comparative trend)

%	1985		1990–91	
0–10	Saudi Arabia	1.7	Saudi Arabia*	0.2
	Rep. of Korea	2.5	Mali*	1.9
	Ethiopia	3.2	Rep. of Korea	3.4
	Mali	3.4	Switzerland	4.1
	Switzerland	4.0	Iran	6.2
	Iran	5.0	Ethiopia	7.0
	Italy	5.9	Germany ex FRG	7.6
	Germany ex FRG	6.3	El Salvador*	9.1
	Austria	6.6	Austria	9.7
	Madagascar	7.4	Ireland	9.9
	United Kingdom	7.7		
	Netherlands	8.4		
	Ireland	9.4		
	Canada	9.6		
	El Salvador	9.7		
	Iceland	9.8		
10–20	Tunisia	10.2	Italy	10.8
	Finland	10.5	Cyprus*	10.9
	Denmark	10.8	Madagascar	11.1
	Morocco	10.9	Sri Lanka*	12.0
	Afghanistan	11.4	United Kingdom	12.0
	Bahrein	11.5	Hungary	12.2
	Trinidad	11.7	Netherlands	12.5
	Mexico	11.7	Poland*	13.2
	Hungary	11.9	Iceland	13.5

**Table 2a Proportion of women in engineering studies
(comparative trend) (continued)**

%	1985		1990–91	
	Egypt	12.7	Jordan	13.5
	Malaysia	13.9	Finland	13.8
	Jordan	14.9	Trinidad	13.8
	Poland	16.8	Canada	13.9
	Turkey	17.1	Malaysia	14.3
	Syrian Arab Rep.	17.2	Egypt	14.4
	Sweden	17.2	Morocco	15.5
	France	18.2	Mexico	15.7
	Honduras	19.2	Turkey*	15.9
	Sri Lanka	19.8	Honduras*	16.6
			Tunisia	16.6
			Norway*	19.5
			Sweden	19.7
			Israel	20.0
20–30	Israel	20.3	France	20.8
	New Zealand	20.6	Denmark	21.7
	Norway	21.5	Arab Emirates*	22.4
	Ex-Czechoslovakia	22.1	Bahrain	23.3
	Portugal	24.0	Ex-Czech.	23.4
	Ex-Yugoslavia	24.4	Syrian Arab Rep.	24.0
	Australia	25.4	Portugal	24.8
	Albania	27.3	Nicaragua*	27.2
			New Zealand	27.2
			Kuwait*	27.2
			Cuba*	27.5
			Ex-Yugoslavia	28.4
			Australia	29.5
			Albania	29.7
30–40	Cuba	31.9	Afghanistan	36.3
	Nicaragua	32.1	Bulgaria*	37.3
	Arab Emirates	34.9		
	Kuwait	36.5		
40–50	Bulgaria	44.4		
	Cyprus	46.9	None	

NB: The sign * designates countries where the female population concerned
is in regression

**Table 2b Proportion of women in
engineering studies (evolution between 1985 and 1990)**

Coefficient of variation	Increase		Decrease	
0–5%	Switzerland	0.1	Israel	0.3
	Hungary	0.3	El Salvador	0.6
	Ireland	0.5	Turkey	1.2
	Malaysia	0.5	Jordan	1.4
	Portugal	0.8	Saudi Arabia .	1.5
	Rep. of Korea	0.9	Norway	2.5
	Germany (ex-FRG)	1.1	Honduras	2.6
	Iran	1.2	Poland	3.6
	Egypt	1.7	Nicaragua	3.9
	Trinidad & Tobago	2.1	Cuba	4.4
	Ex-Czechoslovakia	2.3		
	Albania	2.4		
	France	2.6		
	Sweden	2.9		
	Finland	3.3		
	Austria	3.4		
	Iceland	3.7		
	Madagascar	3.7		
	Ethiopia	3.8		
	Mexico	4.0		
	Ex-Yugoslavia	4.0		
	Australia	4.1		
	Netherlands	4.1		
	Canada	4.3		
	United Kingdom	4.3		
	Morocco	4.6		
	Italy	4.9		
5–10%	Tunisia	6.4	Bulgaria	7.1
	Syrian Arab Rep.	6.5	Sri Lanka	7.8
	New Zealand	6.6	Kuwait	9.3
10–15%	Denmark	10.9	United Arab	
	Bahrain	11.8	Emirates	12.5
+15%	Afghanistan	24.9	Cyprus	36.9

ANNEX Countries Surveyed

Africa

Egypt

Ethiopia

Morocco

Madagascar

Mali

Tunisia

America

Canada

Cuba

El Salvador

Honduras

Mexico

Nicaragua

Trinidad and Tobago

Asia

Afghanistan

Saudi Arabia

Bahrain

Cyprus

United Arab Emirates

Iran

Israel

Jordan

Kuwait

Malaysia

Syrian Arab Republic

Republic of Korea

Sri Lanka

Turkey

Europe

Albania

Germany (Ex FRG)

Austria

Bulgaria

Denmark

Finland

France

Hungary

Ireland

Iceland

Italy

Norway

Poland

Netherlands

Portugal

United Kingdom

Sweden

Switzerland

Ex-Czechoslovakia

Ex-Yugoslavia

Oceania

Australia

New Zealand

Part Two

Better Understanding
Helps Fight Inequality

Chapter 5

Coeducational Classrooms
An Unfinished Process

Nadine Plateau

ABSTRACT: *While secondary schools are coeducational in most Western countries, the masculine model that inspired coed schools has undergone no change. Whether in schools, politics or economics, no true coeducational system, in the sense of one world made possible by equality between the sexes, has been thought out or implemented. The author analyzes how schools are permeated by a logic that tends to reproduce the unequal relations between the sexes and proposes a few guidelines for changing this situation: combatting the hidden agenda, teaching transformed curricula.*

Secondary schools are coeducational in many countries, and yet the masculine model that inspired them remains unchanged. Preparation for a trade, whether it be effective as in technical and vocational education or deferred as in general education, excludes practically all training in the responsibilities of domestic living. As for society, it is said to be not only coeducational but more and more feminized, according to some people. And yet women hold less than 10% of elected offices and continue to do the greater share of housework and child-raising; discrimination against them in the working world is not, as Margaret Maruani (1991) demonstrated, a residual phenomenon, but rather the means by which women enter the labor market.

Consequently, whether in schools, politics, employment or the family, there is no truly coeducational situation, in the sense of one world made possible by equality between the sexes. We live in a world governed by all that is male. If we believe it is fair and just for women to work with men to define the society in which they wish to live, and if we believe that, as in other social areas such as the family, the labor market and the political world, schools are permeated by a logic that tends to reproduce the unequal relations between the sexes, then it is urgent that we create an education system that fits the political agenda.

AN INADEQUATE EDUCATIONAL MODEL

Today's educational landscape has been neutered. With only a few rare exceptions, official documents and studies on the educational sciences no longer mention the presence of girls and boys in a school. All that remains are students, an abstract entity bereft of a body or a private existence and theoretically the equal of all the other students. This has not always been the case.

At the turn of the century, schools offered an education that was differentiated socially and sexually. The division of knowledge was an integral part of the different schools (girls, boys, vocational, technical, general). The post-primary education of boys provided them, according to their social origin, with the knowledge and skills necessary to their integration into the sphere of production (professional work). Likewise, girls were given an education that differed according to their social status. That is all it had in common with boys, because all girls were educated mainly, if not exclusively, as a function of their reproductive role (housekeeping, child-raising).

These divisions largely disappeared as a result of the educational democracy policies that arose in the 1950s. Nowadays, even if differences persist, because not all the streams of education have been unified and not all schools have the same student population, an educational model has arisen which proclaims the equality of all students, regardless of their sex, social status, ethnic origin or religious beliefs. Equality, viewed as a 'given', did not in fact play any role in the model; it didn't determine its definition, and wasn't included as an objective to be achieved. While efforts were made to limit the gap between formal equality and actual equality, as can be seen by the existence of compensation or mitigation policies, little thought was given to the values, preconceptions and biases the model contained.

Let's take a look at this model. First observation: in most western countries, the education made available to the new student bodies is one destined for a privileged social group. The changes brought about by reforms are aimed at adapting to a technocratic society, but question neither the priorities nor the values that inspired a system of education designed for an elite and suited to a male student from an affluent background. The content of the program and means of transmitting knowledge were not rethought to accommodate an egalitarian society. Likewise for the second observation. The result of imposing a coeducational system is to provide girls with access to types of learning previously reserved for boys, which is a good thing, but also, and especially, to encourage the extension of the male education model without modifying it in any way. The proposed education consequently wasn't reformulated as a function of a coeducational society.

The new categories of students, previously excluded, found themselves, given their social situation, experience and background, in a position of inequality compared with the other and faced with two alternatives: integration or marginalization. Let me add that if girls now succeed more often than boys, the extraordinary fact that they have 'caught up' is as much the result of their determination to invest in education at all levels as of their ability to adapt to curricula designed for the male student.

The educational model is therefore not the result of taking into consideration the concrete reality of the new students for whom it was intended, but rather the perpetuation, nuanced by a few alterations, of a model which is effective when aimed at a privileged group but proves totally inadequate in the present context. The contemporary dilemmas of the education system – failure, slow learners, dropout rates, and violence – are the most visible manifestations.

COEDUCATION AND THE REIGN OF THE MASCULINE NEUTER
Two phenomena marked the passage from a gender-oriented education system to a coeducational one. The first was the neutralization of the gender difference. Nicole Mosconi (1989) clearly demonstrated that the transmission of knowledge requires that coeducation be desexualized. She believes both teachers and students feel the need to exorcise sexuality, which they perceive as a threat to cohesion and order. Coeducational schools have banished sexuality, eliminated the feminine gender and imposed the masculine neuter, a term the author sees as signifying the denial of any sexual difference and the affirmation of masculine supremacy.

This is the new mask of male domination referred to by François de Singly (1993). Men have set aside the most noticeable attributes of masculinity; they are edging toward the so-called 'neutral', median values and lending strength to them by adopting them.

A second phenomenon characterizes coeducational education: the disappearance or devalorization of feminine education. This education provided girls with skills useful in domestic life, such as sewing, which they could put to profit in the workplace. What is the present situation? Either such education has disappeared, as in general education, or, when it is relegated to vocational education for girls, it is denigrated to the point that some people feel it should be abolished. The skills traditionally handed down in girls' schools have not been replaced by other skills that make it possible to take over reproduction work validly. Consequently, social acknowledgment of this work has been lost.

Today, education is neuter in gender, yet the masculine model, founded on integration into the professional world, is the standard for all, male and female. A model even more masculine because it places options with the largest number of hours of mathematics and sciences at the top of the hierarchy. Yet girls only obtained access to these fields recently. In fact, from the last century down through the 1950s, the scientific education deemed useful for their schooling was 'simplified' education, adapted to a woman's role and destiny. The present educational system puts emphasis on the subjects historically least familiar to girls. Is this historical 'lag', which lies at the root of the present inequality between boys and girls as regards the teaching of science, simply the result of circumstances? Only if we overlook the patriarchal strategy which consisted initially of excluding women from socially respected areas of knowledge, and subsequently of allowing them postponed access. Yesterday Latin and Greek, today mathematics and science. The feminine 'lag' is thus a socially constructed, organized one, a structural lag.

For over a century, women have concentrated their efforts on obtaining what was kept out of their reach: access to education on a par with that of boys, education that would train and prepare them for an occupation and make them independent. They never dreamed that the price they would have to be pay would be to turn their backs on an entire facet of life, the one for which they assume almost entire responsibility.

Just as education didn't incorporate in its knowledge and pedagogy the new cards dealt out by the massive arrival of students of modest origin, it was also incapable of taking in the profound changes in the relations between the sexes. Girls (as they have proved) want professional, social and family responsibilities to be shared. This implies that boys take on their share of the housework and child-raising. It is extremely disturbing that, at a time when girls demand such tasks be shared, schools reject even the symbolic value attached to this type of work.

THE FEMINIST CORPUS

To help define a coeducational plan, we now have an important body of feminist studies whose contributions and shortcomings can be evaluated in a detached way. In the realm of the sociology of education, which focused on the problem of social inequality in the 1960s and 1970s, feminists raise the question of sexual inequality in education and proclaim loudly that the sex variable is an explanatory variable. For the first time, sex or gender is no longer viewed as a natural category, but rather as one of the organizing principles of society.

All the feminist works on education agree on one fundamental point: school is a place where inequality between the sexes is produced and reproduced. The so-called 'liberal' feminists underlined the inequalities in access to studies and in scholastic paths; they emphasized the consequences in terms of employment. Others, radicals and marxists, studied school in its socio-historical context in order to explain sexual inequality. While liberal feminists believed discrimination could be eradicated by changing the education provided and especially by changing people's mentalities, radical and marxist feminists, trapped in the perception of school as an instrument of producing/reproducing social relations, were unprepared to face their main enemy, whether patriarchy or capitalism.

In the triple conceptual framework of feminism – liberal, radical and marxist – empiric studies flourished on both sides of the Atlantic. Limited to one field of education, these works focus on how sexual inequality is produced in schools and outside of the curriculum taught. This is the 'hidden curriculum', or hidden program of inequalities. The meticulous description of the multiple and subtle processes of sexual differentiation is conclusive. The sexist stereotypes and prejudices of the teachers (male and female), whose representations and expectations of students are positive or negative depending on the student's sex; lower self-confidence among girls than boys even though their grades are similar; monopolization of linguistic and physical space by male students; preferential treatment of boys by teachers; assessment procedures unfavorable to girls; not to mention the verbal and even physical abuse of girls by boys. These are the instruments used in this systematic, though unconscious, action to make girls feel inferior and boys superior which leads to reproducing the sexual hierarchy within the school. The considerable impact of these works can only be explained by the fact that, for the first time, the discriminatory dimension of the learning conditions of girls was revealed at its most concrete, everyday level. The picture painted is a dark one: girls are passive, silent, resigned victims locked in a scholastic universe.

In the 1980s, certain researchers started to plumb the depths of this darkness. These women observed girls' resistance to the roles imposed on them, their opposition to school rules, their negotiations regarding social relations. Their attitude is a new one: girls are seen, not as objects subjected to socialization, but rather as participants who lend a sense to their action. The image they project is totally different; they are active, not stereotyped, and take their fate into their own hands. Recognizing that girls are participants, however, doesn't disprove the theory of the reproduction of gender-based social relations, but the school world is less frozen that was believed; within the constraints, girls have a certain freedom.

The reproduction of the sexual hierarchy is therefore not that mechanical. Sex roles are not imposed irreversibly, socialization is not rampant, sex relations are not defined once and for all, even if they tend to reproduce male domination. This assertion is a basic one, as it opens up a breach through which the prospect of a change can be seen in gender-based social relations. The possibility of a dynamic, historic vision of these relations is born, and with it the possibility of a social change. New concepts are being forged which will take into account that which was previously unexplained. For example, the sex mobility concept introduced by Anne-Marie Daune-Richard (1992), which states that a person can modify his or her position in gender-based relations. A concept that helps explain why certain girls opt for male training; this choice is a strategy for combating their social inferiorization as women.

Consequently, the analysis of scholastic roles in the reproduction of gender-based social relations has been enriched and perfected considerably over the past two decades. A long road stretches from the inevitable sex roles assigned up to the gender-based social relations that are built socially, including in schools. But to date no study has developed a proposal for feminist education. This reflection is not lacking, but appears only in the works of radical feminists who submit proposals in the pages they write. The first of these proposals is to develop another type of knowledge based on the women's personal experience. The foundation of this new knowledge would be arousing awareness of social oppression as a woman and of the priority given to the personal knowledge that comes from life experiences. The corollary to this first proposal is the initiation of non-hierarchized relations between teachers and students; the latter have no less knowledge that the former, and therefore together, as equals and in an atmosphere of cooperation, they will build this new knowledge. The radical nature of these proposals, which reject both the content and the means of transmission of recognized knowledge, explains why radical feminist pedagogy can only be practiced in the specific context of the non-coeducation that characterized certain women's studies programs. In secondary education, it is significant to note that the only way proposed to combat non-egalitarian relations between boys and girls is a non-coed classroom. The radical feminists have not reflected on coeducational pedagogy, nor have they penetrated the coed scholastic world except on an individual basis.

EXPERIMENTATION
Actually, the only true area of experimentation from a feminist viewpoint was that of equal opportunity. By this I mean the policies of emancipation or equal opportunity applied in most member countries of the European Union as a result of the Resolution of 1985. The feminist viewpoint that permeates this resolution is a liberal one, in that it only envisages a revamping of the education system to distribute the resources and benefits of education more equitably between girls and boys. To achieve this goal, it proposes strategies that, in spite of a neuter form (the text always speaks symmetrically of girls and boys), aim essentially at making up for the supposed impediments and deficiencies of girls compared with boys. That the resolution proposes a policy to conform girls to the dominant, masculine, technocratic model is an obvious fact appears in the central theme of Equal Opportunity intervention: the diversification of the options chosen, a formula that means encouraging girls to choose technical and scientific classes, which are traditionally masculine and considered to lead to more promising employment. Practically speaking, this means that research on and positive action in favor of equal opportunity necessarily met this objective, as all of it was funded, partially or totally, by the European Union. A considerable constraint which certainly had a pernicious effect: first it revealed the reputed inferiority of girls in science and technology, then it concealed other discriminatory aspects of learning.

Nevertheless, when we think about the half-heartedness of political determination, about the limited amount of funding earmarked for intervention, and about the resistance of the educational community, the results of the strategies implemented in the context of Equal Opportunity appear to be globally positive. Many projects carried out as part of the diversification of girls' choices have been the occasion for research and experiments strongly marked by the feminist analyses. The most radical experiment, that of the GIST (Girls into Science and Technology) carried out in Manchester by the Equal Opportunities Commission, is exemplary. Initiated and implemented by feminists in order to improve the participation of girls in science and technology, this project includes both research into the causes of girls' failure or under-representation in these fields and intervention aimed at teachers and students. The project's interest lies in the reversal of the approach; instead of changing the girls, it attempts to change the school, to make the scholastic environment 'girl-friendly' by acting on the resources used in the school and the scholastic practices. Documents on women scientists have been included in the manuals, the packaging of science has been changed by including materials and subject that interest girls, a program of visits by women scientists and technicians has been launched to offer girls feminine models, and non-coed subgroups have been created in mathematics and science classes to eliminate competition with boys.

Other members countries of the European Union have carried out studies and action-research within the confined framework of Equal Opportunity. Although they didn't have the expected effect, that is, to diversify girls' choices, they did make it possible to build knowledge and experience that all teachers, male and female, should take into consideration. School manuals were scrutinized under the feminist microscope and concrete proposals were made concerning their content. The European TENET project for school staff training in equal opportunity between girls and boys led to the development of teaching tools and educational strategies similar to those of the English experiment. Most member countries now have extremely rich pedagogical material that may end up in a drawer somewhere, known to only a few initiates unless stringent measures are taken to transform the structure of the education system.

Within the ambient context of sexual neutrality and exclusive attention to social inequality, equal opportunity experiments are the only place where sexual inequality has been recognized and recorded, and where tools to combat it, both in teacher training and in the content of the curriculum and its means of transmission, have been designed and tested. The other side of the coin is that, by exclusively targeting girls, they have become a discriminated group, a group to be assisted, without any reflection or action having been envisaged for the boys' group, even though they sit side by side in class every day. No one would allege that boys have no problems in school and I even think that mitigating policies, although purportedly neutral, are aimed mainly at them because it is they who fail most often. But few people note that their identity and behavioral problems affect the way relations between the sexes evolve in school. Nothing is done to help the boys 'find themselves' in relation to the girls and to their new aspirations, which they perceive as a threat to their virility, especially as girls succeed better and are often more highly esteemed by both male and female teachers. Any project that doesn't include this fact, along with action focused on the boys, can only accentuate the antagonism between the sexes. Consequently, these problems must be taken into consideration if we want to educate boys and girls in a way that enables them to live and work together.

While the result is positive as concerns what has been accomplished, this is due to the quality and militant nature of those who did the work, and not to the pedagogical policy in the countries concerned. Too many experiments were filed away and forgotten; once the contract ended, the action implemented stopped abruptly. Too many experiments were limited in scope because, instead of considering equal opportunity as a priority that required measures to be taken to this end, the only goal pursued was to try to change the mentality by a 'soft' persuasive approach. That is probably why compulsory training in equal opportunity has not yet been included in the program of teacher training institutes. As for information on these experiments, and especially the media coverage that played a significant role in raising awareness among British teachers, it is non-existent in many countries. Isn't this indifference an unconscious resistance to an undertaking that could threaten masculine privileges?

A COEDUCATIONAL PLAN

Criticism of the scholastic system, first from sociologists in the 1960s and 1970s, then from the neo-liberal politicians and economists who came like a flood in the 1980s, finally convinced most people of the schools' inability to fight social inequality and of their ineffectiveness, measured in terms of scholastic failure. A defeatist attitude and loss of confidence in school's emancipating, liberating potential go hand in hand with the growing relinquishing of the curriculum in favor of know-how. This is the depressing context into which secondary education has now moved in the absence of any vision of the future. Isn't there any more ambitious plan for schools? Some people credit schools with having a certain power over society and recognize that schools have an influence on the building of young people's identities, which makes them responsible for what tomorrow's citizens become. From this standpoint, it is possible to design an educational plan that is not limited to merely striving for individual happiness or socio-economic integration, but which, through training and instruction, would lay the foundations for a new society.

Some people, probably a minority, are fighting the dilemmas of teaching which I mentioned above: progressists, teachers, researchers, pedagogues. They are familiar with the prejudices that exist in teaching, denounce the elitist culture taught in school, and criticize pedagogy that ignores life experiences and the material conditions of students' lives. Both theory (I am thinking of the works of Philippe Meirieu) and practice (such as that of teachers who test active methods or intercultural pedagogy) offer a framework of thought and action principles that makes truly coeducational education possible: the recognition of differences as constituting a source of wealth, the inclusion of the social experience of youths, the definition of learning as an undertaking that must have a sense for students so that they assimilate knowledge – provided there is what I call gender consciousness, by analogy with class consciousness. Unfortunately that is not the case. With the exception of feminists, everyone seems to be blind to sex; they only see the social and cultural inequality that crystallizes into scholastic failure.

In this context of blindness to sex in spite of 20 years of coeducation in secondary schools, I believe it is necessary to return to the coeducation plan that was never implemented because it was limited in practice to the co-presence of boys and girls in the classroom. Now we must redefine this project as a function of effective coeducation, by which I mean the introduction and appropriation, in a scholastic environment, of a culture that integrates the contribution of both sexes. Understood from this viewpoint, coeducation links back with the idea of a mixed society that has made progress over the past few years in certain feminist circles. A mixed society that will only become reality when women take part in drafting the laws. A mixed society that, for the moment, is unpredictable in that it still has to be invented by men and women. If we still cannot imagine this society, at least we can envisage a coeducation plan that breaks with the present law of the masculine neuter. We have inherited the feminist research and experiments described above in order to formulate such a plan. The fundamental observation of feminist research in education is that, far from enjoying the same learning conditions as boys, girls are objectively discriminated against, as regards the hidden agenda (by the aspirations, expectations, behavior, etc. of the teachers and boys) and as regards the formal program (through the knowledge taught). Based on this observation, the coeducation plan must, therefore, draw up measures to fight sexism, both in teaching practices and class interactions and in cultural content.

FIGHTING THE HIDDEN AGENDA
A coeducational plan has to develop strategies to fight the hidden agenda which, we must remember, secretes discrimination not only according to sex but also to class, race, etc. These strategies can under no circumstances be limited to taking only the discriminated group into consideration. As I pointed out above, one of the weak points of Equal Opportunity is not to have developed strategies that encompassed both categories of students in order to change the relations between the sexes in the classroom. I also mentioned some disturbing signs in boys' grades and behavior which could lead the authorities and teachers to invest more in the boys by ignoring the question of sexism in the classroom. The only solution to this problem is to think in terms of gender-based social relations and to create new conditions for establishing relations between the sexes.

Let's take the example of violence in gender-based social relations. If we admit that violence is a continuum that stretches from a mere sexist remark all the way up to sexual assault, it is, including in its most attenuated form, the instrument by which sexual hierarchy is reproduced. If a teacher doesn't intervene in the event of a sexist remark, he or she is accepting the affirmation of feminine inferiority. In this case, silence helps create asymmetric relations between the sexes. But any intervention must avoid castrating the boy or overprotecting the girl. One possible solution could be to allow the conflict between the sexes to emerge. All teachers are familiar with such volatile moments when students confront each other about their sexual identities. Instead of repressing such clashes, students could be taught to expresses their differences and control their conflicts.

Finally, if we want to create conditions favorable to egalitarian relations between the sexes, rules must be set for daily living in the school. Rules inspired from values such as respect for others, responsibility toward others, solidarity. Let me add that it is precisely these rules that will enable young people to prepare themselves for their role as citizens in a coeducational society.

TEACHING TRANSFORMED SUBJECTS

The second part of the coeducational plan concerns the fight against sexism in the subjects taught. This fight extends far beyond the denunciation of sexist stereotypes found in school books; it questions their cultural content. This content discriminates against girls because it overlooks the feminine or shapes it after the masculine model, that is by playing down its value. What's more, it doesn't teach girls about themselves nor give them the critical tools to analyze what Monique Haicault (1994) calls the 'sex doxa'. Consequently, neither boys nor girls can understand how the representations of men, women and their relations are constructed in our dominant culture, and even less how to build others based on their experiences.

For over 20 years feminists, by introducing the question of sex and subsequently of gender-based social relations, have criticized the androcentrism of studies and their pseudo-universalism. They took a new look at the 'great men' of our Western culture, from Aristotle to Derrida, and showed how their works are rooted in masculine subjectivity that makes any claim to objectivity and universality a sham. If we refuse to let these men speak on behalf of the entire world and if, generally speaking, we aspire to human production that recognizes sexuation, that doesn't mean we contest its universal importance. You would have to be blind not to recognize that, as soon as they obtained access to learning, women seized upon all within this masculine culture that had any meaning for them. The misogyny of Rousseau or Kerouac did not prevent women of their generations from adopting the message of freedom their works contained even though they interiorized, without (intentionally?) knowing it, the authors' contempt for women.

The coeducational plan must integrate this feminist criticism of learning in the various fields of secondary education. It alone can teach girls and boys the reading habits that will enable them to spot sexist opinions, images and representations contained in books, courses or cultural production in general, including in the media. Moreover, this plan will need to turn to feminist works on women and to the forgotten or concealed works of women in order to transmit more complete knowledge. It is time to show that in spite of obstacles and resistance, some women have made a major contribution to our culture, and that if they were less represented then men, most of them were, as Virginia Woolf describes, like Shakespeare's little sister who didn't write because she couldn't write.

Finally, coeducational education must transmit knowledge that has been transformed. The transformation of knowledge by taking into consideration the question of gender-based social relations is a step toward a more complete culture, one produced by both men and women, a common culture that deserves to be described as universal. That is still a pipe dream, but we can move in that direction through a coeducational plan. For example, teaching the history of the French Revolution by including the feminist viewpoint. This doesn't mean tacking on women's issues as an addendum or a separate chapter, but rather analyzing gender-based social relations at that time, the conflict between male and female interests and the resolution of this conflict by barring women from citizenship. The fact of studying both women and men in their relationship with politics means relating historical truth; it also instills respect for the woman's struggle in boys and the pride of belonging to their sex in girls. It is time for this knowledge to replace the male fantasies of the knitter, the 'pétroleuse' and the suffragette, fantasies that, by denigrating and ridiculing women hungry for their political rights, exorcised the feminine threat.

Likewise, economics could be taught without excluding housework under the pretext that it is done by women for free. Integrating the new knowledge provided by feminists on housework and child-raising within the cultural curriculum transmitted in schools would mean recognizing what we call reproduction in its universal dimension. These tasks are not 'women's work'; they concern everyone. The recognition in courses of this universality of reproduction appears to me to be the best way of compensating for the loss of traditional feminine learning.

CONCLUSION

It is obvious that a coeducational plan is an ambitious undertaking. It presupposes an in-depth transformation of classroom expectations, behavior and practices and an almost total revolution in the lessons taught. And yet I do not believe it is utopian on a small scale, at the local level, in short in the classroom, the 'laboratory' where a teacher can define the rules of the game. We can already create learning conditions that guarantee equality in gender-based relations and encourage solidarity and respect for others. We can see to it that girls and boys learn to live together in the classroom, to understand this microcosm, to find their place in it based on their individual and collective experience, and finally to build it together.

Article published in *Chronique Féministe 53*, Brussel, August/September 1994.

Chapter 6

Orientation and Success in the Scientific Streams

Marie Duru-Bellat

ABSTRACT: *This article seeks to make teachers aware of how to analyze concrete classroom situations in the light of recent research. It gives a synthetic presentation of their results, along with boxes focusing on the action to be carried out on three vital points in classroom living: (1) the implementation of the prescribed curriculum: the organization of work in the classroom, the content of the programs and manuals; (2) student-teacher interaction, assessment practices, interaction between students; and (3) orientation phenomena.*

As the first part of this book indicated, the school careers of boys and girls differ considerably. There are very few girls in the top-level scientific streams. The purpose of this article is to help people in the education system become aware of the concrete mechanisms in daily classroom life which help 'manufacture' such differences. These mechanisms were studied in depth by researchers in the human sciences, particularly by psychologists and sociologists, and especially in the English-speaking countries.[1] Our mission is to convince teachers that these works are far from inaccessible, and can even help them observe these differences in their own classroom. In other words, the objective is to invite them to reflect, without guilt, on their own way of treating the boys and girls in their class, while remembering that what occurs in school is part of a broader social context.

We will focus on three essential factors of life in the classroom, of the student's program and of the teacher's practice in a coeducational context:

---

1   For a synthetic presentation of works in French, see Duru-Bellat (1994), Harlen (1985), Terlon (1985); in English there are many more references (a possible starting point: Kelly, 1987). This article is based mainly on the English-language works.

- the recommended curriculum and its implementation (i.e. the program and the pedagogical resources available), which ranges from relatively formal aspects such as the organization of the system, the programs and the content of the manuals to other more informal ones such as the implicit concepts of teachers and the organization of work in the classroom (more or less directive practices, grouping of students, etc.)

- the actual curriculum followed in the class (i.e. what the students actually experience throughout their school years), through student–teacher interaction (including during evaluations) and interaction between students, with at the core a real 'hidden curriculum' (i.e. what a student actually learns (behavior, information, attitudes, etc.) which goes beyond what is explicitly experienced in the actual curriculum;

- the attitudes toward school work and orientation, the latter to some extent sanctioning the program, although it also reflects an anticipation of the future than extends far beyond the framework of the school.

This last point leads us to conclude by underlining to what a great extent these differences between the sexes, though largely built at school, fit into the framework of the sexual division of labor that is characteristic of a given society.

(1) IMPLEMENTATION OF RECOMMENDED CURRICULUM
(a) Organization of School System and Classes

Students attend school in an institutional context that often seems logical and forms a sort of neutral background. However, international comparisons reveal that success rates and especially orientation can vary considerably between the sexes, depending on how the system is organized. One essential institutional parameter here is *the moment when the first choices are made*, when students can opt out of the study of certain subjects, for instance. The sooner they can choose, the more often girls jump at the chance to drop sciences. In Great Britain, in schools where one common program until age 16 is being experimented, the percentage of girls opting to continue physics in secondary school rose from 10% to 40%, with many of these girls stating that they would have dropped physics as of age 15 if they had been given the choice, as under the former system (Kelly, 1987).

Among institutional factors, *the coeducational or non-coeducational character of classes* in secondary school was the subject of much research. One preliminary point is to find out whether girls and boys obtain *different results* according to whether they attend coed or non-coed classes. During the period 1960–70, English research (summarized in the work by Marsh, 1989) tended to conclude that the academic effects of coeducation were rather positive for boys, without proving negative for girls. As the 1980s, a certain number of works or official reports informed the public of poorer test results in fields such as mathematics or physics among girls attending coed schools (Arnot, 1983; Burgess, 1990; Faulkner, 1991). Nevertheless, taking into account that these two types of schools are attended by students of different social standing and dissimilar scholastic levels (to the advantage of non-coed schools), some studies, such as that of Marsh (1989) in Australia, concluded there was almost no stable, significant inequality in performance.

Social changes could shed new light on this controversial question; one example is the Berlin experiment of a return to a non-coeducational system (Salomon, 1992) which led to a drop in grades among boys due to a degeneration in discipline. Another experiment was carried out for mathematics, consisting of following the progress of girls with a comparable initial level who attended either non-coed classes or coed classes; at the end of a two-year period, the girls' performance in non-coed classes was clearly better than that of the girls in coed classes.

Attitudes are also sensitive to context. Whether for scholastic preferences and options chosen or for images of the fields, youths of both sexes aged 13 to 15 were more conformist in coed schools than in non-coed schools compared with traditional gender-based stereotypes (Lawrie and Brown, 1992; Stables, 1990). When they attend separate schools, boys say they are more attracted to languages, biology and theater and girls to physics and technology. Behind these attitudes lie differences in the students' feelings about their own abilities. Girls tend to underestimate themselves in so-called masculine fields when in the presence of boys; conversely, they emphasize their literary aptitudes in coed contexts (Marsh, 1989). Lower self-esteem is also noted among girls in coed schools than among those in non-coed schools (Faulkner, 1991). This very stable observation of attitudes that are globally more stereotyped in coed schools is found on a more general level in the place the two sexes hold in society. Both girls and boys in coed schools are more favorable to girls investing heavily in their education or in their profession and they have a less traditional opinion of woman's place in society (Faulkner, 1991).

A school's organization can also exert influence by other means, for instance as a function of the way in which students are grouped together for teaching activities. When proficiency levels are grouped to study mathematics in secondary schools, girls with good grades tend to be assigned to the better groups less often than their male counterparts (Hallinan and Sorensen, 1987). This poses a problem, in that research in general points out that more progress tends to be made in the better groups (and less in the slower groups), in which case this means there is an organizational mechanism that is partially responsible for the difference between the sexes.

(b) Curricula and Manuals that Reflect Science
Curricula, manuals and exercises are also capable of causing girls specific problems. Today's manuals which reflect the programs are characterized, especially in the sciences, by an almost total absence of women and/or by their concentration in stereotyped roles (especially a decorative or maternal mission; Moreau, 1994). Although in mathematics women are very present in school books at the kindergarten level (though often in a stereotyped form; Bailey, 1988), given that mathematical activities are generally included in play activities, they later disappear little by little, at the time when boys and girls play very different roles. Girls are less absorbed by problem solving, less competitive, less open with their classmates, but they practice, cooperate, correct... Is there, as Northam underlined in 1987, really 'a parallel between girls' declining investment in mathematics between ages 7 and 16 and the progressive disappearance of girls from math books over the same period?'

An analysis of physics manuals leads to even more unmistakable conclusions. Women appear in certain highly stereotyped roles only and grow increasingly rare as students become older. In secondary education there are two to ten times more men (or boys) than women to serve as examples (Kelly, 1985). Furthermore, surveys of youths have revealed that physics programs accentuate fields traditionally considered to be masculine (mechanics, electricity, magnetism, matter), although putting more emphasis on other fields of physics, such as nuclear physics and radiation or meteorological phenomena and the application of physics to medical or artistic fields, would arouse more interest among girls (Desplats, 1989). Overall, it is clear that, at present, sciences such as physics or mathematics are nearer to the 'cultural heritage' of boys than of girls. After all, don't adolescents themselves describe mathematics using nouns such as logic, abstraction, rigor, research, reasoning, demonstration, etc. (Baudelot, 1991), nouns with a masculine connotation?

Generally speaking, the *dominant representation of sciences* reflects 'an image that includes faultless rationality, common utilitarianism, an obsession with the object to the detriment of the relationship, an exclusion of sensitivity' (Dhavernas, 1992), paradoxical traits, given the traditional cultural identity of women, which accentuates relations with others, imagination, affection, etc. Some British researchers even propose a pedagogy that encourages a feminine vision of science (Bentley and Watts, 1987), affirms the priority of life over economics, underlines the ethical implications of scientific work, gives emotions and subjectivity a role to play alongside intellectual reasoning, etc. Although the attitude toward these questions is not unanimous, these problematics underline the fact that, instead of implicitly considering that girls are 'missing something' in order to succeed in science, it would be wiser to question the socially constructed character of scientific programs (and science itself),[2] drawn up by men and adapted to the interests of boys, even though this is not an unwritten law.

Working from this theory, we can analyze how a 'young' subject such as computer science was constructed as a masculine school subject.[3] If it now appears to be a masculine field, where success helps build a boy's sexual identity. (Culley, 1988; Elkjaer, 1992; Nelson and Watson, 1991), isn't it because it was usually taught by men, who preferred certain types of applications and made reference to uses by professionals generally of the male sex (thus manuals where women are totally absent), against a backdrop of computer games (video games) that are mostly masculine?

Regardless, in daily classroom life, the *content of the exercises* proposed to students is often more in line with boys' interests. Especially as teachers try to get the attention of potentially disruptive students, while they accept that disinterested girls chat or daydream as long as

---

2   It should be noted that women's participation in drawing up scientific information is highly underestimated (Alic, 1986; Peiffer and Dahan, 1982; Phillips, 1985).

3   On this point, see the chapter by C. Terlon in this volume.

they don't disrupt the class (Scott, 1980). This is especially true in the sciences, and it has an effect on success rates. When upper secondary school students are given identical arithmetic problems involving bags of cement or recipe ingredients, the girls' performance is significantly higher in the second case (Leder, 1974). This improved success rate may demonstrate a stronger motivation among students to 'tackle' the problem posed, but it seems that girls truly find it easier to apply proportional logic when they are working with familiar subjects (reductions granted in stores, for example). Thus content does influence the quality of intellectual activity (Linn, 1983). Likewise in CE2 (third year of French primary school), girls are more successful at French language subtests[4] that concern subjects such as health or family life, while boys are more at ease with restoring the chronological order of an automobile race (Baudelot and Establet, 1991). The authors conclude that it is difficult to 'build exercises that measure the verbal skills of students independently of gender-based culture'.

Does this mean that tests are biased? We can speak of *bias* when for example an exercise obviously refers to knowledge or know-how that is unequally assimilated by girl and boy students, so that it is hard to measure the comprehension of a given concept or actual ability. The fact that in natural sciences girls succeed less when tests involve the use of microscopes probably reflects boys' ease in using apparatus in general (Murphy, 1991). Nonetheless, teaching is aimed at students with a past, and the accumulation of different life experiences and expectations can produce real inequality in success rates that reflects actual difficulty in mastering concepts. For example, we know that in physics the mastery of the most abstract concepts is related to the practical mastery of these concept in daily experience (Räsänen, 1992). Consequently, it is hard to decide, based on the results of school tests or examinations, whether we can talk of artifacts that must be corrected by changing the form or content of the exercise, or whether it is a case of real cognitive inequality that can only be attenuated by attacking the underlying processes. Often this choice (or the fact of merely raising this question) is based on stereotyped expectations. We focus on the content if girls do less well in a French test, but less so if they fail a science test...

---

4   Elementary exercise included in a test; test of knowledge.

BOX 1: IMPLEMENTATION OF
PROGRAMS AND USE OF MANUALS

A few questions to ask:

- When I decide to elaborate on an example... Do I make sure that it is also attractive to all the students in the class, i.e. for girls as well as boys, but also for students living in the city and the country, according to their social class, etc.? If necessary, can I broaden the subject so that all the students feels involved? Do I try to explain the relationship between studying sciences and their practical applications?

- When I evaluate student performance... Do I make sure that neither boys nor girls have any advantage as regards a given exercise or test method (due to their extracurricular experiences (games and knowledge acquired outside school)? If I note any systematic differences in success rates, how do I try to interpret them?

- When I write up or choose a text or choose a manual... In what role are the men and women, boys and girls presented, and what image of their future does it project? Are they confined to certain activities and/or behavior and personality traits? Or do I see that as many frightened, gentle boys are represented as ambitious, sporty girls? In the presentation (or illustrations) of exercises, am I able to vary the wording, or is it always 'Pierre's bike', 'Mother goes shopping'? For all these questions use the manual analysis grids presented in Valabrègue (1985) and Moreau (1994).

Examples taken from a 6è mathematics manual (first year of lower secondary school)

Pierre ran the 100-meter race in 14.5 seconds. What is his average speed in km/hr rounded off to the nearest unit?
25 km/hr

Luc swam 50 meters in 17 seconds. What is his average speed in m/sec rounded off to the nearest unit?
3 m/sec

If you pay cash in a supermarket, what coin do you round off to?
5 cents

In a supermarket, Claire buys 2 jars of jelly at 8.75 francs each, a chicken at 32.14 francs and a steak at 12.92 francs. How much does she pay?
62.55 francs

Examples taken from a 2de mathematics manual (first year of upper secondary school)

> In a particular city, 85 out of 100 men are married, 70 have a telephone, 75 own a car and 80 own a house. Out of 100 men, what is the minimum number of men who are married and have a phone, a car and a house?

> A father spends one-third of his salary on housing and various taxes, two-thirds of the remainder on food, half of the remainder on recreation and clothing, and saves the rest, i.e. 1000 francs. What is his salary?

Old problems taken from a 1942 arithmetic manual by Hachette. Reproduced in a 2de manual.

> (1) A housewife in a city has the bad habit of turning on the gas before lighting the match to ignite the burner. So each time the gas is turned on, supplied at a rate of 900 liters per hour, gas flows for 15 seconds for nothing. She only puts the pot on the burner to heat once the burner is lit, which means another 15 seconds wasted. As this bad habit occurs six times a day, calculate the volume of gas wasted each year, and its price at 2.10 francs per cubic meter.

> (2) The peels of 3 kilograms of potatoes are weighed. The result is 0.250 kg when Mother peels the potatoes and 0.375 kg when her daughter peels them. Potatoes sell at 250 francs per 100 kilograms and the family eats 450 kilograms of potatoes per year. Calculate the loss per year:

> 1. in weight of potatoes;

> 2. in money if all the potatoes are peeled by the daughter.

If the content of curricula and evaluations are decisive as concerns the scope of the difference in success rates between the sexes, we would expect the pedagogical *choices of the teachers* to be decisive too. There are still few studies regarding this vital question of the effect of pedagogy. Nevertheless, it appears that certain practices tend to accentuate the inequality between boys and girls, if only because they give students of both sexes the freedom to participate actively, which they do to an unequal extent. In arithmetic (and as of primary school: this study concerns children in the 4th year), when differences between the sexes are usually very limited or non-existent, girls succeed more (and boys slightly less) when teachers encourage cooperation between students than when the encourage competition (Peterson and Fennema, 1985) Inversely, girls' attitudes toward mathematics are more positive in classes where there is a higher percentage of private exchanges between teacher and student than in those with voluntary public exchanges (Eccles and Blumenfield, 1985). The same phenomenon occurs when teachers give more time for individual work, walking up and down the aisles, available for contact, than when they give priority to collective work with long question-and-answer periods (Tobin, 1988).

Finally, students in the classroom are confronted with a *teaching staff* whose disciplinary and hierarchical structure is highly gender-based, all of which sends out a message on the division of labor between men and women. In French secondary schools, women make up half the math teachers and 43.5% of the physics teachers, but less than 5% in mechanical engineering and electricity and over 72% in literature or languages. What may be even more important, and in any case more insidious, is the way in which teachers' personal ideas appear in their pedagogical interaction with students of both sexes. Like all social beings, teachers share current ideas about what is masculine and feminine with their milieu. Therefore they tend to see certain behavior as being natural. Where a certain amount of agitation is considered acceptable among boys, it is particularly upsetting when girls dare to stand up to a teacher (Mosconi, 1989; Robinson, 1992), against a back-drop of pedagogical 'double standards'. Likewise, teachers tend to share the prevailing stereotypes concerning the sexual connotations of subjects, which has an effect on daily interaction in the classroom, a point we are going to study below.

(2) TEACHERS' EXPECTATIONS AND RELATIONS IN THE CLASSROOM: INTERACTION BETWEEN STUDENTS

(a) Student–Teacher Interaction and Evaluation Practices

All classroom observations revealed that teachers in science subjects unconsciously *interact far more* with boy students, whether in contacts initiated by the teacher or in response to the spontaneous intervention (more widespread) of the boys[5] What's more the teacher gives them far more encouragement, and these differences in treatment increase with

---

5   See the analysis of a mathematics class presented by J. Loudet-Verdier and N. Mosconi in this book.

the age of the students. A survey of a high school (2nd cycle of secondary school) geometry class showed that girls received 30% of encouraging remarks and 84% of discouraging remarks, while 70% of 'persistent interaction' concerned boys, who were also the only ones involved in contacts lasting over five minutes (Kimball, 1989). The same trends for physics classes (Crossman, 1987), where there are 50% more verbal exchanges between teachers and boys, three times more criticism aimed at boys and more simple questions addressed to girls.

In particular, it appears that teachers spend more time encouraging boys to complete an incomplete answer or to try to find the right answer, giving them a hint. An in-depth study of how long a teacher waits after a question reveals that boy students are left more time. This is all the more important when you consider that this time affects the quality of the students' answers (Gore and Roumagoux, 1983). These studies of response time are inconclusive, however, and are not found at all school levels (Leder, 1990).

On the other hand, it is admitted that these differences in contacts between teacher and student, depending on their sex, are more marked for good students. Again in mathematics, interaction is far more intense and encouraging for 'good students' if they are boys than if they are girls, which affects the students' confidence in their capabilities (Parsons et al. 1982). As of adolescence, the self-evaluations in mathematics among girls with good grades are not linked with their scholastic level; their confidence in their own capabilities is systematically lower than among boys of a similar level. These 'good' girls are also more sensitive to criticism and start to think that studying mathematics is less important and less useful to them than to boys (Eccles and Blumenfeld, 1985). Other observations show that girls respond when they are questioned, but do not try to answer a question that is not specifically directed at them. And yet students probably learn more from thinking up an answer themselves than from listening to someone else's answer.

Overall, these studies show that, for the same curriculum, boys and girls don't receive exactly the same education, both as concerns quality (as different messages are sent out to them) and as concerns quantity (as pedagogical contacts are more limited). American researchers (Eccles and Jacobs, 1986) calculated that, given the additional time their math teacher spends with them, boys receive 36 more hours of class time than girls between primary school and the end of the second year in lower secondary school.

Lying behind these differences in pedagogical behavior stand the so-called *'expectation effects'* of the teachers. Surveys (mostly English-language) carried out among teachers show that they tend to doubt the abilities of girls as regards sciences and attribute the good grades they get in these courses to their hard work alone. It should also be noted that, according to British studies (some dating back to 1985), secondary school teachers tend to believe that science courses are more important for the general education of boys than for that of girls (Spear, 1987).

Teachers' latent convictions are reflected in the evaluations they draw up. Physics teachers tend to be more tolerant of poor work submitted by girls than by boys (as if, given their sex, girls were 'excused' for not succeeding), while they are more severe with good work submitted by girls, which is probably viewed unconsciously as being 'abnormal' (Desplats, 1989). The same holds true for evaluations. The same assignment, if it is thought to have been submitted by a girl, is judged more favorably for being neat, yet it is praised for its discipline, the richness of its ideas, its scientific correctness and its concision if it is thought to have been submitted by a boy (Spear, 1984). Among students, girls' lack of confidence in their scientific skills explains why they tend to succeed less on standardized tests than on exercises proposed in class. Standardized tests put students in less familiar situations than classroom exercises, are more competitive and require an answer; girls often answer 'I don't know', not hesitating to admit their uncertainty, while boys tend more to 'take a stab' (Kimball, 1989; Linn and Peterson, 1986).

All these observations are valid for both male and female teachers (Dunkin, 1985; Brophy, 1985). This may appear surprising, but teachers of both sexes are part of an implicit global ideological context where certain courses are seen as being 'masculine' or 'feminine' and where the rule, also implicit, tends to give boys a greater value. Going against this rule makes them feel guilty as regards another rule, that of pedagogical neutrality. Proof of this can be found in certain observations made in primary school (Spender, 1982; Whyte, 1984) concerning teachers who tried to correct the imbalance noted by an outside observer, i.e. although the women teachers thought they were being equitable, they actually spent two-thirds of their time with the boys. Those who took this the farthest spent 45% of their time with girls (instead of one-third) yet felt guilty and thought they were showing favoritism. Consequently, the rule of neutrality actually consisted of giving boys priority. And yet the boys in these classes reacted to this 'compensatory' pedagogy by being more agitated and trying to catch and keep the teacher's attention. This is another reason for asymmetric classes, whether the teacher is a man or a woman: the boys have to be 'kept in line' because they demand more attention and have more difficulty adapting to school rules.

Are the differences in the teachers' behavior also *reactions against the students' behavior*, both boys and girls? True, boys are more often the instigators of interaction with the teacher, especially in science classes (Morse and Handley, 1985). This trend grows with age, leading teachers to respond, especially as boys know how to be persistent. In lower secondary school, boys are eight times more susceptible to intervene in an insistent fashion, to speak out or get the teacher's attention (Sadker and Sadker, 1985). To achieve this end, they also know how to use specific strategies (original intervention for example: cf French, 1984).

Globally speaking, certain researchers conclude that the differences in treatment observed among teachers are almost entirely the reflection of differences in the behavior of the students (Brophy, 1985), while others point out that the interaction initiated by teachers is no more equitably distributed between the two sexes than that initiated by the students (Kelly, 1988). Regardless, the dynamics are triggered in the class, between the students – who, through their previous socialization, act in different ways – and the teachers – who, by their reactions, tend to amplify these differences. Thus, when boys cause teachers more disciplinary problems as of kindergarten, the teachers end up paying more attention to them (Morgan and Dunn, 1990), and even becoming more attached to them (Stanworth, 1983). Because girls have a more positive attitude toward school work, they are particularly criticized for their intellectual performance (Dweck *et al.* 1978), given that they cannot be reproached for a lack of diligence. Finally, due to their discretion in the classroom, they are interrogated less, thus giving them less of an opportunity to show that they have something to say and accentuating the idea that it is normal for boys to dominate interaction (Mosconi, 1989; Stanworth, 1982; Scott, 1980).

(b) Interaction Among Students

In a perfectly convergent fashion, *daily relations between boys and girls* in the classroom are another source of reinforcement for gender-based stereotypes. Students, like teachers, find it normal for boys to dominate and girls to take a back seat, for instance when using a microcomputer or carrying out electrical wiring. But supervising the use of equipment more strictly, or providing sufficient material to let everyone participate, thus eliminating the fight for the material which boys win, could minimize the differences in participation in this type of scientific activity (Tobin, 1988).

These daily experiences encourage the progressive emergence among youths of the cognitive categorization[6] of courses or occupations – as well as of one's self or of others – and of daily interactions that are tempered as a result. 'Physics is for boys, so I can't be a girl and do well or compete with boys in this area...' Not only are mathematics perceived as a masculine subject, but they are also the spearhead of scholastic competition in a more general context where femininity implies, among other things, giving up individual competition. If succeeding in this subject is part of the normal behavior expected of boys, we could expect girls to excel more in subjects that are less 'cold', less logical. Consequently, we can infer that girls' reticence to go into the scientific streams is as much a refusal of this stiff competition (for jobs that are highly competitive) as it is a fundamental lack of interest in these subjects.

For what is at stake is becoming and remaining feminine (especially in the eyes of male classmates), which may require adolescent girls to make sacrifices or behave in a very specific way. Meticulous classroom observation demonstrates clearly that apprehension of dissection or an experiment, the refusal to get dirty or protect hair during hands-on lessons, and even some obvious clumsiness are all behavior used by adolescent girls to underline their femininity (Measor, 1983). These psycho-social phenomena help us understand why girls succeed more in mathematics in non-coed schools, where they can exist as individuals and not, first and foremost, as members of a sexually-defined group,[7] for it is especially in coed classes that they fear being rejected as 'not feminine' if they excel in this subject. This holds true for other scientific courses, especially computer science. A recent study (Lage, 1991) states that among girls the passion for computers is associated with negative characteristics (the intellectual totally engrossed by her studies, a lonely

---

6   The idea of any perception or apprehension of reality presupposes interpretation grids that necessarily 'simplify' the situation.

7   The fact that teachers tend to exploit girl–boy opposition in managing their classes is also a factor; a coed context leads them to mobilize the sex stereotypes, whether consciously or not.

wallflower of a girl who seeks refuge in her microcomputer), which is not at all the case among boys. This study also points out that this opposition between the passion for computers and the feminine model doesn't exist at the primary school level, where young enthusiasts of both sexes are perceived positively (as well-rounded, lively young people full of curiosity), even if other studies (Nelson and Watson, 1991) find that at this age boys are encouraged more than girls to play this type of game at home with their father.

Overall, it is striking to note how much the intellectual interests viewed as positive in girls of 10 become incongruous and perceived as paradoxical as regards the feminine identity as of adolescence. A similar trend is observed in countries as diverse as Canada and China. Adolescents in these countries see their interests change over a period of just a few years, girls becoming less positive in mathematics, science and computers and more positive in the written word (Collis and Williams, 1987).

It is, therefore, easy to understand the fear of isolation displayed by girls who continue in this type of interest. Many observations reveal that girls who try to take an interest in subjects considered to be masculine are frequently rejected by their male friends, except if they have other attributes considered to be masculine, such as being good in sports (Archer and Macrae, 1991). Likewise, some girls whose poles of interest are scientific complain they never find girlfriends with whom they can exchange their ideas on these subjects which fascinate them (Lage, 1993). Consequently, it is not surprising to discover, as this study did, that there are so few girls in science clubs. Similar observations are made in the USA, where extracurricular activities (especially math games or chess clubs) capable of proving helpful in succeeding in sciences largely remain, among adolescents, the prerogative of boys (Linn and Petersen, 1986).

Thus it is a multitude of processes, day by day, that build sciences up to be something masculine (Kelly, 1985), and some studies would lead us to believe that all these phenomena explain less the relative non-success of girls in mathematics than their lack of persistence in this subject; in other words, they tend not to continue as soon as they encounter difficulties. This point is probably a central one in education systems such as the French system, where orientation (i.e. the 'management' of their career by students and their families) plays an essential role. (We will come back to the fundamental distinction between success and orientation in the determination of the scholastic path.)

BOX 2: INTERACTION IN MY CLASS

- Where do the students sit in the classroom (and how do I react)? Who sits in front or in back, and does that affect my opinion of them or the attention I pay to them?

- Do I know the names of all the students, and if not whose do I know? What do I call them (first name, Miss, Mr…)?

- How do I go about letting students participate: wait until they raise their hand (and what are my selection criteria if there are several hands raised), call upon them directly,…?

- Do I ask different questions depending on the student (good/poor students, girls/boys…)? Do I encourage them to respond? How much time do I give them? What do I do if they don't say anything? etc.

To answer these questions, nothing is better than a grid you can fill in yourself or have filled in by a trainee or a colleague (cf example below).

- When I have students work in small groups, how are these groups composed? I let them do it and the groups end up non-coed or coed. I intervene to impose a balanced gender mix or I put girls and boys in competition. What affect do these differences have on the group's work? Who leads the group? Who takes notes? Who helps others? etc.

- When I have them work with equipment, do I see that all the students have access (especially girls)?

- When I assign students to little jobs (straightening up, various responsibilities), do I tend to address my requests to boys or girls depending on the type of job?

Example of grid designed and tested by a group of math teachers ('Girls and Math' research action, Academy of Dijon).

		Girls	Boys
1. Work at the blackboard	Volunteer chosen by the teacher		
	Student who goes to the blackboard without being designated by the teacher		
	Non-volunteer designated by the teacher		

2. Simultaneous response of several students	Repetition by the teacher of a response from…		
3. Calling upon a student who didn't volunteer			
4. Absence of any response in the class	Calling upon a student		
5. Speaking up spontaneously	To propose a solution		
	To say he/she didn't understand		
	To ask for more explanation		
	To ask what the point is		
	Other		

ATTITUDES AND ORIENTATATIONS

(a) Self-Selection and its Roots

The orientation choices of youths differ considerably according to their sex; the figures we have seen show this clearly. What is noteworthy is that it is the result of choices made by the students themselves and not the reflection of obvious differences in academic success. Several recent studies on orientation into 1e S class[8] demonstrate this (Duru-Bellat *et al.* 1993; Marro, 1995). Male and female students in the general 2de class end the year with comparable scholastic levels (with even an advantage to girls, including in sciences). For a girl to request this orientation, she must have higher grades in mathematics than boys. Consequently, of students who feel they are average (and they are numerous by defini-

---

8   In the French system, the 1e S year is the section that prepares students for scientific baccalaureates specializing either in mathematics and physics (series C) or in the experimental sciences (series D), series C being the most prestigious. As of 1995 a new range of baccalaureates will be implemented, the objective being to attenuate the domination of the former series C. (Translator's note: The preceding year of general studies is called 2de.)

tion) or who are judged to be so by their teachers, boys envisage 1e S more often than girls.

Therefore, as this is mainly a self-selection, it is vital to understand the logic behind these choices. We will follow two trails: that of 'attitudes' (the reflection of past and present life experiences) and of 'anticipation of adult, professional and family life'.

The most immediate (but probably the most superficial) of these attitudes comes from studying *differences in interest* in mathematics between the sexes, and especially in technology and physics. In France, they are visible as of the start of secondary school (Servant, 1990), even though differences in success rates haven't arisen as yet. Asked what their favorite class was ('even if they're not very good in it'), students in 5e (second year of secondary school) named mathematics second (after physical education) if they were boys, but put it in fourth position if they were girls (after modern languages, French and physical education). Very clear differences of interest in technology were also observed (Terlon, 1990); not only were boys aged 14 far more interested in this subject than girls of the same age, but more of them thought it would be useful socially. As we will see, this difference obviously ties in with the professional projects of both boys and girls, with boys tending to overestimate the importance of sciences in the professions they envisage while the opposite is true of girls (Kelly, 1981). What's more, failure in mathematics, which leads upper secondary school students to see themselves as weak or even hopeless in this subject, doesn't keep many boys from saying they like it 'all the same', as if they had interiorized the social advantage that mathematics represents for them. As Baudelot notes (1991), 'You've got to like mathematics, my son, even if you don't understand it!'

As of age 11 or 12, boys tend to associate subjects deemed 'feminine' with boring subjects, their opinion of subjects being structured chiefly by this 'interesting/boring' dimension. This is not true among girls, who structure their opinions of subjects according to a 'hard or complicated/simple or easy' axis; subjects deemed masculine are also those they feel are hard or complicated (Archer and Macrae, 1991). So it is easy to understand why a few years later more boys choose to study sciences, even if they feel they are difficult, while girls tend to choose subjects they feel are easy (Ormerod, 1981).

Nevertheless, it appears that the stereotyped character of preferences for subjects is declining. One British study (Archer and Macrae, 1991) reveals that among youths aged 11–12 mathematics are now (almost) perceived as a subject as suitable for girls as boys, which wasn't the case in studies carried out ten years previously. Biology or the first foreign language have a less feminine connotation. Still there are subjects with a highly masculine connotation, such as technology, computer science and (to a lesser extent and in spite of a clear evolution toward more 'neutrality') physics. Typing and home economics remain perceived as feminine subjects.

On a more fundamental level, major differences in the *confidence* with which boys and girls confront this subject are constantly observed. Not only are boys less numerous than girls in saying that mathematics and physics are difficult, but they say they are prepared to 'knuckle down' more often, and are more confident in their potential. Girls, on the other hand, doubt their abilities in this area, and are more numerous in believing that you have to have a 'knack' for math, that is that their inability is innate and thus irremediable. Consequently, if we ask upper secondary school students if they feel they are 'gifted' in mathematics (cf the study by the Femmes et Mathématiques (Woman and Mathematics) Association in 1987–88), 28% of boys reply that they feel they are 'not very gifted' (72% feel they are fairly or very gifted) compared with 62% of girls (only 38% feel they are fairly or very gifted). However, when girls succeed in math, they explain this success primarily by their hard work, comparing themselves implicitly with boys whom they feel succeed with less effort and are therefore more 'naturals' (Kimball, 1989). Consequently, there are differences in attitudes between the sexes as of adolescence and these differences create a higher level of anxiety among girls even if their grades are identical (Tocci and Engelhard, 1991).

This evaluation is the underlying reason for the less autonomous, less persevering behavior of girls in mathematics (Fennema and Peterson, 1985). It would appear that, in order to succeed in this subject (especially in some of the fields where following the rules learned is not sufficient), it is necessary to have learned how to undertake highly cognitive tasks and to work autonomously until the problem posed has been solved. The fact that girls are encouraged more toward dependent behavior (which can be seen in the classroom by their often seeking the teacher's approval and tending to apply the algorithms he or she recommends), and that they have low self-confidence or tend to see mathematics as being less useful, are all factors that affect their success through less autonomous learning behavior in this field. Also involved is their conception of math skills as being more innate, as mentioned above. If girls feel that success in mathematics comes from being gifted, they tend to feel that gifted students will find the right answers right away without effort, and therefore if they have to search for the answer it proves they are not gifted. Thus, here again, less tenacious behavior that bears up poorly under the stressful search for the solution.

Other studies focused on the reactions of students when confronted with tasks that require the assimilation of new concepts or new operations (Licht and Dweck, 1984). In such situations, two opposing attitudes are observed: an attitude oriented toward mastering the task (with intensified effort and concentration, increased stimulation that can lead to improved performance) and an attitude of dependence and defeat (with demotivation and poorer performance). These two types of attitude depend heavily on the way in which adolescents have learned to explain their behavior. Those who tend to attribute their failure to their lack of effort are stimulated by difficulty, and are usually boys. Thus researchers draw a connection between the more defeatist attitudes of girls and their difficulties (at the higher levels of the school system) in subjects where new concepts and disconcerting, radically new situations are frequent (which is the case for mathematics, unlike literature where progress is more constant).

As we have seen, teachers themselves tend to react differently to the behavior of their male and female students. Their expectations concord with those of the parents, whose attitudes reflect the stereotyped vision of the potential of the two sexes. American studies show that, for an identical level of performance, the parents of girls (more often than the parents of boys) feel that girls' success is due to their hard work and that mathematics are hard for them. Logically, they expect less in this subject (Kimball, 1989). These parental attitudes are more responsible than the student's grades for the student's anxiety about mathematics.

Overall, these attitudes seem to play a decisive role. A modelized study (Eccles and Jacobs, 1986) represented in figures the specific influence the attitudes of the students and of their parents had on success in mathematics and the choice of a 'mathematized' stream. It showed that, in reality, the previous level in mathematics doesn't act directly on the orientation followed, but only indirectly, as it affects the attitudes of the parents (confidence in their child's potential) and those of the student (confidence in his/her own potential and the feeling that mathematics are useful). It should be noted that this study found that the impact of stereotyped parental attitudes was stronger than that of the teachers' attitudes. The specific influence of these attitudes is more marked in girls than in boys. In other words, more than the initial level of performance, it is the interpretation of this performance by the students and their families which is essential, and heavily marked by gender-based stereotypes.

(b) Anticipating the Future

Along with the image of subjects, there are also representations of professions that are 'suitable' for a man or a woman. It is clear that success in a subject is in some way linked with one's evaluation of chances for success as well as with its future usefulness and profitability in the professional and personal world envisaged. The fact that young women doubt that sciences will be useful in their adult life probably explains why they are less determined to invest in that subject.

As concerns the scientific or technical professions, the *absence of an attractive model* undeniably plays a role. According to the latest French census, of the 20 professions most often entered by women (and which employ 45% of women and 7% of men), none requires technological know-how. Why should girls 'knuckle down' in scientific subjects when the professions they offer access to are only sparsely populated by women? Some studies suggest that having had one or more women math or science teachers during the school years has an effect on university orientation into these branches (Boli *et al.* 1985). These models illustrate that you can be a 'normal' woman and work in a scientific field, a fact that many girl students still doubt.

What's more, girls who hesitate to choose one of the so-called masculine trades are probably aware of the difficulties awaiting them on the *labor market*: difficulties as of the first job, because holding a 'masculine' degree does not eliminate obstacles (far from it);[9] difficulty in keeping a job in a context where the recognition of true ability (for a woman in 'masculine' specializations) remains uncertain.

Generally speaking, young girls are also influenced by *anticipation of adult social roles*, although perhaps not always consciously. It is as if

---

9   According to a recent French survey by the Conférence des Grandes Ecoles, the depressed job market for young engineers affects women first. In 1993 the percentage of engineers with a fixed-duration contract was 28% for men and 39% for women. (The figures were 12% and 17% respectively in 1991.) The recent statistics (summarized in the July 1994 edition of *Le Monde de l'Education*) confirm these difficulties encountered by young women graduates.

girls choose between prestigious but demanding careers (high-level careers that often require mathematics) and compromises in the form of more modest, so-called feminine professions, where part-time employment is possible and work conditions are flexible. This is demonstrated in a recent French survey of students in 2de (Baudelot and Establet, 1991) regarding the criteria for choosing a profession. Free time is given priority by 72% of girls (ranked first or second) and by 11% of boys (who give priority to money, compared with only 49% of girls).

This anticipation of a 'need for free time' specific to women is strikingly realistic. All studies show that the factor that affects women's professional life most is not the nature or value of their scholastic record, but rather their family situation. The actual operation of the family (as defined by 'time budgeting') makes it hard to juggle a strong professional investment with a good family life. Thus it is easy to understand that what appears to be less ambition, a conservative mentality or even fatalism is in fact girls 'choosing' fields where it is easier to 'strike a balance'. If all women were engineers instead of saleswomen or secretaries, the daily life of many families would be endangered! Consequently girls adapt in a reasonable way to their probable future.

BOX 3: WORKING WITH YOUNG PEOPLE ON THEIR PROJECTS

- When a student tells me he/she made a certain choice because he/she is 'motivated': We discuss this motivated choice. (Is he/she seeing it realistically?) I take the time to go over the alternatives he/she eliminated because he/she felt they were too demanding, too distant, too expensive, etc. Is all his/her information on these criteria correct and accurate? Is there any way to get around these difficulties?

- If he/she feels a certain stream is too difficult: Who is he/she comparing himself/herself with? Has he/she thought about what 'price' he/she will have to pay for eliminating this possibility? What are the consequences of taking only minimal mathematics or physics as of upper secondary school? Can he/she cite examples of situations (or professions) where mathematics or sciences are very useful/not useful at all?

- If he/she says that 'it's not for him/her': Isn't he/she afraid of being 'too original' and consequently isolated (to be covered with questions such as 'Have you ever felt you had to hide the fact that you're good in math, and if so why?') Help him/her see that if there is a price to pay for nonconformity, it may also offer advantages... Or has the student thought about a possible future conciliation with family life, and if so will his/her life reproduce what he/she sees around him/her every day? Isn't there a way to make the girlfriend/boyfriend evolve? etc.

These questions can be asked in private or in a group (coed or not). Group sessions can work with 'tools' as shown in the example below (work in Nevers, France, with students in the third year of secondary school), and from the text of Aebischer and Valabrègue in this book.

1. Photobook

No preparation is required. Ten photographs are laid out on a table. Tools used: *Photo-méthode* photobook by Editions du Châtelet and *Plurielles* photobook by CREA, University of Rennes II. Explanations concerning the session: 'I am a guidance counselor and psychologist. We at the C.I.O. are working on how young people see the future. We have come here with your teacher to talk with you and we're going to propose an exercise.' (If the specific goal isn't announced, it's so as not to influence the students.) Instructions: 'Choose the photograph on the table that best represents the life you hope to have later.' (These instructions can be repeated, but not expanded upon. It is possible to add, 'The idea you have of your future'.)

2. Collage

The classes selected for the collage are those for which the chief teacher is part of the sector group. Instructions: One or two weeks before the session the teacher explains, 'We are going to work on how you see your future. For this, I suggest you make a collage that best represents the life you hope to live later on. You can use photographs cut out of magazines, drawings, anything you want, and glue them on a sheet of paper.'

Regardless of what technique is used, the supervisors change, and we set down strict rules to prevent the results from being influenced. During the sessions, the supervisors were asked to stick to the formula defined and ask, 'Can you tell me a bit more?' or 'Would you like to add anything?' The sessions were carried out in the same general way for both techniques used. Each student was given a chance to express him/herself. Once everyone had had a turn, the supervisor summarized what he/she had heard, made remarks and broadened the debate.

An in-depth analysis of child-raising practices in families (especially parental ideas) reveals ambivalent elements. There is both a resolute affirmation of equality between the sexes[10] and the continuation of child-raising practices that differ subtly as of a very early age, with, as we have seen above, boys more frequently encouraged to explore space actively. Parents also seem to have certain profound convictions that could make it hard to bring about this ideal of equality. Therefore women remain basically responsible for raising the children and their professional investment continues to take a back seat to this parental, domestic role.

These implicit contradictions do not escape girls' attention, and in a very crucial way as of adolescence. On the one hand, schools demand more and more work of them, along with an autonomous personal investment. On the other hand, family models (not to mention the media) invite them to invest in relationships with others, to find fulfillment in love, and to put their career on the back burner, as it must never get in the way of their primary role within the family. Perhaps the fact that they are less aggressive, especially scholastically, stems from this growing contradiction between improving their personal worth (and making a major scholastic investment) and being lured toward a destiny that is predetermined by their sex.

CONCLUSION

A few remarks appear necessary. First of all, this rapid review of the results of research on the difference in success in mathematics according to sex clearly demonstrates *the crucial importance of attitudes.* More specifically, attitudes affect performance in mathematics (at the highest levels), the evaluation of this performance, and especially the importance given to mathematics and science in scholastic and professional orientation. Moreover, the difference in success rates, in the strictest sense, is decreasing constantly, *and it is the differences in orientation that are becoming determinant for an identical scholastic level.* This is also true outside of France. Surprisingly similar results are found for countries such as Norway (Stog, 1991), where the differences between the sexes as regards scholastic streams appear to be the result of the self-selection

---

10 In a country such as France it appears obvious that girls and boys must be given the same education, share in housework, envisage a professional career, etc.; Percheron, 1985.

process (less confidence among girls in their scientific level), of the image of scientific courses, and of professional motivations aimed more toward social usefulness than toward prestige and salary. It is easy to understand the choices girls make if we take into consideration this view of reality as seen by girls and their interpretation of the events that concern them. What's more, these choices appear rational (even if they are founded on quite erroneous beliefs), as the girls feel they are less competent in sciences and perceive scientific professions as being difficult (for them) and masculine (Eccles, 1986).

These differences in attitude between girls and boys obviously constitute a decisive factor in masculine or feminine identity. But they are not the result of nature, as many studies show how these attitudes are forged through varied social processes:

- the parents' child-raising practices, and especially their stereotyped expectations as regards success;

- the teachers' pedagogical practices, and especially their more or less implicit convictions and attitudes, which are expressed by different expectations unconsciously communicated to the students, if only through evaluations;

- interaction between students in a coeducational context and at an age where sexual conformity prevails among students.

Overall, through the emergence of these differences in attitude toward science, and especially through an unequal confidence in one's own potential, the progressive development of sexual identity evolves.

Given this conclusion in terms of the *scholastic (and thus social) 'creation' of differences between the sexes*, we can underline the changing nature of these differences according to place and time. They can also be modified by pedagogical action, and a few countries such as Great Britain have developed 'compensatory' programs in scientific and technical subjects (Burton, 1990). These include modifications to make programs more attractive to girls, the founding of science clubs reserved to girls, and contacts with women in scientific and technical professions.

Another British experiment concerns the family context. It consisted of giving training in mathematics to the mothers of girls having difficulty in this subject. After six months, the improvement in the results of girls whose mothers had taken part in the experiment was spectacular. If their mothers could do it, it was possible for the daughters to do it too. These results are easy to comprehend, given the relationships mentioned above between the mothers' attitudes and the daughters' attitudes. In all cases (especially in these Family Maths Programs experiments, cf Rodgers, 1990), by presenting concrete, sufficiently close models, it was possible to foster access to this field of knowledge, from which women feel excluded by their day-to-day experience.[11]

While these two types of observations – the importance of attitudes and the multiplicity of possible intervention – leave little room for contradiction, it is harder to be unanimous as concerns the merits of voluntarist policies or practices in this field. Some people say that concentrating on the attitudes and more generally on the psychology of girls may propagate the idea that there is a 'problem with girls'. The danger in this is not only to 'blame the victims', but also to hide the fact that, if there is indeed a problem, it lies in the social construction of sciences and in the distribution of work and skills between the sexes (Kelly, 1987).

Other people fear that giving girls more access to scientific culture may force them to fit the masculine mold, instead of defending 'equality in difference'. Obviously, it is pointless to talk about girls' disadvantage other than within a given value system. If the fact that fewer girls choose scientific studies is perceived as discrimination, it is because this goes hand in hand with less respected professions. Although we may ultimately feel it is wiser to modify this value system totally, it is still vital that all young people be placed in a situation of equal choice as regards these different professions. As for the concept of 'equality in difference', doesn't that amount to cultivating the difference, because it tends to establish the inevitability of two types (men/women)?

If equality is the right each person has to have all doors open to him/her, and if access to education is precisely what opens those doors, then in the eyes of some teachers the idea of *non-sexist pedagogy* has to become a professional norm (Lempen-Ricci and Moreau, 1987; Valabrègue, 1985). This consists of refusing to draw a necessary link between natural differences and unequal treatment, and is based on the necessary application of equal treatment. It is not a question of denying the existence of natural differences, although we now know that it is useless to try to separate nature from culture, but rather of maintaining

---

11 Synthetic presentations of these numerous pedagogical programs are given in Kelly (1987) and Terlon (1985 and 1990) and in the chapter by Aebischer and Valabrègue in this book.

the objective of equality, if necessary by implementing 'positive discrimination'. For example, regardless of the origin of girls' difficulties in the spatial field, we will try to eliminate these objective handicaps. Consequently, there may be a difference in treatment between the sexes, not to reinforce these differences, but rather to compensate for the limitations that are created, directly or indirectly, in comparison with the possibilities open to the opposite sex. In short, the basic idea of this non-sexist pedagogy is to do away with any gender-based obligations as regards the choice of a life style; and here it may prove to offer men as much freedom as women, as the constraints 'masculinity' places on men are significant (Askew and Ross, 1988).

But the goal is not a utopian pedagogical approach, for it is painted against a backdrop of how society functions globally, whether it be the prevailing concept of science and technology, the stereotypes attached to both sexes, or (especially) the sexual divisions in the workplace that are seen as resulting. Although schools (and the views of the world that students receive there) inevitably reflect this social context, they are not the only factor responsible. Nevertheless, above and beyond the few suggestions (such as 'compensatory pedagogy') discussed above, we feel that schools and those taking part in them cannot remain indifferent to the sexual limitation of choices and scholastic investments that tends to dominate and claim its legitimacy within their walls. If only because the school's message is a fundamentally individualistic one, in which students are invited to cultivate their talents in order to take control of their life, independently of the multiple social constraints to which they are subjected. We will need to strike a balance between the optimistic view, in which everything is the result of conservative thinking that schools can help to evolve, and the pessimist view, which concludes that it is all our fault or it is all decided outside of the classroom.

Chapter 7

The Scientific Education of Girls in China

Yiping Huo

ABSTRACT: *After describing women's condition prior to the founding of the People's Republic, the author presents a few of the characteristics of the present education system in China: spectacular entry of girls into the scientific and technical streams, training of elites, actions to encourage employers to hire women in cutting-edge sectors, but also difficulty in promoting women in the upper echelons of science.*

According to the latest general census in China, carried out in 1990, the Chinese population is 1,130,510,638, including 548,690,231 women or one-quarter of the women in the world.

Throughout the feudal years which lasted several dozen centuries in China, and in the semi-feudal and semi-colonial society which lasted about one century, Chinese women were oppressed, exploited and ill-treated, having no right to take part in political and social life. Being dependent on others, they had neither the right to cultural education nor to an independent personality. After the founding of the People's Republic in 1949, the Chinese government set objectives that include the emancipation of Chinese women and equality between men and women. Implemented through the Constitution, laws and decrees, it guarantees Chinese women the same rights as men on political, economic, cultural, social and family issues.

Masters of the nation and of Chinese society like all other Chinese citizens, modern Chinese women play an active part in all fields of industrial and agricultural production, scientific research, culture, education and public health, as well as contributing to the construction and development of China. For the past 45 years, the social position of Chinese women has gone through radical change.

Along with guaranteeing their political rights and their right to employment, heritage, marriage and family position, as well as all other individual rights, China pays particular attention to guaranteeing Chinese women the right to education. Before 1949, 90% of Chinese women were illiterate and only 20% of Chinese girls attended school.

In 1993, the rate of enrollment of Chinese girls reached 96.8%. The contrast is striking and progress encouraging. The following table, drawn up from statistics gathered by the Chinese National Education Commission in 1994, reflects the present situation of girls' education in China.

Table 1 Number of students in 1994 (unit: 10 thousand)

Schools	Total	Girls	Percentage
Primary	12,822.60	6035.3	47.1
General secondary	4981.80	2207.0	44.3
Technical secondary	209.83	109.5	45.4
Teacher's preparatory	72.20	46.8	59.7
Vocational secondary	405.61	193.8	47.8
University	279.86	96.4	34.5

Moreover, since the restoration of the certificate system in 1982, 22,500 Chinese candidates have obtained a master's degree, including 6,600 girls (26%) and 2,900 obtained a doctorate, including 320 girls (11%).

By the end of 1993, China had 120,000 women teachers in institutions of higher education, or 30.9% of the total number of teachers in these institutions, among which were 2,929 women professors and 20,921 women teaching assistants. All categories combined, China has 174,000 high-level specialists, or 17.3% of the total, of which 7,416 are responsible for the training and orientation of master's or doctoral candidates. Twenty women serve as presidents or vice-presidents of institutions of higher education.

It should also be noted that the country has 1,679 technical and vocational secondary schools for girls and three vocational universities for girls which have opened over 60 streams suitable for women, not to mention the fact that over 1.3 million Chinese women are presently attending institutions of higher education for adults.

As concerns the choice of streams in technical and vocational secondary schools, Chinese girls are concentrated more in sewing, business, accounting, pharmacy, medicine and teaching, due to physiological and psychological factors and to political, economic and cultural influences. In higher education they generally choose literature, history and other human sciences, and shy away from natural and applied sciences, especially agriculture, industry and water and forest resources. This situation is similar to that of many other countries.

The government and schools, at various levels, encourage girls who want to go into scientific fields, especially mathematics and experimental sciences, and create favorable conditions to help them profit fully from their abilities and compete with boys.

As of fifth grade (the next to last year of primary school), Chinese schools organize regional or national mathematics examinations in order to discover and subsequently educate gifted children. According to the results of the past few years, girls rank well. In 1994, two of the ten winners of the mathematics Olympics in Singapore primary schools in the Shanghai region were girls. The Chinese authorities also encourage secondary schools that offer the best conditions to create their own specializations, either in the arts or in foreign languages or in sciences, provided they guarantee a quality education. One example is Secondary School No. 2 in Shanghai under the supervision of the East China Teacher's College, reputed in China for its science program. The best mathematics students in primary schools are grouped together in special classes taught by the school's top teachers. The math classes are accelerated and knowledge in the subject is far broader. In secondary schools, two special science classes were created for the first year and one special class in science respectively for the second and third years, with students recruited not only from all Shanghai but from the rest of the country as well. At present there are 62 boys and 12 girls in the two first-year classes, 37 boys and 6 girls in the second-year class, and 36 boys and 6 girls in the third-year class.

By analyzing the results of the study of these special classes, we find that girls in the special classes are generally above average but very rarely among the top students. In addition to physiological and psychological factors, the girls sometimes lack perseverance and will power compared to the boys. Consequently, the school tries to stimulate the spirit of enterprise and self-confidence, and to encourage them when problems arise. In the international secondary school examinations in mathematics, physics, chemistry and biology organized in 1991, 1992 and 1994, eight students (including one girl) from the special classes of this school won eight different medals, including three gold medals in physics, two gold medals in chemistry, one silver medal in mathematics, and one bronze medal in biology. The girl won the gold medal in chemistry in 1992.

When recruiting students for university, the Chinese education authorities apply the principle of equality based on exam results without favouring nor excluding girls. In order to qualify for and be admitted to universities, knowledge and skills must be of a certain level. As girls in secondary schools always lag behind boys in sciences and as the number of girls enrolled decreases the higher up you go in education, the number of girls entering the scientific streams of higher education has always been lower than that of boys.

As for the employment situation of women graduates, this was not a problem in the past because under the central planning system the State found a job for each graduate. Now women graduates in the traditional science streams, that is, mathematics, physics, chemistry and biology, have more trouble finding a job than male graduates from the same streams. This situation is due mainly to the fact that, with the expansion of the Chinese economy, more human resources are required in the applied sciences and the supply of human resources in traditional sciences exceeds the demand on the job market. It is also due to the fact that, with the transition toward a market economy, companies have greater autonomy as regards staff recruitment. Companies tend to hire men rather than women, as women are soon confronted with real problems such as marriage, child-bearing and child care. Given this social problem, the Chinese authorities have taken a series of measures to guarantee women employment. First, the government intervenes, in virtue of a law protecting the rights and interests of women and children, by obliging companies to employ a given percentage of women on their staff. Secondly, the universities are restructuring their courses and streams, lowering the number of students admitted in the traditional sciences and increasing those in applied sciences, including computer science, agrofood, environment, statistics, accounting and insurance. As graduates of these streams often find a job easily, the percentage of women in these streams increases every year.

As regards promotions Chinese women scientists and technicians rely only on the results of their work and research, competing with men and meeting the same norms. To date, Chinese women still make up a relatively small percentage of specialists, scientists and professors who have reached a top level in their profession. This is chiefly due to the limited percentage of girls in the primary and secondary cycles of universities and especially in the third cycle, that of doctoral candidates. There is also the importance of women's family duties, sometimes because of economic constraints and the lack of social services which prevent them from concentrating their efforts on scientific research. Yet, thanks to their perseverance, many Chinese women have broken into fields of science previously monopolized by men. In 1993, China already had 8.097 million women scientists, 35% of all scientists in China. Of those women, 29 became members of the Chinese Academy of Sciences, or 5.4% of the total. 204 other women were appointed national experts, or 5.7% of the total. 11,374 women received special subsidies granted by the State to specialists and scientists, or 10% of the total. To summarize, today's Chinese women are found in all fields of scientific research and even in many areas of advanced technology, such as nuclear physics, biotechnology, micro-electronics and aerospace.

ANNEX

Table 1: Percentage of girls admitted to selected universities (1982–86)

Universities	1982	1983	1984	1985	1986
HangZhou University (sciences)	17.82	18.72	20.86	22.86	11.14
ZheJiang University (sciences and applied sciences)			20.83	22.47	20.00
ChonQing University (sciences and applied sciences)	21.0	19.8	21.1	22.1	21.3
QingHun University (sciences and applied sciences)	16.8	17.99	18.4	19.59	

Table 2 Situation of students enrolled in Dongnan University (applied sciences) in Nanjing in 1994

Streams	Men	Women
Materials treatment	218	19
Materials sciences	98	15
Electrical and automation systems	290	85
Electrical and automation work	172	81
Industrial automation	283	51
Environment	208	29
Computer science and technology	286	83
Architecture	342	165
Fine chemicals	275	62

Table 2 Situation of students enrolled in Dongnan University (applied sciences) in Nanjing in 1994 (continued)

Streams	Men	Women
Management, mathematics and economics	62	20
Economics	62	31
Bio-medicine	207	55
Micro-electronics	148	34
Telecommunications	1036	183
Physics and electronics	272	42
Instrumentation	168	63
Applied physics	66	12
Mechanical design and construction	283	40
Construction	156	28
Transportation and communications	77	40
Economic management	229	89
Economic management of tourism	11	18
Energy and automation	565	108

Source: Survey by Yiping Huo

Table 3 Situation of students at East China Teacher's College in Shanghai in 1994

Streams	Men	Women
Sciences and applied sciences		
Physics	188	60
Electronics and computer science	214	63
Micro-electronics	20	4
Applied mathematics	111	35
Chemistry	238	125
Biochemistry	31	14
Resources and environmental planning and management	107	43
Environment	112	66
Photoelectronics	28	11
Radiological physics	28	7
Mathematics	189	67
Computers and computer applications	249	80
Biology	230	124
Geography	120	45
Economics, geography and development	107	43

Table 3 Situation of students at East China
Teacher's College in Shanghai in 1994 (continued)

Streams	Men	Women
Literature, human sciences and economics		
Teaching	99	54
Pedagogical management	60	23
Psychology	128	67
Pedagogical techniques	88	36
Philosopy	56	23
Chinese language and civilization	171	102
Chinese for foreigners	102	78
English	178	147
Japanese	66	47
French	33	30
International finance	132	67
Insurance	25	14
Tourism	135	95
Pre-school education	40	25
Sports education	128	36
Special education	24	16
Political science	75	36
History	113	46
Audiovisual teaching	58	39
Teaching of the arts	40	12
Russian	55	41
German	39	31
Economics	165	88
Statistics	116	56
Computer science	135	84
Property	53	28

Source: Survey by Yiping Huo

Table 4 Breakdown of scientists by sector
and by gender in general Chinese census (1990)

Sectors	Total	Men	Women	% of women
Research	198,019	138,616	59,403	30
Engineering and agronomy	4,510,846	3,546,192	964,654	21.4
Aeronautics	134,962	132,591	2371	1.7
Health	4,575,233	1,958,145	2,617,088	57.2

BIBLIOGRAPHY

Files of 1990 general census in China, Volume 2, written by the General Census Bureau of the Council of State Affairs of the People's Republic of China and the Department of Demographic Statistics of the Chinese National Statistics Bureau, published by Chinese Statistics Publishing Office, 1993.

Annals of statistics on education in China, written by the Department of Planning of the National Education Commission of China in August 1994 and published by the People's Education Publishing Office.

Summary of statistics on education in China, written in March 1995 by the Department of Planning of the National Education Commission of China.

Summary table of the number of students enrolled in the College in March 1995, written by the Student Administration Office of the East China Teacher's College.

Statistics by stream and by gender for students at Dongnan University, written by the Student's Office of Dongnan University.

Chapter 8

How Chinese Teachers View Students
A Misleading Advantage for Girls

Anne-Garance Primel

ABSTRACT: *How the model of the 'eternal women' reappeared in the responses to a questionnaire submitted to teachers in Shanghai.*

In a 1994 survey of four professional and vocational upper secondary schools in Shanghai, 120 teachers (72 men and 48 women) filled in a questionnaire. Two of the questions asked them to designate four adjectives that describe girl students (question 1) and boy students (question 2) as concerns studies.

(1) GLOBAL ANALYSIS
The teachers attributed more good points than bad to their students (65.5% of responses are positive adjectives). They concern both girls and boys. Women teachers use more positive adjectives than men teachers, both for girls and boys. Women were a bit less severe or more lenient than men toward the students. While men were just as severe toward girls as toward boys (Table 1), women were more severe toward boys than girls (Table 1).

Table 1 Proportion of positive and negative adjectives describing girl and boy students according to the gender of the teacher (%)

	Question 1: Girls		Question 2: Boys	
	+ adjectives	- adjectives	+ adjectives	- adjectives
Men teachers	62	38	62	38
Women teachers	81	19	65	35

The teachers chose more positive adjectives for girl students than boys. The teachers' opinion is less clear-cut for girls than boys. Girls are held in higher esteem than boys; they have more good points than boys do. But this difference is relatively limited (Figure 1).

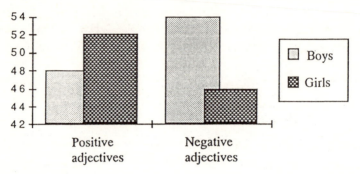

Figure 1 Proportion of positive and negative adjectives describing girl and boy students (%)

Detailed Analysis

When we look at the proportion of responses by adjective (Table 2 and Figure 2), we can see that girls are serious, conscientious, meticulous, studious, persevering,[1] friendly, hard-working, calm and scholarly,[2] while boys are intelligent, studious, dynamic, dexterous, persevering, careless, undisciplined and lazy. The adjectives used for girls are similar in meaning, while those used for boys differ greatly.

Of the first eight adjectives mentioned in at least 5% of responses, the only weakness attributed to girls came last (with 5%), while the three weaknesses attributed to boys rank third (with 12%), fifth (with 11%) and seventh (with 6%).

According to the global analysis (1) and this last observation, we might think girls are more 'privileged' than boys, and that the teachers are far more severe toward the boys. When we compare the strong points found for boys and girls, those attributed to boys are generally considered to be more constructive. Boys are more intelligent (13% compared with 3.5% for girls!) and more dexterous (6.5% compared

---

1   The word 'persevering' also groups the adjectives 'hard-working' and 'persistent'.
2   The term translated as 'scholarly' is negative to Chinese teachers. It signifies an inability to reason alone, a total lack of independence, a rigidity and superficiality in studies.

with 0% for girls). Girls are clumsy and servile, flattering while boys are not at all. Girls are more stupid or incompetent than boys. These feminine and masculine 'portraits' are not specifically Chinese. The fact that these clichés closely resemble those of the West is more than disturbing. The reasons behind these cliches may well vary from one society to the next, but the debate is an international one.

Table 2 Proportion of responses per adjective describing girl and boy students (in % and by decreasing order)

Boys		Girls	
intelligent	13	serious	10.5
studious	12	*conscientious/meticulous*	9.5
careless	12	studious	8.5
dynamic	11	persevering	7
undisciplined	11	friendly	6.5
dexterous	6.5	hard-working	5.5
lazy	6	scholarly	5
persevering	5.5	calm	5
friendly	4.5	dynamic	4.5
serious	3	lazy	4.5
unmotivated	2.5	naive/immature	4.5
average/mediocre	2.5	*disciplined*	3.5
hard-working	1.5	intelligent	3.5
motivated	1.5	motivated	3
determined	1.5	clumsy	3
daring	1.5	unmotivated	3
naive/immature	1.5	undisciplined	2.5
arrogant	1.5	determined	2
scholarly	0.5	stupid/incompetent	2
stupid/incompetent	0.5	*shy*	2
calm	0.5	average/mediocre	2
clumsy	–	*obsequious/flattering*	1.5
conscientious/meticulous	–	daring	0.5
disciplined	–	arrogant	0.5
shy	–	dexterous	–
obsequious/flattering	–	careless	–

Source: The adjectives in italics are those mentioned for one of the sexes only. Teachers used 'shy' for girls only and 'dexterous' for boys only.

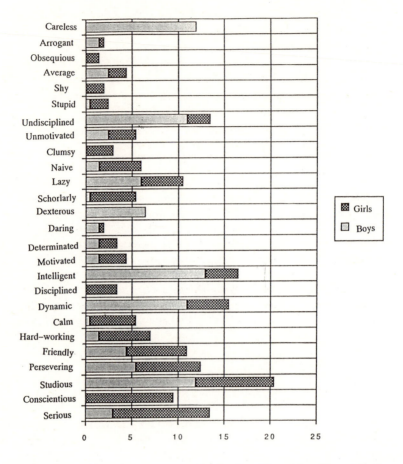

Figure 2 Proportion of responses per adjective describing girl and boy students (%)

Chapter 9

U.S. Women in Science and Feminist Theories

Sue V. Rosser

ABSTRACT: *After describing the situation of women in scientific and technical careers in the US, the author gives a dynamic presentation of the contribution of various feminist currents (liberal especially, but also socialist, African American, radical, psychoanalytical, etc.) in the fight against overt discrimination, both in research and in education. She proposes guidelines for action.*

During the last two decades, women have entered the professions in record numbers. In recent years, women have received degrees in most fields in numbers approaching or exceeding their 51% of the American population. However, the physical sciences, mathematics, and engineering persist as the professional areas where women have not yet broken the gender barrier. Women comprise 45% of the employed labor force in the United States but only 16% of all employed scientists and engineers (NSF, 1992). A 1994 report from the National Research Council revealed that women comprise only about 12% of the employed scientific and engineering labor force in industry. Of 1,647 living scientists elected to membership in the National Academy of Sciences, only 70 are women; in the 1992 election, only five of the 59 honorees were women.

Women scientists are concentrated in the life sciences and social sciences, while male scientists are concentrated primarily in engineering (NSF, 1990). In 1988, women earned 32.9% of the doctorates in the life sciences and 44.0% of the bachelor's degrees. The physical and technological sciences continue to attract scant numbers of women: women obtained only 16.8% of the PhDs and 29.7% of the bachelor's degrees in physical sciences in 1988; in engineering, women earned only 6.8% of the PhDs and 14.5% of the undergraduate degrees that year (NSF, 1990).

Increases in numbers of women in the educational pipeline translate slowly into increased percentages of women in the overall science and engineering workforce. For example, in 1993, women made up only '1 percent of working environmental engineers, 2 percent of mechanical engineers, 3 percent of electrical engineers, 4 percent of medical school department directors, 5 percent of physics PhDs, 6 out of close to 300 tenured professors in the country's top 10 mathematics departments' (Holloway, 1993, 96). Although 41% of working life scientists and biologists and 17% of the members of the American Chemical Society in 1991 included women, in the physical sciences such as physics, geology, and engineering the percentage of women remained even lower (Holloway, 1993).

With the exception of Asian Americans, underrepresentation of minorities in science and engineering also continues to be a serious problem. Although African-Americans and Hispanics comprise 10% and 7% respectively of the U.S. employed labor force, each represented only 3% of all employed scientists and engineers in 1988 (NSF, 1990). A large percentage (44%) of African-American scientists works in the life and social sciences, although a higher percentage of African-Americans (62%) than women works in engineering (Matyas and Malcolm, 1991). Because of the small numbers of Native Americans and difficulties in obtaining accurate reports of heritage on survey instruments, the statistics on this group are problematic. However, based on the limited data which are available, it would appear that Native Americans are underrepresented as scientists relative to their proportions in the overall populations (NSF, 1992).

This dearth of women and minorities in these areas is unfortunate both for the individuals and for science and engineering. Demographers predict that, in the final years of the twentieth century, nearly two-thirds of new entrants into the workforce will be women (U.S. Department of Labor, 1987) and that between 80% and 90% of the workforce growth by the year 2000 will be women and minorities, the groups not traditionally attracted in large numbers to the physical sciences and engineering:

> There will be a larger segment of minorities and women: 23% more Blacks, 70% more Asians and other races (American Indians, Alaska natives, and Pacific Islanders), 74% more Hispanics and 25% more women, adding 3.6 million, 2.4 million, 6.0 million, and 13.0 million more workers respectively. Altogether, these minorities and women

will make up 90% of the work force growth and 23% of the new employees will be immigrants. (Thomas, 1989, 30)

The science and engineering professions typically offer relatively high paying, stable positions which should be particularly appealing in an economy where unemployment and poverty are increasing for women, black and white, and people of colour generally. Attracting these individuals to the physical sciences, mathematics, and engineering would provide them with desirable career access while filling the needs of our increasingly scientific and technological workforce.

Despite relatively low percentages of women in most areas of sciences and engineering, until recently very few programs have directly targeted females. The results of a 1991 study by Marsha Matyas and Shirley Malcolm, which included surveys of presidents or chancellors of 276 colleges and universities and the directors of nearly 400 recruitment and retention programs revealed that less than 10% of the programs included in the study were specifically focused on the recruitment and retention of women in science and engineering. This study reconfirmed similar findings from previous studies that virtually no programs directly target female students or faculty.

A growing body of research documents the need to change the way science is taught in order to appeal to women. Women's studies scholars have explored the ways in which science as it is currently taught and practiced may reflect a masculine approach to the world which tends to exclude women (Keller, 1985; Harding, 1986). This critique has been developed most extensively for biology (Bleier, 1984; Birke, 1986; Fausto-Sterling, 1992; Hubbard, 1990; Rosser, 1986, 1990), but has high applicability to other life sciences and physical sciences.

Liberal feminism serves as the theoretical framework which most accurately embraces the current status of the impact of feminism on science, particularly in curricula, pedagogy and laboratories. This liberal feminist categorization would not surprise those familiar with the theories of knowledge of history and values which liberal feminism shares with the foundations which link government, education, and science in the post-World War II United States.

Growing out of the 18th century Enlightenment and humanist traditions, political scientists, philosophers, and feminists [Wollstonecraft, 1975; Mill (John Stuart), 1970; Mill (Harriet Taylor), 1970; Friedan, 1974; Jaggar, 1983] have described the parameters of liberal feminism. The differences between 19th-century and 20th-century liberal feminists have varied from libertarian to egalitarian, and numerous complexities exist among definitions of liberal feminists today. However, a general definition of liberal feminism is the belief that women are suppressed in contemporary society because they suffer unjust discrimination (Jaggar, 1983). Liberal feminists seek no special privileges for women and simply demand that everyone receive equal consideration without discrimination on the basis of sex.

Most changes in laws with relevance for gender, including Title VII and Title IX, with their enormous impact on education, fought for in this wave of the feminist movement beginning in the 1960s and 1970s, have been won on the basis of equal consideration. Nondiscrimination on the basis of sex is now accepted in most government and educational policies.

Some of the early battles for women in science included revelations of quotas serving to limit the number of women entering medical schools and graduate programs in science, mathematics, and engineering. After formal and informal quotas were removed, researchers concentrated much of their work on documenting the small numbers of women in science, in general, and the particular dearth in some subdisciplines. These statistical data collected now for more than a decade (Vetter, 1994; NSF, 1986, 1988, 1990, 1992, 1994; NRC, 1992; Astin, et al. 1970–93; National Center for Education Statistics, 1994) provide quantitative evidence of systemic overt and covert barriers which have kept women out of science. Careful analyses (Vetter, 1994) document that despite women's increasing participation at every degree level in every field and employment sector, women still face lower salaries at all levels, lower rates of tenure and promotion and higher rates of unemployment in all fields. Less than half the differential between males and females can be attributed to factors such as quality and quantity of degrees held and time in the work force. Since discrimination explains more of the differential, the government directs considerable current funding (NSF, 1993) towards removal of subtle and overt barriers which may account for loss of females from science.

Many feminists have suggested pedagogical changes in the science, engineering, and mathematics classroom and laboratory as a way to remove barriers and make science more female-friendly (Rosser, 1990; 1993). Years of data amassed by the National Science Foundation, reports of numerous professional societies, and meta-analyses such as that provided by American Association of University Women (AAUW) in *How the Schools Shortchange Girls* (1992) furnish a backdrop of documented discrimination which encourages faculty, students, and the public to be more open to changes in teaching techniques which might 'level the playing field for women'.

To the extent that pedagogical changes have been presented as consonant with liberal feminism and its ideals of equal consideration for females, these changes have experienced less resistance. For example, of the approximately twenty teaching techniques I suggest in *Female-friendly Science* (Rosser, 1990), faculty appear most comfortable with techniques such as the following: (1) Incorporate and validate personal experiences women are likely to have had as part of the class discussion or laboratory exercise (i.e. do not use only examples from football, cars, or the military as subjects of math, physics, or engineering problems.) (2) Pair females with females as laboratory partners and provide more hands-on experience with various types of equipment (i.e. male–female pairs of laboratory partners often result in the male working with the equipment and the female taking the data. This is especially harmful for women since NAEP test results (Jones, *et al.* 1992) document that females have less hands-on experience with equipment than males.) These techniques provide no special privileges for female students; they simply serve as a corrective to problems, arrangements, and techniques which may have previously been biased in favor of males.

Changes sought by feminists in curricular content have encountered considerable resistance in science, as in all fields (Maher and Thompson Tetreault, 1994). Although many science and engineering faculty remain at stage 1 – Absence of women not noted – of curriculum transformation and insist that good science and good science teaching are gender-free or gender-neutral, a substantial number have been willing to move to stage 2 – Women as an add-on to the curriculum (McIntosh, 1984). Most faculty do not resist including the names of the nine women who have won the Nobel Prize in a scientific field or medicine (McGrayne, 1993) or other famous women scientists who have made valuable contributions to the experiments that faculty have traditionally discussed in their course. These faculty recognize that adding a couple of women's names provides the women in the class with some outstanding role models. Some faculty will go to considerable lengths to read some of the burgeoning scholarship by the historians of science (Rossiter, 1982, 1994; Schiebinger, 1989) to find excellent female examples to include with the great male scientists and their discoveries. They are relatively comfortable with adding women (and men of colour) on to their course as they have traditionally conceptualized it, particularly because this liberal feminist approach seems fair in that it provides the female students with examples of some women (and men of color) scientists whose accomplishments compare with those of outstanding white male scientists.

Most scientists would assume that the implications of liberal feminism for the sciences extend only to employment, access, and discrimination issues. In fact, the implications of liberal feminism extend beyond this. Liberal feminism shares two fundamental assumptions with the foundations of the traditional method for scientific discovery: (1) Both assume that human beings are highly individualistic and obtain knowledge in a rational manner that may be separated from their social conditions; and (2) Both accept positivism as the theory of knowledge. These two assumptions lead to the belief in the possibilities of obtaining knowledge that is both objective and value-free, concepts which form the cornerstones of the scientific method and the American judicial system. Objectivity is contingent upon value neutrality or freedom from values, interests, and emotions associated with a particular class, race, or sex.

In the past two decades feminist historians and philosophers of science (Fee, 1982; Haraway, 1990; Harding, 1986; 1992) and feminist scientists (Birke, 1986; Bleier, 1984, 1986; Fausto-Sterling, 1992; Keller, 1985, 1993; Rosser, 1988, 1992) have pointed out a source of bias and absence of value neutrality in science, particularly biology. By excluding females as experimental subjects, focusing on problems of primary interest to males, faulty experimental designs, and interpretations of data based in language or ideas constricted by patriarchal parameters, experimental results in several areas in biology have been demonstrated to be biased or flawed. Feminist critiques (Keller, 1985; Harding, 1986, 1992) suggest that these flaws and biases were permitted to become part of the mainstream of scientific thought and were perpetuated in the scientific literature for decades, because virtually all of the individuals who were scientists were men. Since most, if not all scientists were male, values held by most males were not distinguishable as biasing; they became synonymous with the 'objective' view of the world.

In addition to the problems of selective use of species, anthropomorphic and vague language, and universalizing and extrapolating beyond limits of the data, feminist scientists revealed another obvious flaw in much animal behavior research: failure to study females. When females were studied, it was usually only in their interaction (usually reaction) to males or infants. Presumably the fact that until recently most animal behavior researchers were male resulted in an androcentric bias in the conceptualization of design for observation of animal behavior.

Because male researchers had only *experienced* male–male and male–female interactions themselves, their male world view prohibited them from realizing that female–female interaction might be *observed* in their own and other species. Female primatologists (Goodall, 1971; Fossey, 1983) and sociobiologists (Hrdy, 1977, 1979, 1981, 1984, 1986) revealed new information that led to the overthrow of previously held theories regarding dominance hierarchies, mate selection (Hrdy, 1984) and female–female competition (Hrdy and Williams, 1983) by focusing on female–female interactions.

The flaw of failing to study females has also plagued much research on human health, particularly clinical trials of drugs. Since menstrual and estrus cycles may influence metabolism of drugs, it should be important to consider sex differences in drug tests. In a longitudinal study of the effects of cholesterol lowering drugs, gender differences were not tested; the drug was tested on 3806 men and no women (Hamilton, 1985). The Multiple Risk Factor Intervention Trial (1990) examined mortality from coronary heart disease in 12,866 men only. The Health Professionals Follow-up Study (Grobbee *et al.* 1990) looked at the association between coffee consumption and heart disease in 45,589 men. The Physician's Health Study (Steering Committee of the Physician's Health Study Group, 1989) found that low-dose aspirin therapy reduced the risk of myocardial infarction in 22,071 men. A study published in the *Journal of the American Medical Association* surveyed the literature from 1960–91 of studies of clinical trials of medications used to treat acute myocardial infarction. Women were included in only about 20% of those studies (Gurwitz *et al.* 1992). On March 11, 1994, partially due to the efforts of representatives Pat Schroeder and Olympia Snowe, the US Congress declared that women must be included in clinical trials funded by the National Institutes of Health.

These examples of flawed research and other examples resulting from the critiques of feminists have raise fundamental questions regarding gender and good science: Do these examples simply represent 'bad science'? Is good science really gender-free or does the scientific method when properly used permit research that is objective and unbiased?

The liberal feminist answer to these questions is that good science can be gender-free. Liberal feminists suggest that now that the bias of gender has been revealed by feminist critiques, scientists can take this into account and correct for this value or bias which had not previously been uncovered. A liberal feminist positions has two significant implications:

(1) It does not question the integrity of the scientific method itself or of its supporting corollaries of objectivity and value neutrality. Liberal feminism reaffirms the idea that it is possible to find a perspective from which to observe that is truly impartial, rational, and detached. Lack of objectivity and presence of bias occur because of human failure to properly follow the scientific method and avoid bias due to situation or condition. Liberal feminists argue that it was through attempts to become more value-neutral that the possible androcentrism in previous scientific research has been revealed.

(2) Liberal feminism also implies that good scientific research is not conducted differently by men and women and that in principle men can be just as good feminists as women. Now that feminist critiques have revealed flaws in research due to gender bias, both men and women will use this revelation to design experiments, gather and interpret data, and draw conclusions and theories that are more objective and free from bias, including gender bias (Biology and Gender Study Group, 1989).

Liberal feminist critiques of pedagogy, curriculum, and even research in science have achieved limited to moderate success. Sharing the fundamental assumptions of the possibilities of value neutrality and objectivity, liberal feminism does little to challenge the bases of the systems of education, government, or scientific research. Liberal feminism simply asks that females receive equal time and access in the classroom, that their scientific contributions comparable to those of males be noted and that research flawed by the absence of data from female subjects or biased by questions derived from only male experience be corrected.

Liberal feminist demands for equal consideration and access for women appear threatening to some, particularly in times such as these when the Superconductor Supercollider fiasco and military downsizing mean that many US white male scientists and engineers are experiencing problems with access to jobs, research resources, and advancement. However, liberal feminism does not question the fundamental assumptions underlying the scientific method, the link between the government and science, nor the content or methods of science teaching in our educational system.

In contrast, other feminist theories, ranging from Marxist feminism through African-American/womanist feminism and psychoanalytic feminism to radical feminism, including lesbian separatism, spawn pedagogy, curriculum and research methodologies which call into question value-neutrality and objectivity. Since these theories threaten the cornerstones of the scientific method, as well as much about the laws and values upon which the government and educational systems are based, pedagogical, curricular, and research ideas emerging from them have found little acceptance in their pure form from scientists and engineers.

Yet, pedagogical, curricular, and research changes envisioned by feminists working from other than liberal feminist perspectives offer innovations most likely to change the status quo and result in more diversity in the pool of scientists and new visions of science. Although most programs to attract men of colour and/or women to science articulate what might be described as liberal feminist goals, substantial numbers include curricular or pedagogical changes derived from other feminist theories.

Socialist feminists have revealed the extent to which scientific knowledge is socially constructed and reflects the interests in this capitalistic society of the dominant class in terms of which research is viewed as significant and worthy of study (i.e. funding). Since women and women's interests dominate neither in the the political arena, where overall priorities for research funding are established, nor in the scientific establishment, where specific funding priorities are set, subjects of primary interest to women such as breast cancer research have received relatively low priority and funding.

Socialist feminism provides a theoretical framework which might be used to explain several issues that continue to be problematic for women in science classes. For example, mathematics often becomes the gatekeeping course which determines whether or not students will be able to pursue courses in science and engineering. To a student without the full complement of four years of high school mathematics, up to 75% (Sells, 1978; 1982) of college majors, particularly those in scientific and technical fields which lead to higher paying professions with considerable stability, will be closed.

More girls than boys drop out of high school mathematics (OTA, 1987) before they have completed the four year sequence. Studies have shown that girls who drop out of mathematics in high school and women who switch from mathematics or science majors in college do not do so because of poor grades (Arnold, 1987; Gardner, 1986). The grades of the females leaving are as good or better than those of the males persisting in the science and mathematics courses. Whatever they studied, women earned consistently higher grade point averages in college than the men in the class, and the differences were greatest in the traditionally male-dominated fields of engineering, science, and business (Vetter, in press). A variety of factors such as differential responses of guidance counselors, parents (Keynes, 1989) and peers to the desire and discussion surrounding decisions to drop out of mathematics or science may be responsible for the differential persistence rates of males compared to females. For example, parents tend to praise their daughter's hard work in attaining good grades, while attributing their son's success to talent (Keynes, 1989). As a group, parents have lower educational aspirations for their sons than their daughters (Adelman, 1991).

A socialist-feminist analysis of the gender-differentiated drop rates for mathematics despite the superior grades of a female might focus on an analysis of so-called gatekeeping courses in our educational system. In addition to 'weeding out' individuals with out skill in a particular area, other individuals may be removed by differential encouragement (Keynes, 1989; Davis, 1993).

Mathematics courses often serve as such gatekeepers, which control access to more lucrative professions. Some individuals are removed from the pipeline due to lack of ability and/or performance (which may be related to class, given the structure of public schools in the United States). For females, differential encouragement to continue in mathematics, particularly when difficulties arise, may provide an additional filter.

Studies have documented that when computer camps are relatively inexpensive (less than $100), approximately one-third of the enrollees are girls; when the cost exceeds $1000, female enrollment drops to one-sixth (Sanders, in press). This study, coupled with others (Martinez and Mead, 1988; Sanders, 1985) documenting that families buy computers more often for their sons than daughters suggest that families may provide different amounts of money and emphasis upon mathematics, differentiating by gender and possible career goals for their children.

Some projects to attract and retain girls and women in science demonstrate knowledge of the intersection of class with gender as a particular problem. Most projects directed towards kindergarten through twelfth grade girls have a component directed towards encouraging females to stay in mathematics. Staying in mathematics in college provides a direct path to more lucrative livelihoods for women since women achieve near pay equity in some occupations (accounting, management, and engineers) as a correlate of the amount of mathematics they studied in college (Adelman, 1991).

A few programs such as Operation SMART, run by Girls Inc. (Wahl, 1993) target girls from the inner city and lower socioeconomic strata. Their emphases upon science, 'hands-on' activities, and building teamwork through sports represent deliberate attempts to provide girls from urban and lower income families with experiences often available only to boys or to girls from higher income families to develop skills useful for persisting in science and other male-dominated professions. In their recognition of the role of the intersection that class and gender play as barriers for these girls, such programs might be interpreted as adopting a socialist-feminist perspective.

Similar to socialist feminist critiques, African-American feminist or womanist critiques view the scientific enterprise as a function of white Eurocentric male interests. Because they experience the oppression of both gender and race, African-American women have a more comprehensive view of reality and an interest in perceiving problems with the status quo and the scientific knowledge produced by men of the dominant race and class.

In addition to the underrepresentation of African-Americans in science, evidence suggests that science and science education may represent white Eurocentric interests. Despite much more limited funding and other resources, historically black colleges and universities have produced a much higher percentage of African-American scientists (Matyas and Malcolm, 1991) than integrated institutions of higher education. Although such integrated institutions enroll larger numbers of African-American students than historically black colleges and universities, some combination of black role models as faculty, encouragement, and lack of identification of certain majors with a particular race at historically black colleges and universities yields more scientists.

In their survey of programs for women, minorities, and the disabled in science, Matyas and Malcolm (1991) found that most of the programs directed towards minorities had no particular component for women; most of the programs directed towards women failed to attract women of color. Treisman's work (1992) while thoroughly exploring the effects of race on group work in mathematics, fails to address the effects of gender in group dynamics. Similarly, much of the work on gender dynamics in group interactions (Tanner, 1990; Kramarae and Treichler, 1986; Lakoff, 1975) fails to explore the effect of race.

An African-American feminist analysis suggests why African-American women have fallen through the cracks in research and programs to attract and retain in science. Such an analysis also explains why a historically black women's college such as Spelman has produced a disproportionately large number of successful women scientists (Falconer, 1989). With African-American women role models on the faculty and teaching approaches geared towards their students, at Spelman, African-American young women receive the focus and attention missing from other programs to attract and retain in science.

Other feminist theories ranging from existentialism through lesbian separatism provide pieces for the puzzle of why women are not in science and what might be done to change that. For example, the work of Keller (1983, 1985), applying object relations theory and psychoanalytic perspectives, suggests that since the scientific method stresses objectivity, rationality, distance, and autonomy of the observer from the object of study, individuals (primarily males) who feel comfortable with independence, autonomy, and distance will be most likely to become scientists. Some adaptations of science teaching to accommodate the ways women learn more easily as suggested by the research of Belenky et al. (1986) may evolve from individuals who hold essentialist or existentialist feminist theoretical perspectives. The particular interest of females in the social applications of science (Hynes, 1989, in press; Rosser, 1993), the connection of science to human beings (Harding, 1985; Lie and Bryhni, 1983; Rosser, 1990), and feelings for the organism under study (Keller, 1983; Goodfield, 1981) seem understandable in the light of the differences encouraged in males and females by the primary caretaker suggested by psychoanalytic feminism. Programs to encourage women in science that teach females to be risk-takers, strategies that foster competition, rather than cooperation and connection among peers (including female-female peers), and assertiveness training might be viewed as attempts to correct the 'deficit' in female socialization and to equip them to enter the world of scientists in which competition, objectivity, and separation are fostered. The theory of radical feminism might partially explain research (Tidball, 1986; Sebrechts, 1992) documenting the disproportionate number of female scientists who receive their undergraduate education at women's colleges. A variety of factors present in women's colleges such as collective living with other females, a relatively large number of female faculty to serve as role models, teaching strategies geared to a female-only audience, absence of gender role prescription for use of equipment or major selection may account for the success of women's colleges in attracting and retaining women in science. Radical feminism would suggest that the presence of an environment which permits female-only classes and discussions might serve the role of a con-sciouness-raising group, the preferred methodology of radical feminism (MacKinnon, 1987), to influence women in their decision to become scientists.

Several of the strategies such as women in science groups, summer science camps for girls, or afterschool programs to encourage girls in computers or science attempt to provide a female-only experience within the overall context of a coeducational environment. In the female-only environment, concepts can be introduced at the appropriate developmental stage for females. Teaching techniques more in tune with female styles which emphasize interrelationships and connection, and cooperative approaches, rather than competition for equipment with males, may be attempted. These programs seek to duplicate some of the benefits of the single-sex environment for females found naturally at a women's college.

Some changes advocated by feminists grounded in other theories have been adopted by liberal feminists. In several instances, parts or versions of these changes have been accepted by mainstream scientists and educators because they are successful in attracting more females to science or simply because they represent good teaching which is beneficial for both males and females (Rosser and Kelly, 1994).

Typically mainstream science education has failed to acknowledge the connection between the origin of these improvements and women's studies. In some cases, the crucial research on the role of gender and gender dynamics which causes a technique to be successful in attracting and retaining women in science may be lost or fail to be transmitted to the practitioners. The current popularity of small group work in science and mathematics classes provides an example of such a severed connection. Despite the well-documented research from women's studies and the data from Harvard (Light, 1990) underlining the tendency of women to drop out of study groups when they were the only female, if the subject was a nontraditional one for women such as math or science, the role of gender composition has been ignored in most literature on groups in science and mathematics, even when other factors such as race (Treisman, 1992) have been explicitly highlighted.

Some changes advocated as female-friendly in curricular content such as more focus on practical applications, increased information from the history of science, and attempts to place science in its social context, may lose their gender appeal unless undergirded by serious curricular transformation supported through Women's Studies. For example, presentation of certain chemical or drug effects which use the 70 KG white male as the prototype for the effects may do little to reveal side effects or benefits for women in general and women of colour in particular, who may be students in the introductory biology or chemistry course. If Western European white males constitute the only contributors to the history of mathematics discussed in class, the students who have never seen anyone of their gender or race portrayed all semester, may conclude that they have no valuable contribution to make to mathematics, despite the fact that the mathematics course they took included considerable information on the history of mathematics. Environmental geosciences and hydrology courses which focus on the social effects of water resource management policies in third world countries may not be perceived as female-friendly if the impact on women's lives in terms of the distance they must walk each day to obtain water is not considered. Simply adding some practical applications or a bit of history of science to a course, without rethinking the structure and perspective from which the course is taught, may result in cosmetic changes which appear to be female-friendly but represent superficial understanding of the changes needed to attract and retain more diversity in science.

Liberal feminists mollify and modify pedagogical and curricular changes derived from other feminist theories so that they remove barriers for women and men of color and provide equal access to science, mathematics, an engineering. Because changes couched in liberal feminist terms share notions of value neutrality, objectivity, and positivism with the scientific method, they are more easily accepted by mainstream scientists and educators. When liberal feminists downplay the other theories in women's studies and ethnic studies from which the changes really originated, sometimes the focus on gender and/or race is lost and the changes do not benefit men of colour and women. Feminists holding a wide range of theoretical perspectives must constantly monitor curricular and pedagogical innovations adopted by mainstream scientists and educators at the urging of well-meaning liberal feminists to insure that they work to increase diversity in the pool of scientists, rather than maintaining the status quo.

Chapter 10

Girls and the New Information Technologies

Claire Terlon

ABSTRACT: *When personal computers (PCs) appeared, girls found themselves left out of this new technical development of the 1980s, given their reservations about this technological object and the avidity with which boys rushed into this technology, plus commercial supply working in the same direction and reinforcing the trend. The technological evolution itself, however, seems to open up new prospects more favourable to women, both as regards new software developments (hypermedia, virtual reality) and the development of new applications that renew the conditions of access to knowledge and the exchange of information (Internet).*

Between noon and two o'clock, when the PCs are free, the computer room of a Paris high school is buzzing with activity. Thirty-some students are present, all boys. 'Isn't the school coed?' I ask the math teacher supervising the activity. 'Yes, but the two or three girls who came the first few days the room was open were rapidly persuaded not to come back, by sharp elbow jabs, if necessary.' That was in 1981. What might have seemed just an anecdote proved to be a clue as to a general situation, confirmed in the years to come and which, in spite of numerous experiments (mainly English-language) aimed at providing less non-egalitarian access to the new computer resources, has persisted among vast indifference, especially in Latin countries. An attitude used by the computer magazine *Golden* for its French-speaking readers in an advertisement showing a flood of sperm and a slogan written in capitals: 'Your winning instinct made you what you are. Don't let a fax-modem slow you down now.' (*Golden*, February 1994, p. 113)!

THE ADVENT OF THE PC: THE 1980S

What went on in the 1980s? PCs appeared 25 years ago. Two thousand Altaïr 8800 computers, considered to be the first of their species, were sold in 1975. The first computer game, 'Encounter', came out on the market on paper tape and written in assembly language. A year later, Apple I rolled out of the California garage of Steve Jobs and Steve

Wozniak, and in 1977 Apple II set off on a career that left a lasting mark on the microcomputer world. Although the first spreadsheet, Visicalc, was created in 1979, the only real way to use these new machines (that multiplied rapidly, IBM marketing its PCs as of 1981) was to write your own program. So when microcomputerss entered the classroom, teachers had to start learning programming language in order to try to transmit the ABCs to their students. In general, it was the mathematics teachers who took over the programming classes and set up the microcomputerss with CAI (computer assisted instruction) exercises, still used on the terminals that equip many high schools. This situation, linking a new activity with the stereotype that makes mathematics an area where boys succeed more than girls, helps identify computer science as a field from which girls feel excluded and which doesn't interest them. This perception is combined with that of a technological object, an object that boys 'naturally' take over and that girls hesitate to approach. Behavior that can be attributed more to the effects of the differential socialization of the sexes than to any so-called 'natural law'!

The difference in interest in computers that we observe in school, along with the activities performed on microcomputers by girls and boys, are the extension of an extracurricular environment that favors certain social groups. Anglo-Saxon studies rapidly revealed that computers were offered selectively to the male population. Advertising highlights the 'futuristic' side of this new technology in order to promote PCs among young adults concerned with their careers as much as to parents interested in the professional future of their sons. Software is developed around themes aimed essentially at the interests of boys: 'shoot'em up' type arcade games, followed by videogames (Gameboy from Sega, etc.). In fact, it is hard to find a game that is not designed around a theme that implies violence, aggressiveness or competition, none of which interest girls. In the 1980s, these games that flooded the market offered boys an open door to the new computer technology, while girls shied away from the world of computers, perceived as being exclusively masculine. The effect this situation had on the studies chosen and on the resulting restrictions in professional choices were perceived very early on in North America, which saw the danger of creating a new gender gap, once again to the detriment of the girls. Within the American cultural context, the movements for minority rights, along with the studies, publications and courses developed in university Departments of Women's Studies, made public opinion aware of any form of discrimination.

Unequal access to the new computer tool was the subject of numerous investigations which revealed that alienating girls from this technological development would not only severely limit them on the personal and professional levels, but also be a loss for society as a whole. Consequently, a wide range of specific programs aimed at promoting girls' access to the new technologies were tested in the United States.[1] Findings showed that the diversity of pedagogical strategies developed in these programs were also highly useful for children of ethnic minorities (especially Hispanics) and for many boys who were not motivated by the usual approach or for whom it didn't work. For the idea that boys are automatically gifted on a computer is very optimistic. In the early 1980s, programming was said to have eminent virtues for training intelligence, virtues that empiric research never proved, especially for learning that usually remains very basic. At that time it was very hard for studies to recruit a sufficient number of subjects with a functional knowledge of programming language. So when D.M. Kurland's team (Bank Street College, New York) contacted hundreds of high school students to participate in a study, it found only a dozen boys capable of writing a short program correctly. These programs were written in Basic, not in Logo (a language these boys had been taught in school), in spite of a wealth of literature that praised the merits and accessibility of this language derived from the LISP artificial intelligence language and taught as of kindergarten.

What this decade revealed is that a very rapid technological development, for which there was no pedagogical or professional tradition of appropriation, immediately gave rise to a sexist practice regarding the access and use of the new tools that excluded most of the feminine population.

COMPUTER SCIENCE IN THE 1990s: A SECOND CHANCE
FOR WOMEN?

The computer technology of the present decade has evolved so drastically compared to that of the 1980s, both in hardware and software, that we can hope the entirely new applications now available will attract a broader public. Our hypothesis is as follows: spurred by the technological progress made in various areas, PC applications may be created that arouse the interest of potential female users more than in the past, and not just masculine users almost exclusively.

---

1   An analysis of several of these programs can be found in *Les filles et la culture technique (Girls and technical culture)*, Claire Terlon, I.N.R.P.-C.N.R.S., 1985, 150 pp.

In a recent article in *Newsweek* (May 16, 1994, pp 36–44), Barbara Kantrowitz described masculine and feminine behavior toward computers today. She notes that they differ little in many ways from those that arose when microcomputers came out on the market. The American journalist notes that boys brought up in a society that teaches them to dominate or be dominated view computers as something to be mastered, an object that often refuses to execute an order (sometimes even a correct order), which they view as a challenge. Placed in the same situation, girls are inclined to give up, to walk away from this machine that doesn't want to cooperate. The author also notes that girls prefer to work in groups in a non-competitive atmosphere, unlike boys. (The hacker, a programming fanatic, is a solitary person who spends entire nights at his keyboard.) More specifically, men tend to be attracted by the technology itself, while women have a more utilitarian viewpoint; they want applications that are really useful. Kantrowitz rightly detects a 'faster-racecar syndrome' among male PC users. They are fascinated by speed in the automotive world; likewise they have to have the fastest microcomputer. (This is good news for manufacturers, who use this argument to replace one generation of PCs with another more efficient one. Yet we know that most users use only a small share of their machine's resources before a shrewd advertisement incites them to view its performance as being terribly obsolete!)

EVOLUTION IN TECHNOLOGY
One of the driving forces in computer evolution is this race for performance. Microprocessors process information faster and faster. What's more, the price to pay for this performance is governed by Moore's Law: for the same price, performance doubles every 18 months. This makes it possible to develop entirely new software applications and digitize all types of information (images, video and sound, films, magazines, books, phone conversations), thus revolutionizing data storage, processing and dissemination. The explosion in communication technologies thus radically transforms the access to knowledge, along with the work conditions of many professions.

Therefore we can foresee several openings that should interest women more than the computer science of the Eighties ever did. Here are a few examples:

Even in the area of games – which can provide a way of becoming familiar with computer technology – there is a new sophistication that uses the microcomputer's new computation and memory capacities, making it possible to carry out complex modeling (such as the simulation of *Sim City*, where an urban area can be created and managed) or combine graphics with a highly complex plot (such as the superb *Myst*, a deliberate attempt to expand the videogame public). This is a far cry from the games of the 1980s, whose only goal was to exterminate as many adversaries as possible in the shortest possible time. The new games combine multimedia resources with scriptwriting to offer several paths toward a solution. And as studies have shown that girls prefer non-linear games, these new types of game should arouse their interest more.

As of the first experiments, the implementation of virtual reality creation techniques for educational or recreational purposes proved, that girls and boys adapted to these situations easily. More specifically, when virtual reality systems are used to illustrate mathematical or scientific concepts, girls and boys explore the situations proposed with the same interest and absorb these concepts completely. Recently, during a visit to the Computer Museum in Boston (USA), I observed whole classes of high school students moving freely through the various levels of an exhibition. Girls, usually in pairs, sat down for a short trial run on free consoles, but abandoned them if problems arose. They didn't even line up and wait their turn for the most popular experiments besieged by the boys. Yet nothing could get these same girls to give up their seats when they tried the special glasses and gloves used to experience virtual reality. Given the diversity of the applications for this technology in multiple fields, including education – where the spectacular effects of virtual reality experiments on learning are starting to be evaluated – it is highly encouraging to see that this approach arouses such interest in girls.

Perhaps virtual reality, in the sense intended by J. Lanier (1992), one of its pioneers, is only one aspect of what Glover Ferguson, Director of Research for Andersen Consulting, calls the virtualization of the world, made possible by information digitizing and by the telecommunications revolution this digitizing makes possible. The first buds of this virtualization exist. Already millions of subscribers throughout the world exchange information over the 'network of networks', Internet. Its users can simultaneously send dozens of interested individuals electronic messages on state-of-the-art subjects, thus creating 'virtual communities' of people who would never have met otherwise. In companies where electronic mail and software are used by people at different locations to work on the same project, work conditions have been revolutionized. Likewise, the structure of these companies has been transformed radically, as information circulates in a way that is not just hierarchic. However, although studies show that employees using teleconferencing take a more active part in discussions than they would have face to face, even more research shows that, as a general rule, the world of telecommunications is essentially a man's world which women have a hard time entering.

Eighty-five per cent of Internet users are men, and there are scores of anecdotes about women subscribers trying to take part in electronic forums being attacked as soon as they ask a question signed with a feminine name (signature that also generates rather crude questions about their looks and their sexual likes and dislikes). Hence the creation, especially by American women for the moment, of service networks suited to their needs. There are subscribers of both sexes, but most are women and the tone of the exchanges is different. We can only hope that such networks offer their women users the opportunity to become familiar with access to 'on-line' resources in order to make it easier for them to later access the immense resources of Internet and find their niche. Why should women deprive themselves of visiting the virtual museum exhibition (offered this summer on Internet) organized jointly by the Museum of Paleontology of the University of California at Berkeley and the Smithsonian Institute in Washington? The objective is for women not to stand on the sidelines of this extraordinary development in telecommunications, of which Internet is just a forerunner, and which is already working a radical transformation in our learning and work methods and places, not to mention our pastimes...

THE FUTURE IS WIDE OPEN...
'Science Finds, Industry Applies, Man Conforms.' That was the motto of the Chicago World's Fair in 1933. Sixty years later, the concept is reversing. It is society, and not technology alone, that will ultimately pave the way to the computer revolution, and more specifically to the information digitizing revolution in progress. 'All tools are socially constructed,' said David Shields of Georgia Institute of Technology. Lately, the New Jersey Institute of Technology opened a seminar entitled 'Putting technology to work to address society's needs'. This awareness could offer new opportunities to all those – male and female – who have the ideas, energy and creativity to invest in the new developments in information technologies.

Chapter 11

Women, Mathematics and Natural Sciences
Objectives and Results of Learning Among Girls and Boys

Graciela Morgade and Gloria Bonder

ABSTRACT: *As part of the National Program to Promote Equal Opportunity for Women (PRIOM), the Ministry of Culture and Education of Argentina launched the 'Women, Mathematics and Natural Sciences' project. The authors present the results of a survey carried out in primary school and lower secondary school on the images students – girls and boys – have of themselves and their capabilities in mathematics and natural sciences. They put these results, as well as the professional orientations of the older students, into perspective. They close on the notion of '(almost) free choices', which, although indicating the difficulties encountered in equal opportunity action campaigns, kindles great hopes by finding an area of possible freedom.*

Over the past 20 years, especially in the English-speaking countries, mathematics and natural sciences have given rise to numerous studies on differences in behavior between men and women in this area, both in terms of the perception of the social role of these subjects and in the performance of both sexes.

These studies bring to light certain highly significant facts. Overall, by the end of elementary school girls get the same grades as boys, or even better, in mathematics and natural sciences. Yet their performance drops considerably at the end of the first cycle of secondary school, when they lose confidence in their ability to master these subjects and/or discontinue them when these courses become optional.

And even when they have good grades, girls tend to choose a higher education curriculum where sciences are only limited, massively majoring in literature and human sciences in general.

In spite of diverging interpretations of this phenomenon, studies tend to show that it isn't due to a biological predisposition in women and men for a specific type of knowledge, but rather to stereotyped social expectations that differ with sex and are linked to the economic, political and cultural role of women and men in society.

This article presents some of the results of the 'Women, Mathematics and Natural Sciences' project carried out as part of the national program to promote equal opportunity for women (PRIOM) of the Argentine Ministry of Culture and Education. The aim of this study was to verify on a local level the international results of studies on the differences between the sexes as concerns:

(1) the opinion each of the sexes has of his/her own abilities and knowledge in these fields, and the image he/she has of the opposite sex;

(2) the link between these representations and the subsequent professional choices of both.

PRIOM distributed a questionnaire to 8% of students (394 boys and 391 girls) in 7ème classes (last year of elementary school) at 14 public schools in Buenos Aires, as well as to 7% of students (203 girls and 206 boys) at the end of the first cycle of secondary school in public schools of the same neighborhood (three high schools, two commercial training schools and one technical training school).

The criteria used in making up this sample were the sex and socio-economical level of the students, in order to obtain a balanced representation of girls and boys from the various social classes: underprivileged, middle class and wealthy.

The questionnaire covered several areas:

(1) Basic data on the students (girls or boys) in order to pinpoint the dominant social class in the student body;

(2) Student preferences and perceptions, especially in the field of mathematics and natural sciences (at the primary school level), to which were added the exact sciences for secondary school;

(3) Volume of information the students have in these areas;

(4) Choice of secondary school and future projects of the students, boys and girls.

The indicators used to process the information gathered were defined subsequently, based on a quantitative and qualitative analysis of the students' responses.

Correlating school practices and their effects implies two complementary dimensions: one 'material-objective', the other 'symbolic-subjective'. Consequently, both the constraints and conditions of the scholastic structure and the subjectivity of those interacting within that space had to be taken into consideration.

For this reason, school grades constitute an objective 'measurement' (with any notes and remarks on report cards used as the most obvious indicator), as well as a subjective assessment.

Likewise, the subjective way in which each person involved in the education system perceives his/her role also contributes to the difference in results. This perception is built not only on the students' grades (homework, lessons, tests), but also on the 'opinion' the school as a whole and the teacher(s) in particular have of each student, boy or girl. In this model of interpersonal perception, we therefore have to include a 'mirror effect' of the image of the other person, man or woman (Hargreaves, 1979).

The teacher is a 'mirror' for students. Girls and boys evaluate their own image as they see it reflected, so that they often see their scholastic failure as being their fault and accuse themselves, especially of 'insufficient capacity' for assimilating the knowledge that the school wants to transmit to them. In some students, the lack of self-confidence has a negative influence on the image they progressively form of their abilities and chances of succeeding.

The trajectory of girls and boys within the school system follows what Frigerio (1987) calls three types of 'ancipatory biographies' which, depending on the students' scholastic experience are marked by a dominant aspect which is intellectual, emotional or social. We are convinced that, to the student, getting a grade influences his/her choice of optional subjects. This influence is not isolated; it is part of a whole series of differentiating mechanisms that play a part in the interaction between the school and the students.

Students, both boys and girls, also make a personal contribution to the interaction processes in the school and to the effects of these exchanges. The students form an opinion, discuss, give a meaning. As they do not have a privileged position of power in the school, they have a very limited margin of autonomy and consequently an equally limited capacity of negotiation.

As Giddens points out, 'In organized societies, power implies relations induced by the degree of autonomy or dependence of those concerned by the various social interactions. Nevertheless, power-based relations are always reciprocal, even if one of the protagonists (individual or group) is in a position of inferiority. Consequently, power-based relations create a relative dependence for the most autonomous element, while the most dependent individual or group retains a certain margin of autonomy' (Giddens, 1989).

Therefore, without denying the relative autonomy of the students, it must be remembered that, in student–teacher interaction, regardless of the sex of each, the scales are tipped in favor of the teacher.

Here again, this time concerning the influence sex has on the behavior and results of boys and girls during their school years, we can say that the differences observed cannot be explained solely by social pressure outside of the school.

EVALUATION OF RESULTS

In 1993, Argentina created a project to assess the quality of teaching. Among other data gathered were the results obtained by sampling students in their final year of elementary school and of the first cycle of secondary school; this was done for two subjects: mathematics and Spanish.

Table 1 Mathematics
Elementary level

Grade/6	Equivalence 0 to 10	% Girls	% Boys	% Total
6	10	11.34	3.44	7.74
5	8.3	7.04	4.30	5.83
4	6.7	10.31	7.90	9.41
3	5	11.34	13.23	12.74
2	3.3	19.07	18.21	18.65
1	1.7	25.09	26.12	25.98
0	0	15.81	20.96	19.15

First cycle of secondary school

Grade/6	Equivalence 0 to 10	% Girls	% Boys	% Total
6	10	1.33	2.79	1.92
5	8.3	1.33	9.50	5.68
4	6.7	5.10	12.10	8.61
3	5	14.83	18.62	12.74
2	3.3	26.61	26.61	26.92
1	1.7	33.92	20.67	26.56
0	0	21.73	9.68	14.93

The national results obtained using a model set of tests applied to these student samples in twelve regions of the country are shown in Table 1.

The global results proved distressing to the heads of the educational system and for the population in general.

As concerns the subject of this chapter, the following observations stand out:

(1) The percentage of female students given 4 points (i.e. 6.7 on a scale of 0 to 10) or more was 28.69 compared to 15.64 among boys at the end of elementary school.

(2) At the end of the first cycle of secondary school, these results were 7.76% for girls and 24.30% for boys. While the girls' results at the end of elementary school are far better than those of boys, this situation is radically reversed by the end of the first cycle of secondary school.

These observations can be expanded if we compare the results in Spanish class. While girls had better grades than boys at the end of elementary school (40.99% got 4 or more compared with 19.38% among boys), at the end of the first secondary cycle) they confirmed this level, while boys progressed sharply (42.65% among girls compared with 44.75% among boys).

It is obvious that moving on to secondary school causes a differentiation between boys and girls in mathematics.

Representations and Preferences
Favorite Subjects

Boys in the elementary school sample said they preferred the subjects the school put the most value on, the subjects that counted most in the curriculum and in the grades: mathematics, Spanish, human and natural sciences. Subjects such as music, physical education, and manual work were not deemed worthy of mentioning and consequently were almost never cited as favorite subjects.

Mathematics are the favorite subject of students in the sample, chiefly of the boys. They chose mathematics first (45.34%), followed by natural sciences (18.63%) and human sciences in third place (10.54%). Spanish was last, as it is a subject that causes them the most difficulties, as we will see later.

Girls in the sample also chose mathematics first (31.28%). For the other favorite subjects, they chose natural sciences (25.86%), Spanish (17.03%) and human sciences (13.55%).

Consequently, natural sciences come second in order of preference for both sexes. However, as underlined later on, the areas that arouse the most interest in this subject have a low technological content and are clearly linked with the psycho-sexual development of students at this level.

At the end of the first secondary cycle, mathematics are almost universally mentioned. Girls (42.46%) and boys (40%) both rank them first. The most significant differences have to do with social origin. Sixty-five per cent of girls from wealthy families prefer mathematics (48% among boys), while only 21.1% of girls from low-income families choose mathematics (0% among boys).

Hardest Subjects

When we asked students what subjects were hardest for them, we wanted to find out not only what reasons the students gave, but also what those reasons concealed. The students' responses mentioned several options. They attributed their problems to a variety of factors: to themselves, the teaching method used, the skills required, the content of the subject, liking or disliking school. Obviously, we found it very interesting to determine the relative weight of each reason.

At the end of primary school, boys ranked Spanish as the hardest subject (29.57%). In second place they ranked mathematics (17.29%), followed by human sciences (14.54%) and natural sciences last (3.48%).

The difficulties many boys have in Spanish merit particular attention. Generally speaking, the teaching of Spanish in schools consists of teaching 'the art of speaking properly'. For this reason, school gives priority to a mode of linguistic expression different than the one children use in their daily life. Consequently, students are required to express themselves in a language different from that which they use in other places, such as youth clubs, the street, among friends or on the football field, and different from what they hear on the television. In school, bad grammar and bad language are both banned.

The scholastic language thus appears to be 'superior' to others. It gives priority to 'more refined' forms of expression among teachers and students alike. Girls characteristically 'speak better' than boys, so that boys often have more problems in Spanish, because school places more value on and appreciates the 'correct' forms of expression used more by girls than boys. Moreover, in connection with the above, school also emphasizes and takes into consideration the formal aspects of the learning of the language.

'Good penmanship' and good 'oral expression' characterize girls more than boys.

What is particularly interesting in the students' responses is the type of justification they give to explain their learning problems. In both cases, boys and girls, the most frequent reason is their own limitations: 'It's hard', 'I don't understand', 'I don't know how to think it through'. And they don't take into consideration the aspects of the educational process that make it harder to absorb a given subject.

Girls cite this interpretation more often than boys (51.49% and 34.59% respectively). This trend cuts across all the social classes.

At the end of the first secondary cycle, the preference for a given subject becomes less important, as students are more concerned with choosing an orientation from a range of very diverse curricula. It should be noted that only 5% of students (all males) in the technical school mentioned mathematics as the hardest subject, explaining their response by the teaching method and the contents of the program.

Differences between the sexes become clear in the reasons cited by students at this level who have problems in mathematics. The majority of girls feel that 'it's difficult' and that they 'have to work hard', while boys usually mention the poor quality of the teaching or their own lack of work. Moreover, among girls who cited their lack of skills, the large majority (83%) mentioned this reason for mathematics, whereas they attributed their problems in other subjects to insufficient personal work. Mathematics obviously appear to be a subject that calls upon 'aptitude' more than 'the desire to learn', especially among girls.

Usefulness of Mathematics

This question places students in a hypothetical future. At the end of primary school, the highest percentage of responses on the future usefulness of learning math in school concerns the work dimension: 'to have a business', 'to be a good salesperson', etc. This dimension doesn't vary between girls and boys. Another factor of usefulness often mentioned is daily routines: 'to give the right change', 'to go shopping', etc. Girls give these responses a bit more often than boys. 'To continue my studies' is the other dimension mentioned most often and for which there is no difference between boys and girls.

In secondary school, significant differences exist for the three streams observed. In commercial studies, the idea of usefulness in work and higher education prevails, especially for girls (49.2%) compared with 30% of boys.

In the technical section, where there are no girls, a more global vision prevails ('math...is useful for everything'), while at the end of secondary school the university preparation or intellectual aspects of the field are praised ('mental gymnastics', for example) for both sexes. The reason that differentiates the sexes most significantly is linking mathematical knowledge with daily living; there is almost a 10-point difference in favor of women. In other words, girls find a direct practical usefulness for this subject more often than their male friends.

Who Gets Better Grades in Mathematics: Boys or Girls?
If we ask students who does better in mathematics, 25.35% of the entire elementary school sample feel that results are similar for boys and girls: 31% of girls and 22% of boys. The ideas underlying the affirmation of equality in results are expressed in responses such as 'in my class it's even – I think they have the same level', 'both are equal because we are all growing up', 'we are equal because we have the same abilities', 'equal because we know the same things', 'girls and boys because we study', 'it depends on everyone's own intelligence', 'I think it's balanced because no one is a genius or a dunce', 'sex has nothing to do with the subject; all you have to do is understand it'. What's more, we find reasons such as 'I think we are the same; boys are disorganized but intelligent', 'we don't have to work at it very hard and when we have trouble we work harder'.

A significant percentage (nearly 66%) doesn't believe in this equality. To some of the students, boys get better grades in mathematics for the following reasons: 'they're more intelligent', 'they know more', 'they like it more', 'it's easier for them', 'they're better at it', 'boys have more instinct for thinking than for learning'.

Those who consider that girls get the best grades also cite similar reasons: 'girls have a more developed brain', 'girls because they need to know how to count to do shopping and manage the week's money', etc. Moreover, they insist on aspects such as 'they work harder', 'they study more', 'they behave better in class', 'they pay attention', 'they're responsible'. Abnegation, effort, careful studying and work habits are feminine qualities that explain the better grades in mathematics from the standpoint of their boy classmates.

As concerns the secondary level sample, the global assessment of equality of grades is maintained (27.6%), as are the differences between girls (32.2%) and boys (23.1%).

In the sample overall, we note no predominance of one sex over the other. Nevertheless, girls feel they get better grades (33.5% compared with 17% among boys), while boys feel superior (35% compared with 23.72% among girls). The most visible difficulty in the sample appears in the technical school, where 65% of the boys feel that men are better in mathematics. It should be emphasized that the responses least favorable to the equality of the sexes come from girls and boys from an underprivileged background, along with boys from wealthy families. Nevertheless, in the first case there are almost as many responses in favor of girls as of boys, while girls from wealthy families loudly assert the superiority of their sex and their male classmates claim the prize just as forcefully.

Among the reasons cited, there are differences worthy of mentioning. In favour of girls, we noted their hard work and the time they set aside for the work; for the boys, the qualities are their talent and their intelligence. We observe assessments such as 'boys are actually more gifted but more lazy, while girls are less gifted but more responsible'.

In secondary schools, a similar question on physics was added, to which responses were relatively more stereotyped. Thirty-four per cent of the overall sample thought that both sexes achieved the same results (44% of women and 22% of men). Women are obviously far more equitable. Of the sample (the others didn't answer the question) 41.8% is divided clearly into 15% who feel that girls do better (10.8% of girls and 16% of boys, again with the reason being that they work harder) while 26.8% feel that boys do better (13% of girls compared with 55.5% of boys, especially those in the technical school and those from the least privileged school.

To complete this information, the most frequent reason cited remains that of masculine 'intelligence'.

Other Knowledge – Cognitive and Emotional Stimulation
If we accept that there are no innate 'interests' in human nature but only drives or impulses that stimulate people to act or create, we will see that education is the process that generates interests in girls and boys. What's more, it is often education that awakens a 'vocation'.

We analyzed the output, self-perception and prejudices about mathematics, also considering that this school subject is one of the main constituent and epistemological bases of the so-called 'hard sciences'. There is, however, another type of approach to knowledge and procedures involved in these types of knowledge: via the natural sciences.

What Did You Like About the Natural and Exact Sciences?

First of all, it is obvious that 'natural sciences' are not the most 'loved' subject, nor the most 'hated'. Students generally find them interesting. In elementary school, the favorite topic of students of both sexes concerns the question of 'reproduction'. Next, girls prefer 'ecology', 'AIDS', 'the human body' and 'drugs', in that order. Boys choose practically the same topics, but in another order of priority: reproduction, human body, AIDS, ecology... The field in natural sciences that gets the most votes by far is biology.

It is not surprising that, of the scientific streams considered to be 'hard', biology is the most feminized and probably the one generally preferred by women teachers (who make up 92% of primary school teachers in Argentina).

Topics concerning astronomy (the planets, the origin of the universe, etc.), physics and chemistry (which, in the scholastic culture, consists of 'experiments' or 'investigation') is not mentioned by girls as one of their preferences, and only occasionally by boys.

As part of the inventory of opportunities offered to elementary school students to develop their interests and build or 'demolish' gender-based stereotypes, we also must cover aspects that concern contact with machines and instruments. Here it is surprising to note an even distribution of responses concerning the use of a computer or microscope (greater differences between the social classes than between the sexes) and the participation in household repairs. The difference is considerable, however as concerns participation in car repairs; 55% of boys participated compared to 29% of girls, only 14% of whom found it enjoyable.

This trend is found again in the first secondary cycle, and it is interesting to note that both girls and boys like to work in the physics laboratory.

Women and Men Famous for Their Inventions

The question concerned knowledge of famous inventors, men and women, and the responses were predictable but nonetheless discouraging. A large number of students, girls and boys, didn't answer this question, generally due to ignorance. Of the responses obtained 97% concerned male inventors or scientists (Einstein being the most well-known, followed by Edison and Galileo among others). Only a small number mentioned 'the Curies' and under 2% cited Marie Curie.

Role Model

It is obvious that girls have almost no female role model in the fields of natural sciences. So who are the models of girls and boys leaving elementary school? To the question on the person who they would most want to be like, almost two-thirds of girls said that they didn't want to be like anyone 'because I'm happy the way I am'. Of those who named someone, 40% chose an actress, 20% a fashion model and 10% a heroine from a novel. The boys' responses, on the other hand, were more varied; they generally chose athletes, musicians, historic figures and heroes from novels. These trends are found in the first secondary cycle, although with a slightly different breakdown.

Moreover, the data gathered proved eloquent. Neither sex had information on the professional activities of men or women scientists. Girls limited themselves to fashion models and actresses as role models for the future.

Boys have a broader range of possibilities. Each of the masculine choices requires different personal skills and aptitudes to be developed jointly: physical dexterity, creativity and expressiveness, courage, daring, strength, intelligence. For the girls, on the contrary, the image is limited to being beautiful, a little bit stupid, always young...

If we compare these results with the preceding ones, we find the combination of two realities: on the one hand, the weak knowledge applied to physics, astronomy or chemistry, on the other hand the lack of information and contact between girl students and non-stereotyped fields of activity and knowledge. This combination, by omission, gives a 'free rein' to the dominant influence of traditional representations of females.

Enrolment in Secondary Schools and Universities

A breakdown of national enrolment in secondary school by sex indicates that women are concentrated mainly in the baccalaureate sections (63.8%) and commercial sections (57.1%) and are in the minority in technical (21%) and 'agricultural' (28.8%) sections. The breakdown in enrolment is completed by two options – far smaller in number of students – where women are also the majority: artistic sections (70%) and sanitary and social action (75%). This trend in national results is found in the samples observed, although the 'agricultural' component is missing.

Who Chooses the School?

According to the students leaving elementary school, the choice of the secondary school was usually made by the students (girls and boys) with their parents. In second place we find a large number of students (girls and boys) who say they chose themselves. When asked who took part in the choice of the school, this group replied 'me, all by myself'. Here it is important to point out a difference in behavior according to sex; of the 188 students of this second group, 63% were boys and 37% girls.

Reasons for Choosing a School

Both girls and boys say they chose a given school because 'they liked it' (40.1%) without any other details. In second place, the choice made seems to have been based on the fact that it was a good school with good teachers and that it offered a certain specialization. If we look at the breakdown of the responses according to sex, inside each of these groups we find that girls give priority to the fact that it's a 'good school' (60.3%) with good teachers, while boys give priority to the curriculum taught (63.1%). The choices made by the elementary school students, boys and girls, are also based on geographic proximity ('it's near my house') and on the fact that their sisters and brothers attend that school. To a lesser extent, other criteria were mentioned: environment, material conditions, 'atmosphere', no entrance exam.

The Students' Professional Future

When students are asked about their professional future or their future trade, the responses reveal significant differences according to gender at the end of elementary school, although a large percentage (27%) still don't know exactly what they want to do later on. Although girls don't see themselves in careers or positions that involve technical knowledge, many of them mention teaching among their projects. 59% indicate that they will go to university to study literature and human sciences and 37% choose medical school.

This trend is continued in the choice of university studies after secondary school. Table 2 shows enrolment at the University of Buenos Aires, the largest in the country.

	% Men		% Women		Total
Agronomy	1818	68.3	844	31.7	2662
Architecture	6483	52.6	5828	47.4	12,311
Economic sciences	12,926	57.5	9559	42.5	22,485
Exact sciences	2832	51.3	2692	48.7	5524
Social sciences	2852	43	3794	57	6646
Veterinary medicine	1184	48.6	1253	51.4	2437
Law	9898	44.1	12,555	55.9	22,453
Pharmacy	1517	29.4	3637	70.6	5154
Philosophy	2068	30.2	4784	69.8	6852
Engineering	6252	80.1	1549	19.9	7801
Medicine	6655	34.7	12,486	65.3	19,141
Odontology	985	37.2	1661	62.8	2646
Psychology	1467	20.5	5692	79.5	7159
University preparation	20,339	44	26,006	56	46,345
Total	**76,682**	**45.4**	**92,126**	**54.6**	**168,808**

Feminine stereotypes are clearly prevalent in the choice of university
  studies

If we show girls and boys a list of the various fields of specialization,
both sexes see boys as having a broader range of choices (education
and psychology, for example) while girls are almost never seen as being
able to study engineering.

CONCLUSIONS
(Almost) Free Choices
There is always a certain amount of conditioning or a certain form of
determinism involved in a choice, given that the subject has a certain
liberty to make (almost) free choices.

One's personal history, social and scholastic biography and material
living conditions weigh heavily when making decisions about the
future. As we have seen, one key factor is the considerable socio-cultural weight of the images traditionally linked to one sex or the other.

Yet the subject has a margin of autonomy and freedom to go beyond
this conditioning. Therefore, it is important, first and foremost, to bring
together all the conditions necessary to allow students to make their
choice with as much freedom as possible.

Being aware of these conditions, material-objective or those called symbolic-objective here, can open up a whole new range of possible choices to the student. The symbolic dimension depends on perceptions, images, ambitions, expectations and hopes linked with the results obtained during the students' school years. Based on the observations of the images students have of themselves and of the opposite sex as concerns mathematics and natural sciences, we can draw the following conclusions:

(1) Math is 'harder' for women than for men, which is quite clear for all social classes. In most cases, women attribute this difficulty more to themselves, to personal difficulties ('I have to work harder') than to the subject itself or the way it is taught. The mechanisms that create this situation are the result of the socialization of women within the family and at school. To the stereotyped and differentiated expectations according to sex are added the role women and men play in the professional world. Nevertheless, math remains an attractive ('favourite') subject for students, both boys and girls, even if more boys choose it. We can conclude that math mobilizes boys and girls affectively.

(2) Only one-quarter of students in the survey see no difference between the sexes in math results. Here, women have a more equitable vision than men. For the remaining 75%, there are differences, although there appears to be no dominant trend in favor of either sex. In any case, the reason is always closely linked with masculine and feminine stereotypes, emphasizing that 'boys are intelligent' and 'girls are studious'. This division is manifest as concerns physical sciences.

(3) At the end of primary school and the end of the first secondary cycle, the volume of knowledge on the specific contents and the professional field of sciences and technology is extremely limited, and consequently cannot motivate a choice in these orientations. In any case, the school does not complement the social information accessible, which is too limited and stereotyped.

(4) The influence of stereotypes considerably affects students in technical schools and boys from socially deprived families.

(5) In our study, responses on professional future reflect the trends revealed in the breakdown between the school and university streams: women do not go into science or technology. At the end

of elementary school the 'family' has a greater effect on the choices of girls than on the decisions of boys. This leads us to believe that it is the parents who influence the stereotyped choices. At the end of the first secondary cycle, it seems that the stereotypes are even more solidly rooted in girls and boys: 'exact sciences don't suit the feminine character; women can only succeed if they work hard and long'.

It is obvious that schools must evolve considerably if true coeducation is to be implemented.

ANNEX

PRIOM was created by the Ministry of Culture and Education of the Republic of Argentina with the following objectives:

(1) Introduce into scholastic instruction:

    (a) the contributions of women to the economic and cultural development of societies throughout history

    (b) the problems created by their position in society.

(2) Develop an educational experience that encourages:

    (a) the building of relations between the sexes, founded on equality, solidarity and mutual respect

    (b) the active, equal participation of both sexes in community living and family responsibilities

    (c) the integration of women in decision-making positions.

Since its creation, vast progress has been made, such as the integration of the idea of equal opportunity for both sexes in federal legislation on education; the transverse treatment of the theme of 'gender' in the educational curriculum at all levels and in teacher training; the execution of three awareness campaigns among the educational community and the production of a large number of materials for non-sexist instruction.

Chapter 12

Interaction Between Teachers and Students (Girls or Boys) in Mathematics Classes

Josette Loudet-Verdier and Nicole Mosconi

ABSTRACT: *This article describes a study carried out in France in four classes (CM1, 6è and two 5è) on interaction between teachers and students, taking into account the gender of the students and that of the teachers. A one-hour mathematics lesson was filmed on video and analyzed in each class. The analysis used the following parameters: (1) number of times questions where a student's first name was called out, according to his/her gender; (2) number of exchanges for each student; (3) time spent by the teacher in interaction with each student; and (4) content of intervention and instructions. In conclusion, the authors observe that the results of this study confirm those obtained in other countries. Teachers tend to have more – and longer – interaction with boys than with girls. The inequality seems clearer in classes taught by women than those taught by men, but the differences are very subtle ones. All these imperceptible differential elements could be factors that explain the limited self-confidence of girls that the surveys noted regarding mathematics. This article proposes a self-observation method for teachers that is simple to practice, provided a videotape of a class is available.*

Numerous British and American studies have proven that teachers' relations with students differ depending on their gender and that they interact more with boys than with girls, often without being aware of it. These studies also show that boys are encouraged more often than girls, and sometimes criticized more, and that girls are asked simpler questions than boys. These characteristics are even more accentuated in scientific courses, and especially in mathematics.

To our knowledge, few studies have been done as yet to test these results in France. A multi-field team from the University of Paris

X-Nanterre's Department of Educational Sciences[1] set this as one of its objectives. It worked from video and audio recordings of mathematics lessons.

The present article gives the results of four one-hour mathematics classes, one elementary school class (CM1 on writing big numbers) and three lower secondary school courses (one 6è on orthogonal symmetry, one 5èA on the parallelogram and one 5èB on the product of fractions). In the two sequences for 5è, the teachers were men; in the two other sequences, they were women.

For the part of the study on interaction according to gender, we carried out several types of investigation. Initially, we counted the number of times in each lesson that the teacher called out the first name of a student, then the first name of a boy or the first name of a girl. The results were entered in the table on page 148 of this article, with each class characterized by the topic of the lesson, the total number of students, and the number of boys and girls (as an absolute number and as a percentage). On the first line we indicated the total number of names called out by the teacher, on the second and third lines the number by gender (as an absolute number and a percentage). Then, in order to compare the classes in spite of their difference in number and the different proportion of boys and girls, we calculated the number of first names called out per girl or boy student.

In CM1, given the breakdown by gender of students in the class, equity would have decreed that the teacher call out 44% girl's names and 56% boy's names. But the actual proportions were respectively 27% and 72%. Consequently we can say that boys were called on twice as

1   This team was made up in response to a Call for Tender from the Ministry of Research and Higher Education. The title of the study is 'Implicit components in the behavior and language of teachers in mathematics classes and their effect on student learning'. The team, led by Claudine Blanchard-Laville (Professor of Educational Sciences at the University of Paris X), was made up of mathematics didacticians and researchers in the fields of psychosociology, psychoanalysis and ethopsychology. Its members were Jacky Beillerot (Professor of Educational Sciences, University Paris X), Pierre Berdot (Mathematics Lecturer, University Paris VI), Alain Mercier (Doctor of Mathematics Didactics, IREM of Aix-Marseille), Nicole Mosconi (Professor of Educational Sciences, University Paris X), Suzanne Nadot (Educational Sciences Lecturer, IUFM of Brittany, Marie-Hélène Salin (Lecturer, IUFM of Aquitaine), Maria-Luisa Schubauer-Leoni (Professor, School of Psychology and Educational Sciences, University of Geneva).

often as girls. It also verifies a remark that is classical in this type of study: that teachers know the boys' names better than the girls' because teachers never hesitate when they call on boys but when calling on a girl they often say 'Ah... Now what is her name?'

In lower secondary school classes, we didn't find the same disproportion. In the 6è class, a few more girls were called upon, but given the proportion of the sexes in the class this is fairly equitable, with a very slight advantage for the boys. Of the two 5è classes, where the teachers were men, the first was perfectly equitable and the second gave a clear advantage to girls' names, even though they were far more numerous than boys in this class.

We could consider counting names a superficial process for evaluating how girls and boys are treated in a classroom, because the teacher can call upon a student without calling him/her by name. The teacher may also say his/her name several times in a row, as was the case in CM1, and that throws the calculations off. Therefore we tried to count the number of exchanges between the teacher and each student, girl or boy, defining an exchange as a short sequence during which the teacher addressed a student to give an instruction, ask a question or make a comment, and in which the student concerned responded. It can also be a short sequence during which a student made a comment or asked a question on his/her own initiative, to which the teacher responded. For an extended dialogue, each question-and-response pair was counted as an exchange. The instructions or questions addressed to the entire class were not counted. It should be explained that this count cannot be totally accurate, as it was not always easy to see on screen which student the teacher was calling upon or which student was talking or responding. In each class, we had to leave out a few cases where we couldn't identify the interlocutor. The table gives the results of this count below the results for names and using the same presentation. Then, for each class, we simply took the three girls and three boys with whom dialogue was most frequent and added up the number of exchanges between them and the teacher.

In the CM1 class, the disproportion in exchanges between the teacher and students of each sex is more limited than the disproportion in names, but it remains substantial. We find exactly the same proportion as in the English-language studies, i.e. two-thirds interaction with boys to one-third with girls. If we take into consideration the number of exchanges per student, we note that there are major disproportions; for boys this number ranges from 41 to 2 and for girls from 22 to 2. We

Statistical Analysis (Nicole Mosconi)

Class	CM1		6th		5th		5th-2	
Subject of lesson	Writing large numbers		Orthogonal symmetry		Parallelogram		Product of fractions	
Number of students	25		21		23		24	
Number G & B	11 G	14 B	12 G	9 B	12 G	11 B	15 G	9 B
Proportion G & B	44.0%	56.0%	57.1%	42.9%	52.2%	47.8%	62.5%	37.5%
Number of first names called by teacher	194		45		17		74	
First names G & B	54	140	24	21	9	8	57	17
In percentage	27.8%	72.2%	43.6%	38.2%	52.9%	47.1%	77.0%	23.0%
No. per student G & B (*)	(4.9)	(10.0)	(2.0)	(2.3)	(0.8)	(0.7)	(3.8)	(1.9)
Ratio G/B (*)	2.0		1.2		1.0		0.5	
Number of exchanges	309		126		143		169	
Interaction with G & B	104	205	54	72	70	73	120	49
In percentage	33.7%	66.3%	42.9%	57.1%	49.0%	51.0%	71.0%	29.0%
No. per student G or B	(9.5)	(14.6)	(4.5)	(8.0)	(5.8)	(6.6)	(8.0)	(5.4)
Ratio G/B	1.5		1.8		1.1		0.7	
3 G and 3 B with most exchanges	22–14–14	41–37–31	14–10–06	29–9–09	17–12–06	16–15–11	46–11–10	19–14–04
Teacher/student time (in seconds)	725	1489	543	730	598	709	1090	541
(in minutes)	12mn 5s	24mn 49s	19mn 3s	12mn 10s	9mn 58s	11mn 49s	18mn 10s	9mn 15s
Time for one student G & B (*)	65.9	106.4	45.3	81.1	49.8	64.5	27.7	60.1
Times at blackboard	5	8	1	1	0	0	9	4

* The number in parentheses indicates the value of the parameter measured and per student, G or B. This value was used to compare the classes in spite of the different student body. For example, in CM1 one girl was called on 4.9 times (54/11 = 4.9) also note that the woman teacher often interacted with certain students (especially girls) without calling them by name. Should we conclude that relations were more personalized with the boys than with the girls?

In the 6è class, the teacher had far more exchanges with the boys than with the girls, although the number of boys was slightly lower. As the last line of the count indicates, the woman teacher had a large number of exchanges with one boy, as if he monopolized her attention. As in CM1, the first student named is also the one with whom the teacher had the most exchanges during the hour.

In the two 5è classes, the situation was different. In the first, the equity was respected in both interaction and in names called out. The other 5è is an interesting case in that it is an 'aberration' compared to the data of the existing studies: the teacher interacted far more often with the girls (77%) than with the boys, even given the fact that there were more girls in the class (62.5%). One theory that would explain this is that the strong disproportion tends to make boys a minority and therefore relative 'invisible'. When asked, the teacher stated that girls were dominant in this class and boys rather shy.

We can, however, consider that the interaction count is still too inaccurate a procedure, as it doesn't make it possible to evaluate the time the teacher set aside for students according to their sex. It is, of course, very difficult in one class to give equal time to every student, especially as this formal equity would mean a very limited time for each: 60 minutes of class divided between 25 students would mean 2 min 24 sec for each one of them. The time set aside for each might even out over several classes, or over the entire school year. Yet nothing is less sure, and we can just as easily think that the same situations tend to reoccur from one class to the next, even if the most frequent case obviously falls somewhere between the two. Therefore, we can obtain an initial indication by examining the time set aside for each student during one class.

The third part of the table gives the chronometer results. Here again, these results must be viewed with some caution, as timing is a delicate operation. It is sometimes hard to get observers to agree on exactly when an exchange between a teacher and a student starts or ends. We used an average as a reference, calculated based on timing by two different observers.

In CM1, the class started as a series of exercises (five in all) on which each student worked, first individually, then one student going to the blackboard for the correction. The teaching method used was an active one. Children had to find the solution to the problems posed by themselves. If the student at the blackboard made a mistake, it wasn't always rectified by the teacher; sometimes it resulted from a discussion among the students that the teacher merely supervised. Sometimes this discussion was lengthy; the second exercise lasted 27 min and, given the students' questions, sometimes up to four of them went to the blackboard to try to find the solution. But it was during these discussions that the positions of the boys and girls were very unequally shared, as the teacher spent far more time interacting with the boys than with the girls. The boys spent far longer at the blackboard than the girls. In the first exercise, a boy spent 5 min at the blackboard; in the second, two boys spent 20 and 15 min respectively. Finally, a fourth spent 3 min and 30 sec on the fifth exercise. On the second exercise, girls spent 30 sec, 3 min and 9 min respectively; on the third exercise one girl spent 3 min, and another 3 min on the fourth exercise.

In the 6è class, the disproportion for time grew compared with that for interaction. The woman teacher spent one-third more time with boys than with girls. The class was divided up into three lessons, including the first which was mental arithmetic in which the teacher interacted with the entire class at the same time. Only disciplinary remarks were addressed to one student at a time, usually to boys. In a second lesson, where the students corrected two exercises done at home, two students (a girl and a boy) took turns at the blackboard, staying there 2 min and 4 min respectively. Finally, the longest part of the class was set aside for a lesson on orthogonal symmetry, with exercises. It was especially during this lesson that the difference between boys and girls was visible, with the teacher paying more attention to the boys than to the girls. It should be noted that three students in this class (a boy and two girls) were never called upon or addressed by the teacher.

In the 5èA class, it is surprising to note that, although interaction was equitably distributed between girls and boys, a certain disproportion is observed in duration. Exchanges with boys were generally longer than those with girls. Moreover, no one went to the blackboard in this class.

In the 5èB class, we find the same advantage as above for girls as regards the length of interaction. Here we had a class built around a series of arithmetic exercises, where a student did an exercise at the blackboard while the others worked it out at their desks. A fairly large number of students (13) went to the blackboard, with a greater proportion of girls than boys (9 to 4). Moreover, certain girls stayed at the blackboard a long time (we will come back to this later).

Finally, to analyze these differences between the sexes, we used a more qualitative analysis, studying the attitudes of teachers to girls and boys as well as the way both were addressed.

In the CM1 class, instructions and questions were addressed to either sex indiscriminately: 'Read this number' or 'What does it say?'; 'What do you do?' or 'Now do it!'; 'Tell us what to do', or 'Tell us why?' or 'Do you know why?' or 'Do you agree?'. But there were differences, especially in the questions asked of students at the blackboard. Boys were asked to 'explain' what they were doing when they wrote a number and told to 'think' or 'know what to do' (to find the solution). 'Do you understand now?' the woman teacher asked one of them. The girls weren't asked these questions. When they were sent to the blackboard, it was often to resolve a blocked situation. The teacher told them, 'Help me' (to make a table) or 'What do you think?', after which she sent them back to their desk quickly – and often brusquely. As for girls who had problems with an exercise, the teacher didn't tell them 'Tell us' but rather 'Try to tell us' (what you wrote) or 'Try to give me' (the numbers written on your paper) as if she weren't sure that the girl could. Boys with problems were rarely called upon. It was as if 'explaining', 'thinking', 'understanding' and 'comprehending' were reserved for a few boys in the class.

In the 6è class, very few differences were observed between the instructions and questions addressed to girls and to boys. All were asked to 'read the instructions', to 'think', to 'explain' (why there wasn't symmetry). We noted a difference in one point: only boys were told to try to 'imagine' (the superposition of two figures to see if they were symmetric). For responses given by students of both sexes, negative remarks were balanced in number and there were a few more positive remarks for the girls. There is an obvious imbalance only as regards the number of disciplinary remarks. Four of them were addressed at girls and 13 at boys, and of the latter 8 were for the same boy who the teacher feared would be rowdy and was trying to control by constant surveillance. This class also had what could be called 'invisible' girls; they raised their hand for a good portion of the class without being called on. One of them in particular (in the front row) was never called on. At one point, the woman teacher finally noticed her and asked 'Do you want something, Sonia?', to which the student replied 'No, just to go to the blackboard'. But it wasn't time to go to the blackboard and the dialogue stopped there; subsequently she was never sent to the black-board or called on. She wasn't the one who worried the teacher; it was the boy she felt was rowdy and to whom she talked constantly. At the end of the class, she told him she wouldn't put up with his behavior and that they would have to clear that up at the next class. Sonia left right behind him and told the teacher 'Good bye, Mrs. D!' She seemed to be looking for some sign of interest on the part of the teacher, who didn't answer because she was too busy with the boy. She didn't see nor hear the girl.

The 5èA class was a question-and-answer type dialogue between the male teacher and the students. Sometimes they were called on by the teacher, sometimes they answered on their own initiative. The teacher's method was to repeat exactly what the student had said if the answer was correct or to go over the answer and correct it and giving the necessary information and explanations. The exact repetition occurred for 20 of the boys' answers and 13 of the girls'. There were very few negative comments and they were balanced (3 for each sex, plus one disciplinary remark to a boy) and many indications of approval (15 for girls and 13 for boys), among them 'yes' (11 for girls and 8 for boys) and 'yes, but' (4 for girls and 5 for boys). The balance found above was thus reinforced by this more qualitative analysis, with the exception of repeating responses which was in favor of the boys.

We should mention a symptomatic episode in this class. At one moment, a girl excited by the teacher's questions raised her hand to answer, calling out 'ma'am!', which made the others laugh. The teacher snapped back, 'Shall I just call you sir then!' And probably to soften the blow of his remark, he immediately asked her to respond, saying 'Go ahead then!' But the girl didn't answer and sat there without saying anything for a while, as did the girl sitting next to her.

That leaves the last class, where interaction with girls was by far the rule. We saw that girls were sent to the blackboard more often than boys. But this is a relative advantage, given the caustic remarks some-times made to the girls. They concerned their physical appearance as well as their intellectual performance. The male teacher told one girl 'You knew we were being filmed today so you got out your jewelry, didn't you!' A surprising comment, as the start of the film shows that the teacher had forgotten to warn the students at the last class that they would be filmed, as he had been asked to do by the researchers, and so had to inform them at the start of the filming session to respond to their surprised looks. Another girl at the blackboard didn't position the fraction bars and the equal sign correctly and he said 'She's nice, she says yes, but she can't get it right!' While in the middle of multiplication problems, the teacher slipped in a two fraction sum, an operation taught in a previous class and reviewed at the start of this class. Several students were fooled. Among them was a girl, to whom the teacher said 'I was sure I'd catch a few birds. You proved me right!' There were no equivalent remarks for the boys, although there were a few ironic comments. To one of them, he said 'You're splitting hairs!', but this was immediately softened when he told another student 'You can help him because he's lost. That's unusual for Julien...but it happens.' This irony is nothing compared to what happened to Sophie. While everyone was supposed to find 'the sentence that describes what you have to do to calculate the product of two quotients', the teacher turned to Sophie. 'Sophie, you're going to end up under the table... Did you write anything, Sophie? No... I'm not surprised, because you didn't have a dynamic enough attitude to find the right sentence.' At the end of the class, Sophie was sent to the blackboard to reduce a complex fraction to its lowest form. This gave rise to a long dialogue, from which we took the following passages:

TEACHER: O.K. Let's go. Show us what you have to do!

SOPHIE: I don't understand, sir.

The teacher explained again and said:

Go on! Calculate the product. Come on! Apply the rule!

The student panicked and did nothing. The teacher got impatient:

Come on, Sophie. Snap out of it.

She tried a timid answer.

TEACHER: Come on then. Do it! Don't be so shy! Come on! Hurry up!

The dialogue continued in this vein for several minutes. To show her he was bored, the teacher pretended to snore and said 'Come on' 12 times and 'Let's go' 4 times. At the end he sent her back to her desk, saying 'Go on! Shameful!'. To leave the room at the end of the class, Sophie pulled up her coat collar to hide from the camera.

We might wonder which is better for girls: less attention and interest, or this unpleasant type of solicitude.

Generally speaking, we can say that the English-language studies were confirmed. There is a tendency for math teachers, male and female, to interact more with boys than with girls, and especially to spend more time with them.[2] But we also saw that there are exceptions to this tendency. We obviously can't pretend that four classes are representative of anything, and other observations will be necessary to confirm these tendencies. In the four classes studied here, inequality is more evident in those taught by women than those taught by men. We don't know if this tendency is generalized, and although most studies show that the gender of the teacher doesn't cause any significant difference, we need to find out if there is a constant disparity in classes in France. In some classes, such as the 6è, these differences seem linked to disciplinary problems that women teachers have (or fear having) with some of the boys. We also see that the way these differences are manifested is complex and subtle, and changes from one class to the next, with more attention toward girls that doesn't exclude a certain sadism.

We feel we tested a method that allows each teacher to get an idea of his/her behavior and reactions toward the girls and boys in the class. These attitudes and their characteristics are not really conscious ones, which means they are almost impossible to analyze objectively through self-observation alone while the class is in progress.[3]

---

2   The study by G. Felouzis (1994) confirms these results for lower secondary school mathematics classes.

3   cf. Spender (1982)

Part Three

Which Strategies for Change?

Chapter 13

The Difficulty of Changing Social Behaviour

Véréna Aebischer and Catherine Valabrègue

INTRODUCTION

This chapter gives a brief presentation of two pilot experiments carried out in schools, one in France and one in Ireland, and intended to influence the orientation decisions of young girls in favor of occupations in scientific or technological fields. These two experiments were part of a European action program in which Catherine Valabrègue served as consultant, a program aimed at 'stimulating girls' interest and participation in scientific and technical studies, especially in New Computer Technologies'. They were set up in response to the Resolution of June 3, 1985, voted by the Ministries of Education of the member countries of the European Community, regarding equal opportunity between girls and boys. Although a large number of similar initiatives had been implemented in the Western countries as a whole, this was the first time that the Commission of the European Communities decided to launch an action-research program of such scope and carry it out in parallel in nine volunteer member countries.[1]

These two experiments reflect two fundamentally different approaches to the question. In the French experiment, the action's objective was to reach girls on an emotional level, later bringing them to reconsider and even change their initial professional plans (Aebischer, 1988, 1989). In the experiment carried out in Ireland (Gleeson, 1988, 1989), the main objective was to reverse the negative attitudes girls might have about science and technology by teaching them skills in these fields that are generally not very developed in girls. Consequently, the purpose was not to affect the girls' mentalities but rather

---

1   Germany, United Kingdom, French-speaking Belgium, Denmark, Spain, France, Ireland, Italy and Portugal.

their actual behavior. Although carried out with girls and boys in France and with girls and partially with boys in Ireland, these two experiments was essentially aimed at the orientation of girls, putting to one side any orientation of boys toward occupations that were traditionally non-masculine.

As did all the other member countries participating, Ireland and France proceeded by phases: a pilot and development phase in 1986, an initial work phase in 1987–88 to test the experimentation tool, and a second work phase in 1988–89 generally focused on furthering the action and disseminating it throughout the national framework and in other member countries. The first work phase was assessed in all nine countries participating in the program, but it was Ireland and France in particular that monitored the evolution of students' professional plans by administering a pre-project test in preliminary survey form and a post-project test absolutely identical to the first to measure any change. Several projects were still running after 1989. However, with funding from the Commission of the European Communities drying up, they had to be discontinued. The remainder of this article will focus on the work phase assessed.

THE CONCEPTUAL FRAMEWORK

The objective of the French experiment was to reach students, especially girls, on an emotional level, to destabilize any resistance they might have toward a less traditional orientation, and consequently bring more of them to envisage a scientific or technological profession. The system implemented was based on past studies (Lewin, 1946, 1947, 1965), the point of departure of the very concept of action-research (also see Dubost, 1987), all of which indicated that is easier to change the value systems and social behavior of a small number of people making up a group than to change the value system and behavior of the individual. Moreover, for the people in a group to be prepared to change with the group, they must be involved in the change, i.e. they must play an active part.

It might be expected that isolated individuals would be more malleable than groups made up of individuals who think the same way. However, one of the reasons why 'changes brought about by the group' are easier is because individuals, regardless of who they are, are not very eager to stray far from the norms of the group to which they belong. As long as the group's norm remains unchanged, the individual will resist change. If the group's norm is modified, the resistance arising from the relation between the individual and the norm of the group will be eliminated. If a change in a group's state of mind becomes apparent, for example during a face-to-face discussion that allows the participants to express their fears freely and explain why they oppose a change in behavior, then the individual will be more inclined to adopt that change. If properly carried out, discussion can lead to a higher degree of implication than the simple transmission of information in exposé or lecture form, a process in which the audience remains passive.[2] More specifically, there is a vast difference between calling for a decision after an exposé or after a discussion. As a discussion generates the active participation of the audience and gives them the opportunity to express motivations corresponding to various alternatives, the audience is probably more inclined to make a decision such as 'yes, that's an interesting orientation' or 'no, that's not for women' after a group discussion than after an exposé.

Based on these considerations, and after a short pilot phase, the action-research itself was carried out by the Association for Non-sexist Education (14, rue Cassette, 75006 Paris), which co-funded this project with the Commission of the European Communities.

THE FRENCH EXPERIMENT

The first phase discussed here, and which was covered in an assessment, started with a preliminary survey of 231 girls and 238 boys aged 14 and 15 in four secondary schools of the Paris region and in a rural region. Its purpose was to pinpoint their professional plans and their interest in and attitudes toward the subjects taught in the school, their knowledge of and interest in the new technologies, their representations of their capabilities in scientific and technological subjects,

---

2   The dynamics created by group discussion and group decision have been the subject of numerous studies for many years, especially in the field of psychology, and have resulted in highly sophisticated theoretical models. One of the pioneers in the field was undoubtedly the German American psychologist Kurt Lewin, who applied them to a broad range of fields: to change the eating habits of households or the nutrition of babies, in leadership training, and the manufacturing of prejudices, as well as in many fields of rehabilitation, for alcoholics or delinquents for example. So, in spite of the high degree of complexity of contemporary models, whose application to concrete social situations often seems difficult or problematic nonetheless, these works by Lewin provided the main sources of inspiration for the French experiment.

and their images of male/female relations in the couple. It was hoped the responses to these questions could be used to draw a link between the profession chosen and the attitudes expressed.

Overall, the adolescents categorically rejected the idea that abstract intelligence is more a masculine than a feminine trait. The girls felt they were just as gifted as boys for logical and scientific reflection, and just as competent in technological and mathematical fields. They believed that nothing could keep women from becoming famous scientists. Although these responses reflect a globally favorable attitude toward equality between men and women, which remained identical one year later, they contradicted the personal projects of the students. Although, in their attitudes, the girls and boys attributed the same capabilities to both sexes, 57% of the girls (compared with 4% among the boys) planned to enter a 'feminine' occupation: hairdresser, beautician, taking care of children or animals, secretary, sales personnel, assistant. Over 51% of boys (compared with a little under 9% of girls) chose more 'masculine' occupations: pilot, engineer, computer expert, mechanic, technician, that is to say occupations that require a certain technical or technological know-how. Although girls and boys seemed to consider men and women as equals as concerns their capabilities in scientific and technological fields, girls explicitly stated that they didn't want to work in the new information technologies, while boys planned to enter this field massively.

At this point in the experiment, it was, and remains, difficult to know to what extent these responses reflect their true opinions and to what extent they reflect social desirability, that is to say the desire to respond in a way that adults would find suitable and acceptable. Other responses in the preliminary survey may throw more light on the subject. It would appear, for example, that the girls' resistance to occupations requiring a certain technological know-how, traditionally considered as masculine, were linked to traditional man/woman relations, as well as to girls being less attracted to or even rejecting scientific subjects, especially mathematics and physics. Moreover, outside of their school activities, they were less interest than boys in the technical world or in do-it-yourself activities. These results, which seem to coincide with observations made in France and abroad, make it possible to understand why girls eliminate scientific subjects when building their future plans.

The action part concerned 135 girls and 134 boys from the same schools forming the experimental groups, while the remaining 94 girls and 104 boys served as 'control groups'. At the end of the school year, a post-project test identical to the first was given to all students to determine any change in their professional plans in order to assess the impact of the action. It is impossible to judge the evolution of a situation after an action if there is no criterion to evaluate the relation between the effort and the accomplishment. In such a case, erroneous conclusions can be reached and bad work habits encouraged.

To limit any resistance to considering the problems of change and possible alternatives in behavior objectively and without prejudice, the question of orientation and women's work and the problem of changing orientation were discussed in light of on a play or a visit by a young woman employed in a profession that is not traditionally feminine, who came to their school to talk about her occupation. The group discussion led to the explanation of the obstacles that stood in the way of change in general.

Two types of intervention were tested.

(1) Role-playing games, that is to say short plays staged by professional actors who portrayed stereotyped everyday situations (in school, at home, about orientation), situations that tended to confine women to their sexual role and thus place them at a disadvantage. The students (girls and boys) were invited to replace the actors whenever they felt another type of behavior in the situations presented could help open up possibilities. Obviously, the point was not to obtain a finished creation. The accent was placed on the process, that is to say on the dynamics set in motion by the various roles played and by the type of man-woman interaction they might provoke. These role-playing games were meant to encourage girls to become aware of their stereotyped behavior and give them the elements they needed to avoid such behavior. Both the plays and the solutions envisaged by the students were then the center of heated group discussions. Unfortunately, the discussions didn't result in any decision-making on the students' part, probably because of their intensity and the rapid character of these exchanges.

(2) Debates with young 'model' women who had chosen a professional orientation not traditionally feminine, especially in scientific and technical fields. This was meant to make the students aware of promising sectors of activity that could offer women as well as men outlets and prospects for an interesting

career without preventing them from living a full personal life. Moreover, these debates were intended to provide positive identification with the 'role models' and their occupation.

This debate was prepared with at least one teacher, a guidance counselor and a moderator according to a prearranged outline. The debate was conducted to create a true dialogue between the guests and the students. At the end of each session, students had to decide on the advisability of that occupation for women and on its professional and private interest.

All the experimental classes took part in the role-playing games. Due to logistics, the debates with the 'model' women could be organized at two of the schools only.

In order to assess the effectiveness of these strategies for change, the people in charge of the project studied any changes in the professions chosen by the girls. For this purpose, the responses to the first questionnaire were compared, school by school, with the responses to the second, and this result was compared with that of the control groups and the boys. In this way it was possible to detect common trends.

NOTICEABLE RESULTS

Generally speaking, the experiment proved positive, although there were fewer changes in orientation than had been hoped. From a quantitative viewpoint, a drop was noticed in girls' choosing 'feminine occupations' such as hairdresser, stylist, child care and health care nurse in favour of:

(1) another category of 'feminine' occupations: receptionist, tourism agent, 'something with languages';

(2) 'masculine' occupations such as engineer, 'something in computers' or 'in the sciences';

The first of these types of change was observed in all the classes: experimental classes and 'control' classes. The second, on the other hand, was found only in the experimental classes who took part in the role-playing games and had met guests who were women scientists. The variations range from 1.6% to 10.2%. They were stronger in managerial families and less strong in factory worker and office employee families. In schools where only role-playing games were tested, the changes observed in the experimental groups were the same as in the control groups.

From a more qualitative viewpoint, taking the spontaneous observations of the principals, teachers and students into consideration, it appeared that although the role-playing games didn't lead to changes in orientation, they made the students speak out more freely, stimulated imagination and creativity and sometimes led to spectacular upheavals in the hierarchy reigning inside a class with students who were least gifted but good actors becoming leaders). But it was particularly the debates with scientific women that met with positive echoes among the young women. Many of the girls talked about them with great pride whenever given a chance.

These changes prove that it is possible to make girls aware of occupations that call upon technological know-how. The action probably should have been accentuated even more. Especially as the predominance of 'feminine occupations' among girls and 'masculine occupations' among boys persisted. Although, as the teachers concluded, the combined actions were able to modify the classroom experiences of the students and bring girls as well as boys to communicate better, two major criticisms can be made. The experiment was addressed at girls chiefly, to encourage them to go into so-called 'masculine' occupations, and almost nothing was done so that boys would choose so-called 'feminine' orientations. That means that the experiment as a whole accentuated the man/woman rift instead of attenuating or eliminating it. In order to build their identity and structure their character, adolescents need to become different, especially sexually. It appeared clear that coeducation in schools and classrooms is often not true coeducation (see Mosconi, 1989). When watched by the boys, girls exacerbate their conformity to suit the image they think the boys have of them, and vice versa. During this important period of adolescents' lives, when they structure their personal identity, the affirmation of their sexual identity often seems to involve the confirmation of tastes and interests recognized as being 'masculine' or 'feminine'. By perpetuating this rift between orientation and masculine or feminine careers, the action didn't allow the girls and boys to find other areas in which to affirm their personal and sexual identity.

Another problem concerned the implementation of decision-making, which was not carried out with enough rigor. The extremely lively discussions after the role-playing games didn't lead the girls and boys to make decisions. Yet the studies on which this experiment was based underline the importance of decision-making. Moreover, the decisions made after the debates with young 'model' women were too general for the girls to apply to their personal case, while crucial decisions on personal professional plans had to be made alone at the end of the year in a context that was not the same. Thus perhaps it isn't surprising that a relatively limited number of girls actually decided to change their orientation.

THE IRISH EXPERIMENT

The main idea for the experiment carried out in Ireland consisted of working directly on the behaviour of girls, teaching them in a given way to handle tools and technical objects. This instruction was intended to bring them indirectly to have more skill and confidence in their capabilities in order to foster their interest and participation in the technological field.

This approach, which was unique in the European action program, had been influenced by the results of the Girls into Science and Technology (GIST) program in the UK (Kelly, Whyte and Smail, 1984). In this project, carried out with groups of 11-year-old students among others, the girls were weaker than the boys in spatial and mechanical reasoning. The fact that the girls were given instruction in these specific fields helped improve their spatial aptitudes considerably.

The originality of this project can also be explained by its context. In Ireland, many schools are not coeducational. In all-girls schools, the curriculum isn't exactly the same as in all-boys schools. In one of the experimental girls' schools, there were no physics, advanced mathematics, metal or wood working or industrial and technical design classes offered and outside resources had to be called upon to fill this need. Likewise, in many coed schools, certain classes, especially technology, were reserved for boys. This fact, combined with a very broad system of options in the curriculum, didn't encourage girls to choose scientific or technological subjects. The development of initiation to technology modules, added on to the usual programs, were therefore particularly interesting and pertinent.

Working closely with the guidance counselor and with at least one teacher per experimental school, as well as with a counselor from the 'Curriculum Development Unit of Trinity College in Dublin, the director of the national program[3] drew up five initiation modules for technologies, both old and new. Cooperation between the teachers

---

3   Maureen Bohan, Education Ministry, Dublin

concerned was vital for the development of a five-module program, each lasting about seven weeks, with 80 minutes per session per week. The modules were carefully prepared for each of the sessions, with specific objectives: tasks to be executed, know-how to learn. They concerned:

(1) the use of the media and audiovisual equipment to enable students to become familiar with tape recorders, overhead projectors, VCRs, video cameras, slide projectors, etc.

(2) the use of computers, knowing that fewer girls than boys use one or have access to one, even though this tool is now part of the landscape in a large number of professions

(3) electrical material (soldering systems, fuses, magnets, clothes irons, etc.) that students have to learn to disassemble, repair and reassemble

(4) modelling (technical and industrial drafting, construction of cardboard models, etc.) that help improve visual and spatial reasoning and aptitudes, as well as practical know-how

(5) the multidisciplinary applications of the computer, for example in the telecommunications field.

Each module also was to have two sections on 'awareness of the equality between men and women in the technological fields' and 'awareness of sexual roles in society', the latter combined with information focused on prospects for careers in the fields covered in each module. Due to work overload and cost, this latter aspect of the second sections became operative only in the second phase of the experiment, especially in the form of visits to industrial sites and visits of 'model' young women to the school.

The teachers received in-depth training during the preparatory phase and met at regular intervals during the first phase of the experiment to review the modules and report on progress achieved.

As in the French experiment, the first phase started with a preliminary survey of 86 girls and 9 boys in four experimental secondary schools (two girls' schools and two coed schools), and in four identical 'control' schools, among a student body aged 12 to 15. In three of the schools, students came from working class urban centers with a high unemployment rate. (In one of the classes, 80% of the fathers were unemployed.) The fourth school included students from both urban and rural communities. The preliminary survey focused on student attitudes toward the place and role of men and women in the workplace and at home, and their own implication in so-called 'masculine' and 'feminine' household chores, in leisure activities and in activities linked to the use of computers. Two questions concerned their professional plans. As in the French experiment, a post-project questionnaire was handed out at the end of the project year in order to assess the effectiveness of the measures taken in terms of any change in the students' attitudes and in their orientation plans.

Several other evaluation tools were supposed to identify the reactions of the students and teachers regarding the project, the attitude of the parents and that of the teachers regarding the role and place of girls and boys at home and in the workplace. Most of these tools were introduced during or after the experiment.

Generally speaking, the experiment met with an enthusiastic welcome from students and teachers alike. If we compare the responses to the questionnaire after one year of the experiment to those in the preliminary survey, we note that the experiment built a greater general awareness among all students of the importance of equality between men and women and more particularly a favorable evolution in attitudes toward the implication of women in the new technologies. The students' representations became far less stereotyped, even though the change was less noticeable among boys than girls. It was the students who participated in the project, and more specifically girls from the experimental schools, who expressed less traditional attitudes as concerns that woman's place in society and in the home, and whose interest in computers grew most. At the end of this experiment, girls and boys felt that girls should be encouraged to do metal and wood working and use computers.

Regardless of their degree of enthusiasm for the project, there were no significant statistical differences between the 'control' groups and the experimental groups as concerns their attitudes toward the job market, and the students' orientation choices and professional plans were not affected greatly. A larger share of girls, both in the experimental schools and the 'controls', expressed less stereotyped professional plans, but the change was only slightly greater in the experimental group. As the teachers and other participants in the project remarked, professional orientations remained traditional among girls and unchanged among boys. At this point, it seemed difficult for girls to transform their enthusiasm into personal projects in the scientific and technological fields.

The introduction of these five modules providing instruction not usually available to girls was made possible thanks to the cooperation and enthusiasm of the school teachers and principals. They had to make a considerable effort to find the time necessary within an existing teaching program, either by partially eliminating music and physical education classes or by integrating the modules into the science courses. This approach forced the teachers concerned to take time from the subjects normally planned in the teaching programs. However, the first obstacles for this pilot experiment were having to juggle constantly between the compulsory school program and an experimental program, even though it was welcomed, the resulting feeling of guilt among teachers, and the feeling of not properly accomplishing what was compulsory. The integration of the experimental project in the existing time schedule thus seems to be a necessity in order to make the experiment viable, and what's more transposable.

Yet integrating the experiment into a regular scholastic framework might make the project lose its spirit and eliminate one of its main reasons for existing: creating awareness of the equality between men and women in the technological fields and awareness of sexual roles in society. Several project participants felt that not only would the development of the 'acquisition of technological skills and know-how' side be achieved to the detriment of the training of educational staff and their reflection on equal opportunity, but also it could assign a back seat to orientation itself, i.e. visits to worksites, and the awareness of occupations that accompanies the five modules. The tug-of-war between the various functions (teaching, orientation and awareness raising) could make them appear contradictory. Moreover, focusing on girls' orientation could appear a luxury, given the urgency of helping adolescents from often underprivileged backgrounds find jobs, an urgency marked by the concern for teaching them a trade.

CONCLUSION

These two pilot experiments demonstrate that it is possible, in a relatively short period of time, to make students aware of the equality between men and women in the technological and scientific fields, and to promote a greater awareness along with more positive attitudes toward this topic. Yet they also reveal the difficulties inherent in the very nature of these two approaches which, in spite of their differences, both had the same objective, which unfortunately was imperfectly attained: influencing the orientation choices of girls in favour of occupations in the scientific or technological fields.

The first surprise was to note the absence of any correspondence between personal behavior and mentality. As demonstrated by the French action-research, for example, it is possible to have a generally favourable attitude toward equality between men and women and toward women holding jobs in scientific and technical fields and not to adopt this attitude personally. And as the Irish experiment demonstrated, even if relatively conservative attitudes may change through practical experience and become more egalitarian, this change is expressed on a general level and doesn't affect the students' personal choices.

The second surprise was to see that there was a contradiction between the two objectives: encouraging equality between men and woman and inciting greater numbers of girls to move into the sciences. This contradiction first appeared evident to the guidance counselors, torn between two objectives: orienting all children toward a professional future than would satisfy them and focusing on girls. The contradiction became even more obvious in the work on equality between the sexes, which placed emphasis on the sexualization of occupations, thus highlighting differences between the sexes. Moreover, by inciting girls to go into so-called masculine occupations (and never the opposite), a hierarchy was immediately created between masculine at the top of the ladder and feminine at the bottom, thereby also reinforcing sexual differentiation in relations. Which means that the experiments could well have reinforced the man/woman rift instead of attenuating or eliminating it.

In conclusion, we can ask ourselves whether the development of a taste for science and technology shouldn't be taught in a context that makes them appear, not as a finality and a possible area for building a personal and sexual identity, but rather as a means of achieving other, more general, priority objectives, in keeping with the ambition of growing as a woman or a man. From this point of view, the computer, for example, will become a tool as indispensable to working well in school or on the job as the lowly pencil. It is up to men and women to find other areas to affirm their personal and sexual identity!

Chapter 14

Sex Differences in the Study of Science in Scotland and England

Mary R. Masson

ABSTRACT: *By choosing a range of fields broader than that of boys, Scottish girls leave themselves the option of choosing a profession as late as possible in their scholastic career. The results are highly encouraging as concerns scientific and technical careers.*

This chapter is not about a change in curriculum, but instead it concerns differences in the numbers of girls studying sciences that result from the different education curricula in Scotland and England.

In 1984, as a result of the 'Women into Science and Engineering 1984' initiative, it was noted that the 1983 pure science intake at Aberdeen University included 53% of women, which seemed significantly higher than the UK average of around 30%. The 1983 figure for women in science proved to be slightly anomalous, but nevertheless, the percentage of women in science at Aberdeen has remained relatively high (generally over 40%) compared with national figures (e.g. 31.3% of 1992 science graduates in Great Britain were women).

We found from a survey done in 1984 that our women students tended to have offered a wider spread of subjects at entrance than the men students, and also that many had not decided to study science until relatively late in their school careers. We suggested that women students appeared to want, more that the men, to be able to keep their options open for as long as possible, and that more women ended up studying science because of the Scottish system of examinations, in which pupils aiming for higher education normally take five or six subjects at Higher level, and so can take a mix of 'science' and 'arts' subjects. By contrast, English pupils normally study for just three subjects at A-level, and are therefore forced to choose between 'science' and 'arts' at age 16 or earlier.

Study of the published data on examination results for Scotland and England has provided some insights into the magnitude of the differences between subjects choices for the two sexes.

A study of sex differences for individual subjects at Higher grade for school leavers in 1987/88 includes much interesting data. Subjects were ordered according to the ratio of girls to boys or boys to girls (Table 1). Girls were found to predominate in a larger number of subject closest to parity between the sexes. Girls predominated in all modern languages, music and art, and boys in physics and engineering subjects by at least a factor to two. Girls predominated in English more than boys predominated in maths. Within science subjects, chemistry was closest to parity.

The same study includes information about subject combinations taken by boys and girls, some of which has been summarized in Table 2. Although the number of girls with Higher passes in English, maths and science is not as high as the number of boys, it is still a very significant number.

Table 1 Ranking of subjects by sex differences *

Subject	Ratio of Girls to Boys	Total with Higher Pass	Average number of Higher held	
			Boys	Girls
Secretarial studies	54.8	3355	3.03	2.71
Home economics	22.9	1164	2.78	3.02
German	3.74	1056	5.05	4.97
French	3.09	4071	5.24	4.78
Art and design	2.01	4427	3.17	3.30
Biology	1.95	6629	4.70	4.8
History	1.41	5754	4.22	4.45
English	1.39	19,967	4.22	3.91
Modern studies	1.24	3465	4.55	4.61
Accounting	1.18	2067	4.72	4.53
	Ratio of Boys to Girls			
Maths	1.15	11,629	4.77	4.94
Geography	1.25	6247	4.28	4.36
Chemistry	1.30	8291	4.90	5.17
Economics	1.43	2185	5.23	5.34
Physics	2.20	7417	4.87	5.44
Technical drawing	14.73	1578	3.30	3.92

* Data are included only for subjects passed by over 1000 pupils

The data concerning numbers of Higher passes held (Table 1) reveals that girls who have passes in subjects in which boys predominate have, on average, a greater number of Higher passes than the boys taking these subjects. Conversely, boys with passes in subjects dominated by girls tend to have a greater number of Higher passes than the girls. The same trend is seen in the comparative pass rates. That is, the pass rates are higher for girls than boys in a subject dominated by boys, such as physics, and vice versa. The trend is observed for six out of eight of the subjects shown (English and chemistry are the exceptions).

These observations suggest that the better pupils are selecting subjects with less influence from the forces that cause gender-stereotyping. It is more likely to be the weaker pupils who choose mainly subjects in which their own sex predominates.

It has proved to be interesting to compare the sex ratios for subjects at Scottish Standard Grade and Higher Grade with the same subjects at English GCSE and A-level. The data listed in Table 3 and 4, show that for most subjects the sex ratios are rather similar for Scottish and English pupils at the Standard grade/GCSE. However, at Higher/A-level stage, the sex ratio is usually much bigger for the English students. The effect is particularly pronounced for English (where the boys have dropped the subject) and for maths and physics (where the girls have dropped the subject). That is, in England, there is a strong tendency for girls to give up subjects dominated by boys, and for boys to give up subjects dominated by girls. The effect is very much less in Scotland, mainly because the pupils are not forced to drop so many of their subjects.

Table 2 Combinations of subjects held by school leavers with at least one pass at Higher grade

Subject Combination *	Boys	Girls
English, maths, science	4600	3730
English, science, no maths	1038	2016
English, maths, no science	699	1172
Maths and science, no English	772	171
Maths, no science, no English	291	194
Science, no maths, no English	570	387
No maths or science	4460	7104
Total with at least one Higher	12,430	14,774

* Most pupils held Highers in addition to the combinations listed

Table 3 Sex differences for Scottish examinations

Subject	Standard grade + O grade*		Higher grade	
	Girls/Boys	Total passes	Girls/Boys	Total passes
French	1.68	17,233	2.51	4043
Biology	2.38	14,121	2.06	7616
History	1.56	9507	1.40	5315
English	1.24	35,797	1.33	20,425
	Boys/Girls		*Boys/Girls*	
Maths	1.07	26,409	1.11	12,462
Chemistry	1.07	18,279	1.21	8088
Geography	1.18	11,989	1.14	6112
Physics	2.03	17,035	2.43	3004

* O-grade has been replaced by Standard grade, but in 1992 significant numbers still took O-grade in some subjects

The overall outcome is that in Scotland, very many more girls leave school with qualifications that will permit them to study science, among other options. Thus, they are able to make the decision about their university specialization at a much later stage when they have more than a superficial acquaintance with possible subjects. This seems to result in more girls deciding to study scientific subjects.

Table 4 Sex differences for English examinations

Subject	G C S E		A-level	
	Girls/Boys	Total passes	Girls/Boys	Total passes
French	1.56	124,400	2.40	20,137
Biology	1.03	36,800	1.60	25,684
History	1.21	98,500	1.20	27,334
English	1.34	263,100	2.28	55,918
	Boys/Girls		*Boys/Girls*	
Maths	1.06	205,500	1.81	35,413
Chemistry	1.47	36,300	1.43	24,411
Geography	1.17	113,600	1.19	28,133
Physics	2.087	36,700	3.50	23,745
Single science	1.50	19,000		
Double science	1.03	128,700		

There is one encouraging note in the English figures (Table 4). The new Double Science GCSE course seems to be attracting almost equal numbers of girls and boys, and around 70% of the the total numbers of candidates chose this option. The effects upon the A-level figures in subsequent years remain to be seen.

Finally, it is interesting to note that in 1968, the Dainton Report, which had the aim of trying to find ways of increasing the numbers of students (of both sexes) studying science and technology, stated as follows:

'174. First and foremost:

I. We recommend a broad span of studies in the sixth forms of schools; and that, in consequence, irreversible decisions for or against science, engineering and technology be postponed as late as possible.

II. We therefore recommend that normally all pupils should study mathematics until they leave school...

V. We hope that care will be taken by those responsible for the Scottish educational system to see that recent changes in the examination structure do not cause any serious departure from the traditionally broad base of Scottish education.'

Chapter 15

A Few Examples of National Strategies

Huguette Bergeron

ABSTRACT: *Based on information supplied by teachers and representatives of the Ministries of Education and Social Affairs of developing countries (Senegal, Cameroon) and industrialized countries (Spain, Portugal, Belgium, France, New Zealand), the author presents a synthesis of the national strategies implemented to change the present situation.*

Many countries are concerned with the education of young women and their access to scientific and technical occupations. Governments are motivated either by the evolution of education systems increasingly open to girls (prolonged compulsory school attendance, coeducational classrooms) or by action taken by the United Nations (Decade for Women, 1979 Conference on Science and Technology for Development) or because they understand the interest they have in not leaving by the wayside part of the human manpower indispensable to their development.

But the problems they face differ in their state of development and their sociocultural specificities.

IN DEVELOPING COUNTRIES
The same observation is made everywhere
The education of most girls is limited to literacy, at best to a primary education and/or domestic and agricultural training. The number of girls attending school drops as of the end of primary school and becomes minimum by the end of lower secondary school, even if their absolute number is on the rise.

Those who reach higher education are generally found in literary, legal or economic studies or in pharmacy or medicine, and in these fields they mainly are trained for jobs at intermediary levels: nurse rather than doctor, secretary rather than manager, primary school or early secondary school teacher rather than university professor.

Thus most women are eliminated from highly-skilled occupations with a high social status and a good salary. And this observation, which is true for all activities, is even more true for scientific and technological occupations.

What are the causes of this situation?

First of all, there is one general cause. The economic crisis that has hit the developing countries, directly or indirectly, has slowed government action. In Senegal, for example, the Education Commission drew up a New Schools plan late in the Seventies. The crisis caused budgetary restrictions, a shortage of teachers, and a decrease in school supplies which impeded the development of the program planned. Again, it is the economic crisis that incites families with moderate or low incomes to give boys an advantage by giving them priority in education.

The weight of traditions is also a heavy handicap for girls. Their major contribution to domestic and agricultural chores, excessively early marriage and repeated pregnancies, and the illiteracy of a large percentage of the female population, especially mothers, all hamper the development of the education of girls and young women. And those who manage to get sufficient instruction see their professional career blocked by ignorance of the possibilities for its development, insufficient business training and resistance to geographic and professional mobility. Traditions also create a psychological environment unfavourable to girls and foster the idea that they are not meant for certain occupations, especially scientific or technological ones, but rather for occupations where manual dexterity, social contact and dedication count.

To all this must be added, for certain nations or groups, sociocultural specificities that are hard to overcome. Although social equality causes profound differences in orientation and chances for success everywhere, these differences are even more accentuated in countries such as India, where highly differentiated social statuses exist, *de facto* if not *de jure*. Likewise, strong Islamic traditions can hinder the education of girls. A report by Mrs. Tsague-Nguemo points out that in Cameroon the enrollment ratio among girls, in a population with a Moslem culture, is particularly low. And in India Moslems have specific school legislation that does not favor girls. But the fundamental problem of school attendance among girls and women's access to all levels and sectors of the working world is only one manifestation of women's inferior socioeconomic status.

As the FEMED bulletin[1] points out, 'Countries can only achieve the objective of education for all if they ensure that girls have access to education. But the combined efforts aimed at having all children attend school must go hand in hand with appropriate strategies to keep them from dropping out of school (…) Most young women leave school for reasons linked to the education system.'

Possible Strategies

All studies on the problem of women's unequal access to the professional world, and especially to technical and scientific occupations, underline that no solution is possible without a strong government policy.

- The first step of any government action must be to identify and pinpoint obstacles: discriminatory practices, sociocultural problems, perverse effect of modernization that doesn't lighten a woman's workload but relegates her to inferior jobs due to a lack of schooling.

- Then nations must design a legal arsenal that will give women equal opportunity, in education as in employment: coeducational education, i.e. the same curriculum for boys and girls; sometimes the creation of 'special' schools which, as in India, enable girls to make up for shortcomings in their schooling upon entry into higher education; multiplication of teachers, laboratories and scientific institutes, because the rarer the schooling possibilities, the more they exclude girls; quotas for girls in scholarships grants, enrollment in schools and employment in order to encourage girls in scientific and technological occupations; making parents aware of family discrimination through television and radio programs; help and support for informal actions which work directly on-site to help girls and young women all the way from learning to read through advanced professional training that enables them to progress technically and career-wise; reflection on scientific programs, schooling and careers. The first obstacle encountered in many countries is the language barrier; children, both girls

---

1   FEMED Bulletin: bulletin of the working group from the DAE (sponsoring educational programmes in Africa) about the participation of women in education.

and boys, are blocked by the esoteric nature of abstract language and work harder to translate into their own language than to comprehend the scientific concepts, as Mrs. F. Sow (Senegal) so justly points out.

Moreover, international aid can and must support such government action. The aid often concerns teaching women in general. That is what organizations such as the D.A.E. (African Education) and G.T.P.F. (Women's Participation Working Group) do; both of these organizations took part in UNESCO's international conference on education (October 5–8, 1994). This is also the field of activity of F.A.W.E. (Forum for African Women Educators), which received UNESCO's Comenius Award for its activities. A.A.S. funds a research grant program on the education priorities of young women. NORAD is more specifically interested in science and mathematics studies for girls, for which it created a 'special convergence group' whose goal is to accentuate efforts in this field. It is intended to reassess scholastic programs, retrain science and mathematics teachers and inspectors, and improve teaching conditions.

The similarity of the problems that arise in African and Asian countries has been underlined: vast illiteracy, large proportion of the population under age 16 (at least 50%). For each of these aspects, the women's education problem has been spotlighted, the goal sought being to help selected African governments determine the financial, technical and human resources necessary to accelerate the participation of young women in science and mathematics courses. The Ouagadougou Declaration (1993) also spurred governmental action in twenty-some African and Indian Ocean countries.

But in addition to these government actions, women conscious of the problem are mobilizing so that women will have an equal opportunity, so that all branches will be accessible, so that overt and covert discrimination is brought to an end. They develop their own defenses by creating regional, national and international networks that scrutinize the values and practices of modern science. The newsletter published by United Nations Development Fund for Women (UNIFEM News) wrote about their work in its August 1994 issue. It was in this issue that the Indian physicist Jayshree Mehta underlined that 'a durable change requires not only more women scientists, but also access to the fundamental notions of science and technology for more women (...) The type of science we learn in university distances us from the people because it is not made for the people.' Mrs. Mehta is a member of several non-traditional institutions and takes part in numerous projects, as does Mrs. Byanyima, an aeronautical engineer and founder of the Association of Women Engineers of Uganda. Women scientists are creating more and more professional networks to handle questions concerning their own situation and are uniting their efforts with those of international networks. Such professional networks presently exist in over 15 African countries.

Mrs. Mehta is presently organizing the Eighth World Conference on 'Women, Science and Technology' to be held in Ahmadabad (India) in 1996 and which will serve as a forum to follow up on the 1995 Fourth World Conference on Women.

What is striking in these networks is the desire to reshape professional priorities by aligning them on the daily needs and life of individuals. Their leaders ask their colleagues to 'reformulate science and technology so that people can understand their immediate environment, solve their everyday problems, become self-sufficient and improve their quality of life.'

In conclusion, we can say that developing countries face a double series of difficulties in the field of educating girls for scientific and technical occupations. Their school system, often inherited from the colonial period, suffers from implicit discriminatory measures in women's education and employment. And as we saw above, to this heritage are added additional obstacles due to the specific cultural traditions of each country and to the limited means available to their governments. But international action such as that of women's networks is working to pinpoint problems and find a solution outside of the traditional channels used to date by the developed countries.

IN THE DEVELOPED COUNTRIES

Although here again we find the same inequality of access to scientific and technological instruction and occupations, and although here again the same discrimination exists, especially covert, and although here again unjustified traditions weigh heavy in the balance, the problem is not exactly the same. Governments have implemented coeducational classes and equal schooling, and everyone has access to all professions. Therefore manoeuvering to keep girls and women out of scientific occupations, whether voluntarily or not, can and must be denounced with vigor, sometimes with some chance of succeeding.

The scientific community is concentrating on this problem, especially in studies and research, some of which are covered in this book.

Although study and experimentation means have been limited by the economic crisis, they have made it possible to continue research and even to create new projects. At all levels of the educational system, people are starting to be acutely aware that the problem exists, orchestrated by the vigorous action of action groups, not all of whose members are women.

Nevertheless, inequalities subsist, due either to a misinterpretation of the problem or to tacit, but effective, resistance. Consequently, the action must be continued at all levels:

- among the individuals themselves. Girls have to be persuaded that scientific and technical occupations are meant for them as well as for boys, that their capabilities are equal to those of boys, and that learning and practicing these trades will in no way make them any less feminine;

- in families. Parents, especially those with modest resources, have to be persuaded that girls are the equals of boys, that they have the same opportunities, and that it is unjust – and perhaps even dangerous for the family itself – to give priority to their sons' schooling. Here again, the mothers must be made aware of the problem;

- in schools. Information, and even training, must be created or continued among principals and teachers of technical and scientific subjects;

- among employers, so that they do not practice discrimination, whether tacit or not, under the pretext of 'feminine absenteeism', which only exists if family chores are unfairly shared or because the social system is not adapted to the constraints of salaried work. It is especially inappropriate to blame women for having to take off work if they cannot find sufficient aid, for instance to take care of their children.

The governments obviously have to take this problem into consideration. If necessary, they must add to their legal arsenal in order to enforce equality; but they must also promote studies and experimentation in this field. That is the policy many countries adopted several years ago.

Several types of action have been taken to achieve this goal and can be used as models. Awards have been created for girls, counting on the incentive of the examples of women who work in scientific and technical fields. They are accompanied by financial aid to allow the winners to continue lengthy studies, whose cost is often dissuasive:

- In Quebec, the Irma Levasseur Award, created by the Ministry of Women's Affairs, rewards the best project presented at Panquebec Expo-Sciences;
- In France, the Scientific and Technical Vocation Award, attributed by the Department of Women's Affairs, is awarded annually to 480 upper secondary school students who submit a project in these fields. Encouraged by this example, regional councils, associations, and businesses are imitating this state aid.

Information plays a vital role in the orientation policy for girls, of course, both to show them the range of possibilities open to them and to fight accepted ideas and obsolete images. Many countries use this vector to reach all the publics concerned. It can provide media coverage for actions carried out in the field, or give girls the feeling that they can obtain access to a wide range of knowledge and professions, or make parents consider other perspectives for their daughters' schooling and professional future, as well as promote action between institutions. As an example, let's take the Belgian campaign called 'The occupation that's not meant for girls hasn't been invented yet' or France's '100 occupations for girls'. The latter includes posters and a brochure with testimonials by women in non-traditional occupations. This material was designed by the Department of Women's Affairs and by ONISEP (Office of Information on Education and Professions). It can be used in classes as well as at Information and Orientation Centers. It was the subject of debates in scholastic information programs, but has also been used in certain courses (history, geography, economics, civics, technology, sciences). Students have had the opportunity to consult individually, and it has been used for information forums and exhibitions on occupations.

In addition to these major, but 'one-shot' actions many countries have also designed more global policies. The following are a few examples:

- In New Zealand, the government made a global, explicit attack on the problem of underprivileged groups (the Maoris and South Pacific populations, the handicapped and women) as regards access to scientific and technical occupations in order to 'overcome inequality due to sex, race, providence or social environment'. This action is governed by official texts and implemented or assisted by government departments, especially the Ministry of Women's Affairs, the Labor Ministry for the private sector, the Council of Technical Education (where a specific section handles the instruction of women workers), and the Commission for Equal Opportunity Employment in the public sector.

This desire led to numerous actions, certain aimed at facilitating the organization of working women's work time: day care centres, reduced hours, flextime or shared time, aid to women entering or re-entering the work force, law on maternity leave granting the right to return to work at the end of leave. Another series of actions was implemented for girls in order to encourage them to choose 'non-feminine' occupations, using targeted information and training courses and seminars. This is the direction taken by the development of adult education, called 'second chance education', which concerns a growing number of women, as well as the funding of school tutoring and aid for reconversion, especially into new technologies (computers, management, telecommunications) or traditional technologies (mechanics, engineering drawing), and encouragement for employer incentives for apprenticeship, on-the-job training, specialization, training for managerial jobs. Employers have launched training actions in electronics, radio and television technology and in the petrochemical industry (actions often linked to manpower problems in the sector concerned).

The government was also concerned with women's promotion to managerial positions and in 1979–81 carried out an extensive study of the limited number of women in high positions in the education system. It appointed women to managerial positions and encouraged the private sector to do so as well. Finally, it tried to change attitudes and social behavior through action directed at the families and those in charge of orientation.

This represents a global policy, i.e. one at all levels, in all the fields concerned, in the public sector as well as the private sector. The medium- and long-term results would merit assessment.

- Flemish Belgium developed a highly targeted project, which is described in detail in this book. Essentially it is centered on the problem of student orientation.

- The Iberian Peninsula, for its part, focused on teacher training and information. The project coordinator is the Commission for Equality and Women's Affairs (Portugal). This commission and the University Seminar on Non-sexist Education (Spain) are the organizers. Also working on the project are various universities, teacher training centers and the Women's Institute (Spain). The purpose was to consider the problem of equal opportunity between girls and boys, which is starting to concern the leaders of education systems. The project's aim is to create the conditions of equality, plus dynamics based on networks of teachers who will take action in the classroom, in school councils, among parents, and in initial and continued teacher training. Studies will be carried out on equality and sexist stereotypes in the education of adolescents.

   A Summer University was held in Lisbon in 1994. A publication was launched in the spring of the same year, and the second Summer University (1995) is presently being prepared. Material from these activities will be published in autumn 1995. These are the conditions for the implementation of both theoretical reflection and practical research.

- For quite a few years, France has pursued a policy of equal opportunity for girls, at the instigation of the Ministry of National Education and the Junior Ministry in charge of Women's Rights. In the 1980s, inter-institutional action for the equality of girls and boys in school and the broadening of professional choices have taken the form of pluriannual plans and programs for the Academies. As indicated in an official document, the objective is to better prepare girls for economic and social changes by helping raise the level of their skills and broaden their professional choices, thus improving their employment prospects.

   Another objective is to better understand – and thus regulate – girls' schooling, by specifically studying the reproduction of sexual differentiation in family and social roles and in professions, a reproduction which influences girls' orientation choices and their overall plans for life, and which is also perceptible in the instruction offered. Separately or jointly, the two ministries implemented actions, a certain number of which are described in this book. A review of these actions is made by the academic authorities at regular intervals and a national report is published, signed jointly by the two ministries of National Education and Social Affairs, the latter having taken over responsibility for the women's affairs sector. The last review examined the progress made toward the four goals set in the Agreement signed in 1983 by the Junior Ministry in charge of Women's Rights (then in existence) and the Junior Ministry in charge of Technical Education within the Ministry of National Education. The four objectives set were:

- to prepare girls and their families to build a diversified training project, especially through specific information and the creation of remedial classes. This is the project that included the greatest number of actions;

- to stimulate awareness among all the leaders of the education system. This objective also mobilized much activity;

- to create school conditions favorable to girls. This means both everyday material conditions and reflection on differentiated pedagogy, and even aid to girls having difficulty in schools where they are in a small minority;

- to facilitate the professional insertion of young women with an industrial technology diploma by raising employer awareness and setting up a monitoring system for graduates in certain regions.

The latest report noted that the last two objectives required more effort and concluded, 'Equal opportunity does not exist between boys and girls and, contrary to what is believed, giving girls "priority" is not a sexist measure. It is merely a just decision aimed at creating equality between the two sexes (...) Much remains to be done (...) especially as the difficult period we are going through is not favorable to the creation of measures concerning women's employment.'

CONCLUSION

Once the principle of equality has been clearly recognized by law, its application must be respected. While the setting of quotas may prove useful if the existence of the problem has not been clearly understood, and in societies where the concept of equality between human beings is not part of the customs, traditions and laws, it is not recommended in the opposite case. As Mrs. Evelyne Pisier, Professor at the University of Paris I, wrote in Le Monde (February 8, 1995), 'equality under the law is the only idea that makes it possible to fight the prejudice that, in many fields..., helps justify the inferiority of women (...) To combat inequality, the fight for equality must continue.'

We must underline the major role played in France by ONISEP, which has been responsible for a national agency for youths, families and educational teams for 25 years.

It contributes significantly and in many ways (written publications, audiovisual and multimedia tools, regular TV programs) to the mission of equal opportunity for all. Working jointly with the Department of Women's Affairs, it created information instruments specifically designed for girls, in order to draw their attention to all the possibilities they were overlooking, especially in scientific and technical careers. Within other information media (videocassettes, CD-ROMs, TV programs, miscellaneous publications), it includes images of women working in these occupations in order to make girls aware of the possibility of future employment. It creates documents for teachers, including information to help them better understand the specific behavior of girls in their orientation choices, and to inform them of studies carried out on this problem and thus make them particularly attentive to this question in the classroom.

This written and visual image of equality between girls and boys in scientific and technical instruction and professions contributed considerably to enriching the information made available to girls and their families and to helping them draw up their professional plans.

There are two reports on the pilot period, published in Dutch and available from the Conseil Consultatif flamand pour l'Education.

Report for the School Year 1992–93.

Report on the External Conference on the Project – May 27, 1994.

The external assessment report of the project, carried out in 1993–94 by Mrs. K. Roels of the University of Ghent for the Education Ministry, will be available by the end of 1994.

This general study is based chiefly on the contributions of: Mrs. Yvette Cagan, ONISEP, France; Mrs. Tsague-Nguemo, Department of Mathematics, School of Sciences, University of Yaounde I, Cameroon; Mrs. Fatou Sow, sociologist, research assistant at CNRS, associate researcher at the Fundamental Institute of Black Africa, University Cheikh Anta Diop, Dakar, Senegal.

It also worked from: the Report of the Commission for Equality and Women's Rights, Portugal; the Report to promote access among girls and women to technical and technological instruction, written by Mrs. Doris MacDonald, Department of Education, Wellington, New Zealand; several reports and memoranda from the Ministry of National Education and the Junior Ministry in charge of Women's Rights, France; brochures published by UNESCO in the 'Studies in Technical and Vocational Education' collection.

Chapter 16

Proposed Diversification for Choosing a Stream in Secondary Technical and Vocational Schools

Josée Desmet-Goethals

ABSTRACT: *This text presents the various phases of a nationwide project to diversify the professional choices of young women. By emphasizing the methodological aspects of such a project, the author will interest all those who want to create a coherent set of actions to help education systems progress. She accentuates the need for international cooperation.*

(1) IDENTIFICATION

The diversification project is an intervention project based on the 'Diversification' action and research program implemented in the Flemish- and French-speaking communities of Belgium in 1990–91.

The present Education Ministry of the Flemish Community approved the organization of the project and integrated it in the priority policy of the Flemish Community in the field of education. The project is financed by the Flemish Community of Belgium and co-financed by the European Commission. It is coordinated by the Flemish Advisory Council for Education.

Target

The project concerns the curriculum for full-time technical and vocational instruction in secondary education.

Goal

The project is aimed at encouraging girls to enroll in technical sections.

Procedure

- Action and research at five schools (1990–91) to analyze obstacles found in mentalities and structures.

- Pilot project concerning 16 schools (1992–94) benefitting from a certain number of additional hours for teachers participating in the project. Evaluation of the pilot period by an evaluator (1993–94).

- Project execution phase (1994–96) with the participation of 32 pilot schools (16 additional schools). This extension was decided by the government of the Flemish Community on July 20, 1994.
  The upcoming specific two-year mission will propose models for the integration into the school project of the materials and methods employed and the diversification activities carried out.

- The European Commission co-funded the project pilot period.

- A new proposal has just been submitted for the organization of a 16-school network (4 Flemish, 4 Dutch and 4 Irish) to develop a pedagogical model to stimulate the sociocultural independence of girls and boys aged 15 to 18.

(2) OPERATIONAL STRUCTURE AND METHODS OF PROJECT

(a) Three Priorities in the Pilot Phase and a Fourth in the Execution Phase

The project must face numerous stereotypes in mentalities and education systems, as well as in segregation attitudes and prejudices in the labor market which influence girls' (and boys') choices of streams and careers. This project is aimed not only at increasing the number of girls in the technical instruction sections, but also at improving the conditions they find in the schools and curricula, and when they enter the labor market. In this context, it is obvious that simplistic strategies do not work! That is why the project was built around three priorities, each focusing on a series of interconnected factors:

(i) *non-traditional education and career choices among girls and boys:* approach to stereotypes in attitudes and mentalities in students, teachers and parents;

(ii) *aid to girls enrolled in technical sections:* representing an infinitesimal minority in technical sections, girls haven't reached the critical mass considered 'normal recruitment' and consequently need to be encouraged to continue in this stream they have chosen, as well as helped to stand up to any discrimination;

(ii) *the switchover to higher education and the world of employment for girls with technical qualifications:* approach to professional segregation and conventional attitudes;

(iv) a fourth priority intervenes during the execution phase: *the integration of diversification within the school project.*

(b) The Project Method Follows Two Action Guidelines

During its pilot phase (1992–93 and 1993–94) the project drew up action guidelines at three levels:

- *Coordination level:* Working with the teachers from 16 pilot schools, the experts developed pedagogical material to be used in class ('modules').

  Experience from the TENET program revealed that many teachers hesitated tackling a complex topic, or tackled it incompletely or from the wrong angle. The teachers felt their involvement in the concrete development of 'diversification' offered them effective refresher training or retraining. Thanks to this involvement, the pedagogical material is very similar to the curriculum and can be used immediately.

- *School level:* A series of specific activities and analyses related to the three priorities were carried out simultaneously. The ultimate objective was to integrate awareness activities in the school project.

- *European level:* Cooperation with similar programs created new inspiration and dynamics while rendering a comparative evaluation possible.

As concerns the development of teaching material, the Diversification project owes much to the Irish FUTURES project and to Dutch projects and publications on relations between girls and technology. In the future, teaching material will be created through direct cooperation between 20 teachers from at least three European member countries.

The project experts participated in European conferences in Ennis (Ireland), Athens (Greece) and Leewarden (Netherlands). The project organized various workshops for Flemish and Dutch professors, as well as internal and external conferences focusing on the European side of the program.

Three pilot schools in the project organized exchanges with three Irish FUTURES schools. The three action guidelines included:

- the development of the curriculum with the materials to be included;

- refresher training for teachers as part of the 'equal opportunity policy' carried out in various European countries (bibliography, conferences with European participants, student exchanges) and as part of the diversification process for school programs;

- awareness actions aimed at parents, orientation counselors, representatives from the working world and decision-makers in the broadest sense of the term;

- research activity at the school level;

- advice to decision-makers.

(3) RESULTS OF PILOT PERIOD

At the end of the 93–94 school year, project results were as follows.

(b) Main priority: Broadening and Diversification of Choices of Streams and Careers for Girls and Boys

(i) A 'General courses' module was published in May 1994. It was developed by teachers working jointly with Ireland, and A. Deketelaere was put in charge of its definition, editing and publication. It presents some 15 different activities to be added to the curriculum of various general courses offered during the first two years of secondary education. These activities are intended to inform secondary students (girls and boys) about all the existing possibilities (including the least traditional) in the field of education and occupations.

This module focuses on three objectives:

- enlightening young people by showing them the present state of existing professions and careers (professional segregation due to sexist prejudices and its origin), as well as other alternative, non-traditional options;

- eliminating prevailing ideas (and their inaccuracy) in the technical field and that of related professions;

- developing modern prospects for the future among young people as concerns private life, professional life and social obligations.

Three methods were used:

- an analysis of the present situation;
- becoming aware of one's own preconceptions and stereotypes;
- examples showing how to break habits and images based on sexist prejudices.

(ii) A module on 'Technological instruction – Topic: electricity' was published in September 1994. This course is essential in the Diversification program approach. It is part of the 'basic education', but is taught in a very different way, as a function of the different types of schools (of masculine or feminine culture) and forms of education. The module developed by the Diversification project is a practical manual on electricity. It puts into application the results of research on the image of technology, the initial situation, the types of instruction, and the interest and work methods of girls. Its objective is to make the technological class as attractive and profitable for girls as for boys.

(iii) A module including hands-on practice for primary school students: The Education Ministry of Flanders recently introduced into its policy some objectives to be achieved in primary education which specifically concern technological instruction and the fight against stereotypes in attitudes.

The creators of the project, working with primary and secondary teachers, developed a large number of topics to be used by primary students on experimentation days. They also drew up a module including a selection of experiments designed to familiarize young children with technology and give them a positive image of technical activities in the broad sense of the term, as well as of non-traditional roles. All the experiments were designed with the specific goal of fighting stereotypes.

Present Situation
All the module experiments have been carried out and assessed by teachers and education experts. The module was also presented to representatives from the professional world with activities in the technical sector. It is scheduled for publication by the end of the 1994–95 school year.

A new series of experimentation days for primary school students will be organized by schools taking part in the 'Diversification' project. This project is working with other Flemish projects to promote and develop technology in primary education. Exchanges have been organized with similar experiments in the Netherlands.

(b) Second Priority: Aid to Girls Enrolled in Technical Sections
Project participants continued the development of a 'technical and practical subjects' module (see the activity report for 1992–93). This module is intended for schools whose technical section student body is mostly boys and for technical instruction teachers, most of whom have girl students in their classes for the first time. As designed, this module is a manual with instructions on how to introduce an assistance structure into technical schools. It has a theory part that analyzes the differences in situations between girls and boys in technical sections and a practical part with instruments that can be used by the teachers. The theory part was prepared by J. Desmet essentially from two sources: Bontius (1991) and Byrne (1993).

For the schools, the strength of the Diversification project lies in its practical, cooperative approach. Consequently, the Diversification module developed practical instruments jointly with the technical instruction teachers:

- models to analyze problems concerning girls and technology and to propose solutions
- a questionnaire to help teachers detect particular 'loopholes' in the general knowledge and interests of girls and boys based on their technical curriculum
- a student questionnaire to assess their position on coeducational classes
- instructions for a beginner's course in job-seeking, paying special attention to social behavior and non-traditional situations in this activity
- information to expand the concept of 'technology and technical functions' beyond functions strictly limited to the industrial context.

The practical part is being prepared by K. Dries jointly with technical instruction teachers. The module is practically completed and will be published in mid-1995.

Visits by teachers and representatives of technical sections were also organized as part of this module. In February 1994, a workshop was organized in Ninove (Belgium) subsequent to an organized trip to Utrecht in September 1993.

(c) Third Priority: The Switchover to Higher Education and the World of Employment for Girls with Technical Qualifications

The search for diversification that leads girls to choose technical sections means it is necessary to examine the consequences of education's stimulus on the labor and job market. The project worked on several points of entry onto the labor and job market.

First of all, a study was made based on Flemish and Dutch reports on 'qualified women in technical jobs', the attitudes and opinions of women, employers and other employees. This study was carried out thanks to cooperation between the Flemish and Dutch technical sectors, which made it possible to obtain better results, both quantitatively and qualitatively, than if it had concerned only the Flemish part of Belgium. The Flemish Advisory Council for Education entered an agreement with the University of Ghent to publish the results.

Then six pilot schools organized a survey of former women students in order to determine how they had entered higher education or the labor market. J. Desmet consigned the results of this survey in her Report on the project for the 92–93 school year.

Moreover, contacts were organized with the commerce and industry sectors: with local factories and businesses for pilot schools, and with representatives of the social partners for project coordination. A cooperation action was implemented recently between the project coordinator and the Emancipation of the Public Service Sector of the Flemish Community, so that women qualified in the technical field fill a greater number of jobs in the public sector.

Finally, a survey was made of companies requesting women trainees with technical qualifications, and the results are presently being processed.

(d) Fourth Priority (of the Execution Phase): Introduction of Diversification in the School Project

One short-term objective consisted of developing a transferable strategy to introduce diversification definitively in the school project.

When asking company executives and pedagogical teams to take steps to promote greater diversity in the choice of streams and careers, it must be remembered that the profile of the company, the pedagogical team and their relations with the sociocultural and socio-economic environment influence the type of process and the method used for its implementation. A structure was created to manage this diversification process in pilot schools, including an in-house coordinator assisted by an internal organization group.

Although the coordinator is a teacher first and foremost, he or she must apply a middle management approach. Most of them will need additional training in the diversification and management of coordination within their schools. A standard program for refresher training courses is being drawn up jointly with the in-house coordinators in office and a foundation specializing in training.

It is clear that concrete tools are necessary to prepare and implement a permanent diversification policy in schools of a different type. Thus a set of internal and external analyses and models for in-house strategies will be developed with a group of partner schools in the project.

Since the 1993–94 school year, a group of experts in pedagogy belonging to educational networks have been kept informed at regular intervals and associated with refresher training courses on diversification. The point of this is that in the future they will be adequate partners to monitor the implementation of the diversification strategies in the schools.

(4) IMPLEMENTATION AND CONTINUATION OF THE PROJECT IN THE EDUCATIONAL POLICY OF THE FLEMISH COMMUNITY

(a) Upon the proposal of the Flemish Ministry of Education, the Government of the Flemish Community decided to extend the Diversification project for two years.

(b) The Flemish Ministry of Education sent all secondary schools a memo explaining the content, strategy and products of the project and announcing the possibility of joining the group of 32 pilot schools.

(c) The Flemish Advisory Council for Education organized a promotion campaign for the two project modules already published (module for general courses and module for technological instruction) and for the minutes of the study day on May 27, 1994. A large number of students and teachers have procured these minutes. A. Deketelaere was invited to present the modules to groups of experts in pedagogy, teachers and orientation counselors.

(5) CONCLUSION OF THE COORDINATOR

As concerns equal opportunity between girls and boys in the education field, one-dimensional strategies do not work. By introducing teaching materials aimed at both boys and girls (generally grouped in coeducational classes) during the activities scheduled in the program, it is possible to make them aware of a non-traditional behavior and to diversify their choice of a stream and a career. The personal approach is useless, however, if nothing is done about the structural obstacles that exist in the education system and about the prejudice and covert – but real – discrimination that exists on the labor market. The projects and strategies drawn up in direct cooperation with the schools and teachers will only have a chance of producing long-term results if decision-makers in education and employment make a serious assessment of equal opportunity, the mechanisms of control and sanctions.

After approximately ten years of an equal opportunity policy (cf the Resolution of the Council of European Education Ministers of June 3, 1985) and numerous analyses, the implementation of joint cooperation among different countries in the European Union to draw up projects at the base level (schools, teachers, programs) finally seems possible. Actually, only close cooperation with teachers can effectively guarantee that concrete projects and strategies will be carried out. All projects need a well-defined operational structure, a clear methodology and Europe-wide cooperation. This cooperation has made rapid progress as concerns concrete achievements and an improved assessment of strategies and instructions.

Nevertheless, the more results are obtained in the field of education, the more equal, just and equitable treatment on the labor market becomes urgent. In this area, education is dependent on the social partners in the labor market. Guarantees that the trend toward diversification in education will be respected are still required.

Chapter 17

Girls and Sciences
Examples of concrete action

Yvette Cagan

ABSTRACT: *The author presents a series of actions carried out at different levels (regional, national and local) in order to change educational practices. Independently of the singular nature of the actions described (most of the experiments were carried out in countries in the European Union), the reader, whether teacher, principal or director of educational policy, can use these examples to define his or her own action plans as a function of his or her context and level of intervention. Teacher training is covered briefly. It is probably on this important area that the international community will have to focus in the coming years.*

In order to facilitate girls' access to scientific and technological knowledge, four major types of action have been carried out, at the initiative of national governments, the European Union, associations (women scientists, teachers, etc.) or local bodies:

(1) *National actions* having a major impact and ripple effects: scientific awards for girls in upper secondary schools or universities, information campaigns for girls and families;

(2) *Educational actions in schools:* at the level of a region, a school district, a class; on-site as part of national or local programs, on-site at the initiative of local bodies, and possibly leading to media coverage locally, regionally, and in some cases nationwide for actions of an exemplary nature;

(3) *Teacher training and awareness actions;*

(4) *Actions concerning the production of ad hoc teaching materials.*

The actions carried out in schools and in the classroom concerned scientific and technological subjects. They were usually built around a group of interdisciplinary educational actions involving the staff in charge of student orientation and working toward a general objective of equal opportunity between girls and boys as regards knowledge and know-how. Several of the actions grouped science and technology teachers in a class project or school project.

(1) NATIONAL ACTIONS
(a) Scientific Awards for Girls
Several countries attribute scientific awards or scholarships to girls in secondary schools or universities in order to enable them to continue their scientific studies.

(i) Prix de la Vocation Scientifique et Technique des Femmes (France)
The 'Prix de la Vocation Scientifique et Technique des Femmes' is attributed annually by a regional jury to 480 girls in their last year of secondary school for a scientific or technological professional project. This award has incited other partners (regional councils, associations, businesses) to join in and attribute a financial grant to candidates with good credentials (interesting projects and good grades) but who were not chosen by the regional juries.

(ii) Scientific Scholarships for Women (Ireland)
These scholarships are attributed through a competition to girls in their second university cycle who want to go on to the third cycle.

(iii) Irma Levasseur Award (Quebec)
By creating this award, which bears the name of a Quebec woman scientist, the Minister of Women's Affairs of Quebec (a woman) sought to promote the scientific vocation of young women by encouraging them to erase the image of scientists as necessarily males. It rewards the best project submitted by a girl to the Pan-Quebec Expo-Sciences.

(b) Information Campaigns
Several countries have organized information campaigns on scientific and technical occupations in order to familiarize girls and their families with the range of schools and jobs that exist in these fields. These campaigns have reached a broad public through intense media coverage on radio and television. Their goal is to make girls realize that they can obtain access to knowledge and varied occupations they thought were not suitable. The campaigns also open up new perspectives to parents and potential employers. Finally, they encourage inter-institutional actions, for example in the fields of education, employment and health.

(i) *'The occupation that's not meant for girls hasn't been invented yet'* campaign (Belgium)

(ii) *Information campaign on the results of pilot projects to broaden the professional options of girls (Germany, Ireland, Denmark)*

(iii) *'It's technical. It's for her' campaigns (France)*

In 1991–92, the Junior Ministry for Women's Affairs and the Ministry of National Education launched a first nationwide information campaign on this topic. It led to seminars and group discussions throughout France that brought together decision-makers from the National Board of Education, teachers, guidance counselors, and women's rights representatives. This campaign accompanied the National Education Campaign in favor of technical education.

Different teaching tools were created for guidance counselors and teachers: a videocassette with portraits of women technicians and scientists, a poster presenting various occupations, a technical notebook for the class containing information on the role of girls in training or employment, occupational fact sheets, practical information.

A second 'It's technical. It's for her: 100 occupations for girls' followed in 1992–93. Using the same theme, this time it placed the accent on the life experience of one hundred professional women working in science and technology. A brochure presenting their experiences, along with a series of twelve posters for the classroom and for career information rooms, was published by the Department of Women's Affairs and ONISEP (Office of Information on Education and Professions), the French agency that processes information on studies and occupations and distributes it to young people, families and educational teams. Designed use in the classroom, this material was distributed directly to schools and information and orientation centers, as well as to all newsstands. It was used in different ways by teachers and orientation staff in lower and upper secondary schools:

- in the classroom, as part of scholastic and professional information, in debates on professional images and the role of women in 'other' occupations;

- in the classroom in history, geography, economics, civics, technology, and science classes, and as part of reflection on the role of men and women in the work force, the economy of the country, etc.;

- as part of information forums organized jointly with information and orientation centres;

- in student projects on occupations as part of their schoolwork.

(2) EDUCATIONAL ACTIONS IN SCHOOLS
(a) *Actions in Primary Schools*
(i) In Europe

Prior to any action among students on the specific topic of sciences, it is necessary to promote awareness of the respective situations of men and women, the differences that exist between them and the way in which these situations are experienced by both.

To this end, the Commission of the European Union promoted the emergence of the representation of such situations among primary and secondary students by organizing a poster competition in four countries (Spain, Greece, Ireland, Portugal). Its objective was to stir up debate at school and in the home on equality between men and women. National juries selected the winners and gave awards for the best poster; one award was attributed by the Commission. The best posters were distributed widely in all the schools in these countries. In Greece they were printed in calendar form and distributed to youth organizations, and the Commission of the European Union published a deluxe brochure with the most interesting posters.

(ii) Initiation of Nursery School Students to Technology (France)

Men and women teachers at the Longueville-sur-Scie nursery school had their students work on a discovery project creating small technical objects, to initiate them in technology. This action, which enabled both girls and boys to carry out technical observation and creation work, was crowned by an exhibit of the objects made.

(iii) Orika Project (Luxembourg)

The Orika Project invited girls and boys in their last year of primary studies to take part, with their teachers, in technical initiation workshops and courses in a upper secondary technical school. Four two-hour sessions in limited groups enabled them to become familiar with technology, carry out experiments, create a project and learn how to use a computer.

*(b) Action in Secondary Schools: Student Images of Science
and Equality Between Men and Women*

(i) Reflection Workshop on Professional Orientation
(Academy of Grenoble, France)

In these workshops, run by a scholastic and professional orientation staff, students worked with photobooks and videocassettes. The 'Plural Lives' photobook is a teaching tool created by a team of researchers at the Academy of Rennes to incite reflection on professional images. The designers[1] describe the tool in these terms: 'Support which, through the personal selection of one or more photographs and the explaining of this selection in front of the class, makes it possible to understand oneself better, to compare viewpoints, and to explore, engage and discuss the different images group members have. The photographs are chosen through reflection on professional images and an analysis of the gender-based image of professions, searching for the most striking social images of men and women.' Five parameters were retained to choose the photographs:

- corporal space (interior/exterior);

- corporal extensions (tools, machinery, etc.);

- corporal technique (gestures, etc.);

- corporal appearance (clothing, etc.);

- corporal organism (physical force).

(ii) Science and Technology Discovery Classes for Lower
Secondary School Students (France)

These one- or two-day courses in vocational or technical high schools offer students in their last two years of lower secondary school (prior to orientation choices) an opportunity to discover scientific or technical training. Their objective is to make students (especially girls) aware of technical occupations and life in a technical school.

They proceed as follows:

- greeting of the students;

---

1   Annie Junter-Loiseau *et al. Orientation des filles et égalité professionnelle –
Former pour innover (Orientation of girls and professional equality – Training to
innovate)*, Paris, CNDP.

- presentation of the school and the range of subjects offered, either by girl students in the scientific or technical streams or by the projection of a videocassette filmed in the school;

- discovery class in technical shops (2 hrs) or in classes in several specialized fields planned for this occasion;

- debate with girls enrolled in these courses;

- evaluation with lower secondary school students and personalized assessment (often in questionnaire form).

A tour of a business may, in some cases, prove a useful complement to these discovery classes, but first they should be organized by the students concerned.

In France, numerous actions of this type accompanied the regional or nationwide information campaigns on industry and technical trades ('Youth-Industry', 'All Pros').

(iii) Theatre Techniques (France)

The use of theatre techniques for lower secondary school students offers interesting results as concerns the expression of stereotypes, the resolution of conflicts in terms of orientation choices or role games, and the discovery through theatrical games of alternatives other than those the students had in mind. The techniques used are those of the Théâtre-Forum (Academies of Dijon and Grenoble, especially). The theatre company working with the students uses Augusto Boal's interactive Opprimé Theater methods: placed in a dead-end situation enacted on stage by the company, spectators 'are asked to find a solution to the problem posed, by enacting "their solutions" in the stead of the person who is in the dead-end situation (a girl facing her employer in this specific case). They will then improvise with the actors and the spectators (young people in this case) will judge how acceptable the solutions are.'[2]

Moreover, a Théâtre-Image of Technical Occupations was organized for students in 4è (one year before their orientation choice). Its objective was to trigger exploratory behavior in students so they would look into technical occupations. This theater action was led by an actor/actress, a guidance counselor, and the technology professor.

---

2   Activity report of the Three-year Action Plan for the Orientation of Girls, Academy of Grenoble.

Repercussions from these theater actions were followed by educational actions in the classroom:

- the study of texts on women's employment;
- courses on women's employment and its evolution;
- reflection discussions on women and employment, women and the sciences, women and technology, images of masculine and feminine roles and the role of men and women in society.

(iv) 'Girls and Science' Action-Research (France)
This was carried out in Dijon and Auxerre (Academy of Dijon) and was aimed at instituting new pedagogical procedures that could interest girls in lower and upper secondary school in mathematics and physics.

(v) Action Within the School Project on Girls and Science (France)
In four lower secondary schools in Lorraine, France has carried out action-research on how to stimulate girls' interest in science and technology. Led by teams of educational volunteers, it involved the class (girls and boys), teachers, guidance counselors and document researchers. The work was carried out under the supervision of a psychosociologist, Vera Aebischer, over a two-year period in classes in the last two years of lower secondary school (which precede the orientation choices prior to entrance in the professional cycle or general and technical studies in upper secondary school). It included several phases:

- a student questionnaire on their knowledge and vision of science and technologies;
- reflection by the sociologist and teachers on their images and attitudes in the classroom towards the girls and boys;
- discovery of model women scientists of the past and present, leading to the creation by the students of short documents (poems) and to interdisciplinary action centered on the staging of a play (with the students as the actors) about a man and a woman scientist from the past. The interdisciplinary action required research on women scientists with the science teachers, work to write up the script with the literature teacher, the creation of the costumes in manual skills class, etc.;
- meetings with contemporary women scientists (especially women engineers);

- information research on a wide range of scientific and technical occupations, with a debate on masculine/feminine roles and images;
- the creation of a scientific or technical object: construction of a gymnastics apparatus, construction of a telescope.

(vii) School–Business Links (Luxembourg)

Technical upper secondary schools built relations with several businesses in order to organize 'Industry and Crafts Seminars'. During these seminars, students got a close look at the economic reality of a business and could modify their negative prejudices regarding certain occupations (especially the girls). Several training courses and visits to businesses completed this initiative.

(3) TEACHER TRAINING AND AWARENESS ACTIONS

These actions took on different forms according to the local reality and needs.

(a) Awareness Actions

(i) Awareness Days (One to Three Days)

These are prerequisites to any action in favor of equal opportunity between girls and boys. What's more, they enable teachers and educational counselors to become aware of a certain number of factors involved in the education of girls and boys, the socialization of young people, relations with scientific and technical subjects, teacher-student interaction, and women's employment situation.

(ii) Seminars and Colloquia

They create links between university professors having studied these issues, women graduates' associations, and educational counselors. The following were organized:

- in Germany, conferences for educational communities and business executives;
- in Denmark, conferences for directors of technical and business schools;
- in Spain, seminars for teachers;
- in France, seminars for resource people in charge of girls' orientation in the different regions and academies;

- in Ireland, colloquia for teaching school personnel;
- in Portugal, colloquia for teachers and pedagogy supervisors.

(b) Actual Training Actions
(i) Training modules in the form of one or more days focusing on one or more specific topics and shedding light on problems or implementing actions to remedy a problem encountered in class.

Module 1: four days to train relay people in charge of organizing actions in schools (France: Academy of Antilles-Guyane).
First day:

- theoretical contribution through the analysis of what levers to use;
- quantitative and qualitative contributions on the role of girls in education and of women in employment (data to build awareness of the importance and urgency of the action).

Second day:

- workshop to build a personal project for a young women: Theoretical comprehension data and practical aspects.

Third and fourth days:

- review of the present year's actions with the participants in the field;
- prospects.

Module 2: three-day forum-theater for teachers (France: Academy of Dijon)

- How to work on attitudes daily, in script form with interactive techniques inciting the youths and guidance counselors to think about girls' orientation.

Module 3: one day

- data on girls' orientation
- women and employment
- national program to diversify the professional choices of girls: objectives and work guidelines.

(ii) Theater workshop fashioned after Augusto Boal's Opprimé Theater, enabling the teachers to apply a logical process through role-playing to solve problems, and providing them with a technique for working with their students in the classroom.

(iii) Training modules within teacher and professor training courses, especially for new teachers and professors.

(iv) Summer universities

All these actions are also useful to the information and orientation staff working with girls and their families. Moreover, many information documents (guides, teaching files, information newsletters) complete this consciousness raising of the educational personnel.

(4) Teaching Materials
(a) Textbooks
Work was carried out in several countries to revise scientific textbooks as a result of studies showing that girls also assimilate scientific and technical knowledge by 'living' examples, through situations with which they are more familiar. This revision had a certain effect on the feminine public and the teachers.

(b) Revision of Mathematics and Physics Teaching Materials to Make Them More Accessible to Girls (Denmark, Spain, Netherlands Eespecially)
In Denmark and the Netherlands, the teaching of mathematics, natural sciences and computer technology was revised in depth in order to help motivate girls. Denmark also created new teaching materials to teach physics in primary schools.

In the Netherlands, assessment materials (tests, examinations) were reviewed 'in order to detect any aspects that repel girls' and introduce certain gender-linked errors into the assessment process.

These revisions of textbooks and teaching materials were often made during the revamping of a curriculum or a reform of the education system (Spain).

(c) Teaching Materials: Exhibitions (France)
The interactive 'Bearing: Orientation. Profession: Future' exhibition was created by a scientific and pedagogical team from the Academy of Orléans. It is interactive in that it includes several hands-on displays

that encourage the student to become a participant. It can also be used in schools to lead into classroom work. The main topics covered are:

- 'At the source of work';
- 'I, you, he, she, work': the daily jobs of men and women yesterday and today;
- 'The training cruise': an exciting adventure;
- 'Knowledge and Training': the reign of technology, the impact of science;
- 'Professional activity': from the country to the city, from one revolution to another;
- How to choose?': getting aboard, exploration;
- 'From choice to decision': information to be processed according to personal criteria;
- '3, 2, 1, Action': my strategies, direction the future

USEFUL ADDRESSES

UNESCO United Nations Educational Scientific and Cultural Organization

Ms Wassyla Tamzali
Coord. Unit, Activities Relating to Women
1 Rue Miollis
F 75732 Paris Cedex 15
FRANCE
Tel: (33)1.45.68.38.24
Fax: (33)1.45.07.71.51

UNIFEM United Nations Development Fund for Women

Dr. Marilyn CARR
304 East 45th Street, 6th Floor
New York, N.Y. 10017
Tel: (1–212) 906–6289
Fax: (1–212) 906–6705

UN/CTSD United Nations Commission on Science and Technology
   for Development

Gender Working Group
Dr. E. McGREGOR
IDRC
250 Albert Street
P.O. Box/B.P. 8500 Ottawa
CANADA:

Tel: (1–613) 236–6163
Fax: (1–613) 238–7230

UN/CSW
United Nations Commission on the Status of Women

Division for the Advancement of Women
Center for Social Development and Humanitarian Affairs
Vienna International Center
P.O. Box 500
A – 1400 Vienna
AUSTRIA
Tel: 43.1.211.310
Fax: 43.1.232.156

COMMISSION OF THE EUROPEAN COMMUNITIES

Equal Opportunity Unit
Direction générale 5 13
27 rue Joseph 2
1049 Brussels
BELGIUM
Tel: (32)2.295.20.93

TWOWS
Third World Organisation for Women in Science

Ms. Lydia P. MAKHUBU, President
c/o International Centre for Theoretical Physics (ICTP)
P.O. Box 586
34014 Trieste
ITALY
Tel: (39)40.22.40
Fax: (39)40.22.45.59

CWAST
China Women's Association for Science and Technology

Mr. WU GANMEI, Secretary-General
c/o Department of International Affairs
54 Sanlihe Road
Beijing 100863
CHINA
Tel: (86)1.25.75691
Fax: (86)1.25.75692

FRENCH NATIONAL COMMISSION FOR UNESCO

Ms Renée Clair
34/36 rue la Pérouse
75775 Paris Cedex 16
Tel: (33)1.43.17.66.61
Fax: (33)1.43.17.67.73

In France, a Public Information Agency, under the supervision of the Ministry of National Education, has worked for 25 years to provide nationwide information on schooling and professions to youths, families and educational teams. ONISEP (Office of Information on Education and Professions) contributes extensively, and in various ways (publications, audiovisual and multimedia tools, TV programs, etc.), to the educational mission that champions equal opportunities for all:

- by creating (jointly with the Department of Women's Affairs) information products especially designed for girls, to attract their attention to all the professional opportunities they overlook, especially in science and technology (example: the brochure and posters for the 'It's technical. It's for her: 100 occupations for girls' campaign);

- by including images of women working in these occupations using other information media (videocassettes, CD-ROMs, TV programs, publications) or messages aimed especially at girls to make them aware of their potential in these occupations;

- by creating fact files for teachers, including information that improves their understanding of the specific behavior of girls in their orientation choices and informs them of the studies carried out on 'girls, sciences and technologies' in order to make them better listeners when these questions arise in the classroom.

References

Adelman, C. (1991). *Women at Thirtysomething: Paradoxes of Attainment*. Washington, DC: U.S. Department of Education Office of Educational Research and Development.

Aebischer, V. (1988) 'Pour une orientation des filles vers les nouvelles technologies et les services.' Report prepared within the Commission of European Communities' research-action programme *Egalité des Chances et Nouvelles Technologies de L'information*. Paris: Ministère de l'Education Nationale, Direction des Lycées et des Collèges.

Aebischer, V. (1989) 'Pour une orientation des filles vers les nouvelles technologies et les services.' Report prepared within the Commission of European Communities' research-action programme *Egalité des Chances et Nouvelles Technologies de L'information*. Paris: Ministère de l'Education Nationale, Direction des Lycées et des Collèges.

Alic, M. (1986) *Hypathia's Heritage: A History of Women in Science from Antiquity to The Last Nineteenth Century*. London: The Women's Press.

American Association of University Women Educational Foundation. (1992) *How Schools Shortchange Girls*. Washington, DC: AAUW Educational Foundation.

Archer, J. and Macrae, M. (1991) 'Gender perceptions of school subjects among 10–11 year olds.' *British Journal of Educational Psychology 61*, 99–103.

Arnold, K. (1987) 'Retaining high achieving women in science and engineering.' Paper presented at Women in Science and Engineering: Changing Vision to Reality Conference sponsored by the American Association for the Advancement of Science. University of Michigan, Ann Arbor, MI.

Arnot, M. (1983) 'A cloud over co-education: an analysis of the forms of transmission of class and gender relations.' In S. Walker and L. Barton (eds) *op cit*.

Askew, S. and Ross, C. (1988) *Boys Don't Cry: Boys and Sexism in Education*. Milton Keynes: Open University Press.

Astin, A., *et al*. (1970–1993) *The American Freshman Annual Series, 1970–1992*. Los Angeles: Higher Education Research Institute.

Bailey, A. (1988) 'Sex-stereotyping in primary school mathematical schemes.' *Research in Education 39*, 39–46.

Baudelot, C. (1991) 'Aimez-vous les maths?' *Journal de la Société de Statistique de Paris 132*, 2, 5–15.

Baudelot, C. and Establet, R. (1991) *Allez les filles*. Paris: Le Seuil.

Baudelot, C. and Establet, R. (1991) 'Filles et garçons devant l'évaluation.' *Education et Formations 27–28*, 49–66.

Belenky, Field, M., Clinchy, McVicker, B., Goldberger, N.R., and Tarule, M.J. (1986) *Women's Ways of Knowing*. New York: Basic Books.

Bentley, D. and Watts, M. (1987) 'Courting the positive virtues: a case for feminist science.' In A. Kelly (ed)

Biology and Gender Study Group. (1989) 'The importance of feminist critiques for contemporary cell biology.' In N. Tuana (ed) *Feminism and Science*. Bloomington, IN: Indiana University Press.

Birke, L. (1986) *Women, Feminism and Biology: The Feminist Challenge*. New York: Methuen.

Bleier, R. (1984) *Gender and Science*. New York: Pergamon.

Bleier, R. (1986) *Feminist Approaches to Science*. New York: Pergamon Press.

Boli, J. *et al.* (1985) 'High ability women and men in undergraduate mathematics and chemistry courses.' *American Educational Research Journal 22*, 4, 605–626.

Bonora, D. and Huteau, M. (1991) 'L'efficience comparée des garçons et des filles en mathématiques.' *L'Orientation Scolaire et Professionnelle 20*, 3, 269–290.

Bontius, I. *et al.* (1991) Begeleidingsmodel. Gerichte begeleiding door samenwerking tussen praktijkopleiders, consulenten en decenten, 's Hertogenbosch, C.I.B.B. Dutch Training and Development Centre.

Brophy, J. 'Interactions of male and female students with male and female teachers.' In L.C. Wilkinson and C.B. Marrett (ed) *op cit.*

Burgess, A. (1990) 'Co-education: the disavantages for schoolgirls.' *Gender and Education 2*, 1, 91–95.

Burton, L. (ed) (1990) *Gender and Mathematics*. Exeter: Cassell Education.

Byrne, E. (1993) *Women and Science: The Snark Syndrome*. London, Washington, DC.

Coll (1992) *Le Sexe des Sciences*. Paris: Editions Autrement.

Collis, B.A. and Williams, R.L. (1987) 'Cross-cultural comparison of gender differences in adolescents' attitudes toward computers and selected school subjects.' *The Journal of Educational Research 81*, 1, 17–27.

Crabbe, B. *et al.* (1985) *Les Femmes dans les Livres Scolaires*. Bruxelles: Editions Mardaga.

Crossman, M. (1987) 'Teachers' interactions with girls and boys in science lessons.' In A. Kelly (ed) *op cit.*

Culley, L. (1988) 'Girls, boys and computers.' *Educational Studies 14*, 1, 3–8.

Daune-Richard, A.M. (1992) 'Rapport social de sexe et conceptualisation sociologique.' *Recherches Féministes 5*, 2, 2–30.

Davis, C.S. (1993) 'Stepping beyond the campus.' *Science 260*, 414.

Deem, R. (ed) (1980) *Schooling for Women's Work*. London: Routledge and Kegan Paul.

Deketelaere, A., Desmet-Goethals, J. *et al.* (1996) *Equal Opportunities in Socio-cultural Education of Girls and Boys*. Brussels-Dublin-Utrecht.

Desplats, M. (1989) *Les Femmes et la Physique*. Thèse NR Sciences de l'Education, Université de Strasbourg.

Dhavernas, M.J. (1992) 'Je ne suis pas celle que vous pensez.' In Coll *op cit*.

Dubost, J. (1987) *L'Intervention Psychosociologique*. Paris: Presses Universitaires de France.

Dunkin, M.J. (1985) 'Teacher sex and instruction.' In T. Husen and T. Neville-Postwaite (eds) *op cit.* .

Duru-Bellat, M. (1990) *L'école des Filles. Quelle Formation, pour Quels Rôles Sociaux?* Paris: L'Harmattan.

Duru-Bellat, M. (1995) 'Filles et garçons à l'école, approches sociologiques et psycho-sociales: 1. Des scolarités sexuées, reflet de différences d'aptitude ou de différences d'attitudes?; 2. La construction scolaire des différences entre les sexes.' *Revue Française de Pédagogie 109*, 111–142.

Duru-Bellat, M. and Jarousse, J.P. (1993) *La Classe de Seconde: une étape Décisive de la Carrière Scolaire*. Dijon: Cahiers de l'IREDU, no.55.

Duru-Bellat, M., Jarousse, J.P. *et al.* (1993) 'Les processus d'auto-sélection à l'entrée en 1ère.' *L'Orientation Scolaire et Professionnelle 22*, 3, 259–272.

Dweck, C.S. *et al.* (1978) 'Sex differences in learned helplessness: the contingencies of evaluative feedback in the classroom.' *Developmental Psychology 14*, 3, 268–276.

Eccles, J.S. (1986) 'Gender roles and women's achievement.' *Educational Researcher 15*, 6, 15–19.

Eccles, J.S. and Blumenfeld, P. (1985) 'Classroom experiences and student gender.' In L.C. Wilkinson and C.B. Marrett (ed) *op cit*.

Eccles, J.S. and Jacobs, J.E. (1986) 'Social forces shape math attitudes and performance.' *Signs 11*, 2, 367–380.

Elkjaer, B. (1992) 'Girls and information technology in Denmark. an account of a socially constructed problem.' *Gender and Education 4*, 1, 25–40.

Falconer, E. (1989) 'A story of success: the sciences at Spelman College.' *SAGE VI 2*, 36–38.

Faulkner, J. (1991) 'Mixed-sex schooling and equal opportunities for girls: a contradiction in terms?' *Research Papers in Education 4*, 3, 197–224.

Fausto-Sterling, A. (1992) *Myths of Gender*. Second edition. New York: Basic Books.

Fee, E. (1982) 'A feminist critique of scientific objectivity.' *Science for the People 14*, 4, 8.

Feingold, A. (1988) 'Cognitive gender differences are disappearing.' *American Psychologist* February, 95–103.

Fennema, E. and Leder, C. (ed) (1990) *Mathematics and Gender: Influences on Teachers and Students.* New York: Teachers College.

Fennema, E. and Peterson, P. (1985) 'Autonomous learning behaviour: explanation of gender-related differences in mathematics.' In L.C. Wikinson and C.B. Marrett (ed) *op cit.*

Fennema, E. and Sherman, J. (1977) 'Sex related differences in math achievements, spatial visualisation and affective factors.' *American Educational Research Journal 14.*

Fossey, D. (1983) *Gorillas in the Mist.* Boston: Houghton Mifflin.

French, J. (1984) 'Gender imbalances in the primary classroom: an interactional account.' *Educational Research 26,* 2, 127–136.

Friedan, B. (1974) *The Feminine Mystique.* New York: Dell.

Friedman, L. (1989) 'Mathematics and the gender gap: a meta-analysis of recent studies on sex differences in mathematicals tasks.' *Review of Educational Research 59,* 2, 185–213.

Frigerio, G. (1987) *Aportes para la Transformacion Democratica de la Educacion.* Buenos Aires: FLACSO.

Gardner, A.L. (1986) 'Effectiveness of strategies to encourage participation and retention of precollege and college women in science.' Ph.D. Thesis, Purdue University.

Giddens, A. (1989) 'Una teoria de poder en educacion.' *Revista Propouesta Educativa.* Buenos Aires: FLACSO/Mino y Davila.

Gleeson, J. (1988) 'Action-research project designed to stimulate the interest and encourage the participation of girls in school activities related to the new technologies.' Interim external evaluation report, Limerick, Ireland: Thomond College of Education.

Gleeson, J. (1989) 'Action-research project designed to stimulate the interest and encourage the participation of girls in school activities related to the new technologies.' Interim external evaluation report, Limerick, Ireland: Thomond College of Education.

Goodall, J. (1971) *In the Shadow of Man.* Boston: Houghton Mifflin.

Goodfield, J. (1981) *An Imagined World.* New York: Penguin.

Gore, D.A. and Roumagoux, D.V. (1983) 'Wait time as a variable in sex related differences during fourth grade instruction.' *Journal of Educational Research 26,* 273–275.

Grobbee, D.E., Rimm, E.B. Giovannucci, E., Colditz, G. Stampfer, M. and Willett, W. (1990) 'Coffee, caffeine, and cardiovascular disease in men.' *New England Journal of Medicine 321,* 1026–1032.

Gurwitz, J.H., Nananda, F. Col, and Avorn, J. (1992) 'The exclusion of the elderly and women from clinical trials in acute myocardial infarction.' *Journal of the American Medical Association 268*, ii, 1417–1422.

Haicault, M. (1994) 'Doxa et asymétrie sociale des sexes.' ('Doxa and social asymmetry between the sexes.') *Programme de Recherche en Sciences Sociales*. Point d'appui ULB. Brussels: Federal Department of Scientific, Technical and Cultural Affairs.

Hallinan, M.T. and Sorensen, A.B. (1987) 'Ability grouping and sex differences in mathematics achievement.' *Sociology of Education 60*, 63–72.

Hamilton, J. (1985) 'Avoiding methodological biases in gender-related research.' In Women's Health Report of the Pubic Health Service Task Force on Women's Health Issues. Washington, DC: US Dept. of Health and Human Services Public Health Service, VI, 62.

Haraway, D. (1990) *Primate Visions*. New York: Routledge.

Harding, J. (1985) 'Les jeunes filles et les femmes dans l'enseigne ment scientifique secondaire et supérieur: peu d'élues.' *Perspectives 15*, 4, 605–618.

Harding, J. (1985) 'Values, cognitive style and the curriculum.' In *Contributions to the Third Girls and Science and Technology Conference*. London: University of London, Chelsea College.

Harding, S. (1986) *The Science Question in Feminism*. Ithaca, NY: Cornell University Press.

Harding, S. (1991) *Whose Science, Whose Knowledge?* Milton Keynes: Open University Press.

Harding, S. (1992) *The Racial Economy of Science*. Bloomington, IN: Indiana University Press.

Hargreaves, D. (1979) *Las Relaciones Interpersonales en la Educacion*. Madrid: Narcea.

Harlen, W. (1985) 'Les filles et l'enseignement des sciences au niveau primaire: sexisme, stéréotypes et remèdes.' *Perspectives 15*, 4, 591–603.

Holloway, M. (1993) 'A lab of her own.' *Scientific American 269*, 5, 94–103.

Hrdy, S. (1977) *The Langurs of Abu: Female and Male Strategies of Reproduction*. Cambridge, MA: Harvard University Press.

Hrdy, S. (1979) 'Infanticide among animals: A review, classification and examination of the implications for the reproductive strategies of females.' *Ethology and Sociobiology I*, 3–40.

Hrdy, S.B. (1981) *The Woman that Never Evolved*. Cambridge, MA: Harvard University Press.

Hrdy, S. (1984) 'Introduction: Female reproductive strategies.' In M. Small (ed) *Female Primates: Studies by Women Primatologists*. New York, Alan Liss.

Hrdy, S. (1986) 'Empathy, polyandry, and the myth of the coy female.' In R. Bleier (ed) *Feminist Approaches to Science*. Elmsford, NY: Pergamon Press.

Hrdy, S. and Williams, G.C. (1983) 'Behavioral biology and the double standard.' In S.K. Wasser (ed) *Social Behavior of Female Vertebrates*. New York: Academic Press.

Hubbard, R. (1990) *The Politics of Women's Biology*. New Brunswick, NJ: Rutgers University Press.

Husen, T. and Postwaite, N.T. (eds) (1985) *The International Encyclopedia of Education*. Oxford: Pergamon Press.

Hyde, J.S. and Linn, M.C. (eds) (1990) *The Psychology of Gender: Advances Through Meta-Analysis*. Baltimore: Johns Hopkins University Press.

Hyde, J.S., Fennema, E. and Lamon, S.J. (1990) 'Gender differences in mathematics performance: a meta-analysis.' *Psychological Bulletin 107*, 2, 139–155.

Hynes, P. (1989) *The Recurring Silent Spring*. Elmsford, NY: Pergamon Press.

Hynes, P. (in press) 'No classroom is an island.' In S.V. Rosser (ed) *Teaching the Majority*. New York: Teachers College Press.

Jaggar, A. (1983) *Feminist Politics and Human Nature*. Totowa, NY: Rowman and Allanheld.

Jones, L.R., Mullis, I.V.S., Raizan, S.A., Weiss, I.R. and Weston, E.A. (1992) *The 1990 Science Report Card: NAEP's Assessment of Fourth, Eighth and Twelfth Graders*. Washington, DC: National Center for Educational Statistics.

Kandel, L. (1974) 'L'école des femmes et le discours des sciences de l'homme.' *Les Femmes s'Entêtent, Temps Modernes, 333–334*.

Keller, E.F. (1974) *Reflections on Gender and Science*. New Haven, CT: Yale University Press.

Keller, E.F. (1983) *A Feeling for the Organism: The Life and Work of Barbara McClintock*. New York: W.H. Freeman and Company.

Keller, E.F. (1992) *Secrets of Life, Secrets of Death*. New York: Routledge.

Kelly, A. (ed) (1981) *The Missing Half: Girls and Science Education*. Manchester University Press.

Kelly, A. (1982) *Summary Report, Sex Stereotyping in Schools*. Lisse: Council of Europe, Swets and Zeitlinger.

Kelly, A. (1984) 'Women's access to education in the third world: myths and realities.' In S. Acker (ed) *op cit*.

Kelly, A. (1987) 'Some notes on gender differences in mathematics.' *British Journal of Sociology of Education 8*, 3, 305–311.

Kelly, A. (1987) 'Traditionalists and trendies: teachers' attitudes to educational issues.' In G. Weiner and M. Arnot (ed) *op cit*.

Kelly, A. (1988) 'Gender differences in teachers-pupils interaction: a meta-synthesis review.' *Research in Education 39*, 1–24.

Kelly, A. 'The construction of masculine science.' *British Journal of Sociology of Education 6*, 2, 133–145.

Kelly, A. (ed) *Science for Girls?* Milton Keynes: Open University Press.

Kelly, A., Whyte, J. and Smail, B. (1984) 'Girls into science and technology.' Final report. Manchester: University of Manchester.

Kelly, G.P. (1987) 'Setting state policy on women's education in the third world: perspectives from comparative research.' *Comparative Education 23*, 1, 95–101.

Kessler, S., Ashenden, C., Connell, G. and Dowsett, E. (1985) 'Gender relations in secondary schooling.' *Sociology of Education 58*, 34–48.

Keynes, H.B. (1989) University of Minnesota Talented Youth Mathematics Project (UMPTYMP); Recruiting girls for a more successful equation. ITEMS. University of Minnesota Institute of Technology. Spring.

Kinball, M.M. (1989) 'A new perspective on women's math achievement.' *Psychological Bulletin 105*, 2, 198–214.

Klein, S.S. (ed) (1985) *Handbook for Achieving Sex Equity Through Education.* Baltimore: Johns Hopkins University Press.

Kramarae, C. and Treichler, P. (1986) *A Feminist Dictionary.* London: Pandora Press.

Kruse, A.M. (1992) '…We have learnt not just to sit back, twiddle our thumbs and let them take over. Single-sex settings and the development of a pedagogy for girls and a pedagogy for boys in Danish schools.' *Gender and Education 4*, 1, 81–105.

Lage, E. (1991) 'Boys, girls and micro-computing.' *European Journal of Psychology of Education 6*, 1, 29–44.

Lage, E. (1993) *Lycéens et Pratiques Scientifiques.* Paris: L'Harmattan.

Lakoff, R. (1975) *Language and Woman's Place.* New York: Harper and Row.

Lanier, J. (1992) 'Virtual reality, the promise of the future.' *Interactive Learning International 8*, 275–90.

Lawrie, B. and Brown, R. (1992) 'Sex stereotypes, school-subject preferences and career aspirations as a function of single/mixed sex schooling and presence/absence of an opposite sex sibling.' *British Journal of Educational Psychology 62*, 132–138.

Leder, G.C. (1974) 'Sex differences in mathematics problem appears as a function of problem context.' *The Journal of Educational Research 67*, 8, 351–353.

Leder, G.C. (1990) 'Gender and classroom practice.' In L.Burton (ed) *op cit.*

Lempen-Ricci, S. and Moreau, T. (ed) (1987) *Vers une Education non Sexiste.* Lausanne: Réalités sociales.

Lewin, K. (1946) 'Behaviour and development as a function of the total situation.' In L. Carmichael (ed) *Manual of Child Psychology.* New York: John Wiley and Sons Ltd.

Lewin, K. (1947) 'Frontiers in group dynamics: concept, method and reality in social science; social equilibria and social change.' *Human Relations 1*, 5–42.

Lewin, K. (1965) 'Décisions de groupe et changement social.' In A. Levy (ed) *Psychologie Sociale. Textes Fondamentaux Anglais et Américains.* Paris: Dunod.

Licht, B.L. and Dweck, C.S. (1984) 'Determinants of academic achievement: the interaction of children's achievement orientations with skills area.' *Developmental Psychology 20,* 628–636.

Lie, S. and Bryhni, E. (1983) *Girls and Physics: Attitudes, Experiences and Underachievement* (pp. 202–211). Norway: Contribution to the Second GASAT-conference.

Light, R.J. (1990) *Explorations with Students and Faculty about Teaching, Learning, and Student Life.* Cambridge, MA: Harvard University Press.

Linn, L.S. (1983) 'Content, context and process in reasoning during adolescence.' *Journal of Early Adolescence 3,* 63–82.

Linn, M.C. and Petersen, A.C. (1986) 'A meta-analysis of gender differences in spatial ability: implications for mathematics and science achievement.' In J.S. Hyde and M.C. Linn (ed) *op cit.*

MacKinnon, C.A. (1987) *Feminism Unmodified: Discourses on Life and Law.* Cambridge, MA and London: Harvard University Press.

Maher, F.A. and Thompson Tetreault, M.K. (1994) *The Feminist Classroom.* New York: Basic Books.

Mahony, P. (1994) 'Sexual violence and mixed schools.' In Jones and Mahony (ed) *Learning Our Lines, Sexuality and Social Control in Education.* London: The Women's Press.

Maizels, J., Masson, M.R., Payne, D.R. and White, J. *Report on WISE' 84 questionnaire for Aberdeen AUT women's group.* Aberdeen: Aberdeen University.

Marro, C. (1995) 'Réussite scolaire en mathématiques et en physique, et passage en 1ère S: Quelles relations du point de vue des élèves et des enseignants?' *Revue Française de Pédagogie* (forthcoming).

Marro, C. and Vouillot, F. (1991) 'Représentation de soi, représentation du scientifique type et choix d'une orientation scientifique chez des filles et des garçons de seconde.' *L'Orientation Scolaire et Professionnelle 20,* 3, 303–323.

Marsh, H.W. (1989) 'Effects of attending single-sex and coeducational high schools on achievement, attitudes, behaviors and sex differences.' *Journal of Educational Psychology 81,* 1, 70–85.

Martinez, M.E. and Mead, N.A. (1988) *Computer Competence: The First National Assessment.* Princeton, NJ: Educational Testing Service.

Maruani, M. (1991) 'Feminisation et discrimination: évolution de l'activité feminine en France.' ('Feminization and discrimination: evolution in women's activities in France.') *L'Orientation Scolaire et Professionnelle 20,* 243–56.

Masson, M.R. (1986) 'Women in science in the 1980s.' *Chemistry in Britain 22,* 319–322 and 339.

Matyas, M. and Malcolm, S. (1991) *Investing in Human Potential: Science and Engineering at the Crossroads*. Washington, DC: American Assosciation for the Advancement of Science.

McGrayne, S.B. (1993) *Nobel Prize Women in Science: Their Lives, Struggles and Momentous Discoveries*. New York: Birch Lane Press.

McIntosh, P. (1984) 'The study of women: Processes of personal and curricular re-vision.' *The Forum for Liberal Education 6*, 5, 2–4.

Measor, L. (1983) 'Gender and the sciences: pupils' gender-based conceptions of school subjects.' In Hammersley and Hargreaves (eds) *Curriculum Practice: Some Sociological Case Studies*. London: The Falmer Press.

Mill, H.T. (1970) 'Enfranchisement of women.' In A.S. Rossi (ed) *Essays on Sex Equality*. Chicago: University of Chicago Press.

Mill, J.S. (1970) 'The subjection of women.' In A.S. Rossi (ed) *Essays on Sex Equality*. Chicago: University of Chicago Press.

Moreau, T. (1994) *Pour une Education Epicène*. Lausanne: Réalités sociales.

Morgan, V. and Dunn S. (1994) 'Management strategies and gender differences in nursery and infant classrooms.' *Research in Education 44*, 81–91.

Morse, L.W. and Handley, H.M. (1985) 'Listening to adolescents: gender differences in science classroom interaction.' In L.C. Wilkinson and C.B. Marrett (ed) *op cit*.

Mosconi, N. (1987) 'La mixité dans l'enseignement technique et industriel ou l'impossible reconnaissance de l'autre.' *Revue Française de Pédagogie*, 78.

Mosconi, N. (1989) *La Mixité dans l'Enseignement Secondaire: Un Faux Semblant?* Paris: Presses Universitaires de France.

Multiple Risk Factor Intervention Trial Research Group. (1990) 'Mortality rates after 10.5 years for participants in the Multiple Risk Factor Intervention Trial: Findings related to a prior hypothesis of the trial.' *Journal of the American Medical Association 263*, 1795–1801.

Murphy, P. (1991) 'Assessment and gender.' *Cambridge Journal of Education 21*, 203–214.

Myers, K. (ed) (1992) *Genderwatch! After the Education Reform Act*. Cambridge University Press.

National Center for Education Statistics. (1994) *Earned Degrees Conferred by Institutions of Higher Education, 1950–91, Reported in Professional Women and Minorities: A Total Human Resource Data Compendium*, 11th Edition, pp. 66–68. Washington DC: Commission on Professionals in Science and Technology.

National Research Council (1991) *Women in Science and Engineering: Increasing their Numbers in the 1990s: A Statement on Policy and Strategy*. Washington, DC: National Research Council.

National Research Council (1992) 'Summary report 1992: Doctorate recipients from United States universities.' Washington, DC: National Academy Press Series.

National Research Council (1994) *Women Scientists and Engineers Employed in Industry: Why so Few?* Washington, DC: National Research Council.

Nelson, C.S. and Watson, J.A. (1991) 'The computer gender gap: children's attitudes, performance and socialization.' *Journal of Educational Technology Systems 19*, 4, 345–353.

Northam, J. (1987) 'Girls and boys in primary maths books.' In G. Weiner and M. Arnot (ed) *op cit.*

NSF (National Science Foundation) (1986) 'Report on women and minorities in science and engineering.' Washington, DC: Author.

NSF (National Science Foundation) (1988) 'Women and minorities in science and engineering.' (NSF 88–301). Washington, DC: Author.

NSF (National Science Foundation) (1990) 'Women and minorities in science and engineering' (NSF 90–301). Washington, DC: NSF.

NSF (National Science Foundation) (1992) 'Women and minorities in science and engineering' (NSF 92–303). Washington, DC: NSF.

NSF (National Science Foundation) (1993) 'EHR Activities for women and girls in science, engineering, and mathematics' (NSF 93–126). Washington, DC: NSF.

NSF (National Science Foundation) (1994) Personal communication from Lola Rogers.

Ormerod, M.B. (1981) 'Factors differentially affecting the science subject preferences, choices and attitudes of girls and boys.' In A. Kelly (ed) *op cit.*

OTA (Office of Technology Assessment) (1987) 'New developments in biotechnology background paper: Public perceptions of biotechnology' (OTA-BP-BA-45). Washington, DC: Author.

Parsons, J.E., Kaczala, C.M. and Meece, J.I. (1982) 'Socialization of achievement attitudes and beliefs: classroom influences.' *Child Development 53*, 322–339.

Peiffer, J. and Dahan, A. (1982) *Routes et Dédales. Histoire des Mathématiques.* Paris: Blanchard.

Percheron, A. (1985) 'Le domestique et le politique. Types de familles, modèles d'éducation et transmission des systèmes de normes et d'attitude entre parents et enfants.' *Revue Française de Science Politique 35*, 4, 840–891.

Peterson, P.L. and Fennema, E. (1985) 'Effective teaching, student engagement in classroom activities, and sex-related differences in learning mathematics.' *American Educational Research Journal 22*, 3, 309–335.

Phillips, P. (1985) *The Scientific Lady. A Social History of Woman's Scientific Interest: 1520–1918.* New York: Saint Martin's Press.

Ränäsen, L. (1992) 'Girls and learning of physical concepts.' *European Education.* Autumn. 83–96.

Robinson, K.H. (1992) 'Classroom discipline: power, resistance and gender. A look at teacher perspective.' *Gender and Education 4*, 3, 273–287.

Rodgers, M. (1990) 'Mathematics: pleasure or pain?' In L. Burton (ed) *op cit.*

Rosser, S. (1986) *Teaching Science and Health from a Feminist Perspective: A Practical Guide.* Elmsford, NY: Pergamon Press.

Rosser, S. (1988) *Feminism within the Science and Health Care Professions: Overcoming Resistance.* Elmsford, NY: Pergamon Press.

Rosser, S. (1990) *Female-friendly Science.* New York: Pergamon Press.

Rosser, S. (1993) 'Female-friendly science: Including women in curricular content and pedagogy in science.' *The Journal of General Education 42,* 3, 191–220.

Rosser, S. *Biology and Feminism: A Dynamic Interaction.* New York: Trayne Publishers.

Rosser, S. and Kelly, B. (1994) 'From hostile exclusion to friendly inclusion: USC System model project for the transformation of science and math teaching to reach women in varied campus settings.' *Journal of Women and Minorities in Science and Engineering 1,* 1.

Rossiter, M.W. (1982) *Women Scientists in America: Struggles and Strategies to 1940.* Baltimore: The Johns Hopkins University Press.

Rossiter, M.W. (1994) 'History of women in science from 1945–1972.' Presentation at National Women's Studies Association Meeting at Iowa State University. June 17.

Sadker, D. and Sadker, M. (1985) 'Is the OK Classroom OK?' *Phi Delta Kappa 66,* 5, 358–361.

Salomon, E. (1992) 'Girls don't move up.' *European Education 24,* 3, 57–60.

Sanders, J. (1985) 'Making the computer neuter.' *The Computing Teacher.* April. 23–27.

Sanders, J. (in press) 'Girls and technology: Villain wanted.' In S.V. Rosser (ed) *Teaching the Majority.* New York: Teachers College Press.

Schiebinger, L. (1989) *The Mind Has No Sex.* Cambridge, MA: Harvard University Press.

Scott, M. (1980) 'Teach her a lesson: sexist curriculum in patriar chal education.' In D. Spender and E. Sarah (ed) *op cit.*

Sebrechts, J.S. (1992) 'Viewpoint: The cultivation of scientists at women's colleges.' *The Journal of NIH Research 4,* 22–26.

Sells, L. (1978) 'Mathematics – A critical filter.' *The Science Teacher 45,* 29–39.

Sells, L. (1982) 'Leverage for equal opportunity through mastery of mathematics.' In S. Humphreys (ed) *Women and Minorities in Science.* Boulder, CO: Westview Press.

Servant, A. (1990) 'Apprentissages fondamentaux en fin de 5ème: nature et évolution des acquis, liens avec le vécu et le cursus scolaire.' *Education et Formation 24,* 31–43.

Singly, F. de (1993) 'Les habits neufs de la domination masculine.' ('The new clothes of the masculine.') *Masculin Féminin,* November, 55–64.

Spear, M.G. (1984) 'The biasing influence of pupil sex in a science marking exercice.' *Research in Science and Technological Education 2,* 55–60.

Spear, M.G. (1987) 'Teachers' views about the importance of science to boys and girls.' In A. Kelly *op cit.*

Spender, D. (1982) 'The role of teachers: what choices do they have?' In A. Kelly (ed) *op cit.*

Spender, D. and Sarah, E. (ed) (1992) *Learning to Lose. Sexism and Education.* London: The Women's Press.

Stables, A. (1990) 'Differences between pupils from mixed and single-sex schools in their enjoyment of school subjects and in their attitudes to science and to school.' *Educational Review 42,* 3, 221–229.

Stanworth, M. (1983) *Gender and Schooling: A Study of Sexual Divisions in the Classroom.* London: Hutchinson.

Steering Committee of the Physician's Health Study Group (1989) 'Final report on the aspirin component of the ongoing physicians health study.' *New England Journal of Medicine 321,* 1026–1032.

Stog, B. (1991) 'Girls' avoidance of "hard" science subjects: protest or rational choice?' *Scandinavian Journal of Educational Research 35,* 3, 201–211.

Tannen, D. (1990) *You just don't Understand.* New York, NY: Ballantine.

Terlon, C. (1985) 'Filles et garçons devant l'enseignement scientifique et technique.' *Revue Française de Pédagogie 72,* 51–59.

Terlon, C. (1990) 'Attitudes des adolescent(e)s à l'égard de la technologie: une enquête internationale.' *Revue Française de Pédagogie 90,* 51–60.

Thomas, V. (1989) 'Black women engineers and technologists.' *Sage 6,* 2, 24–32.

Tidball, M.E. (1986) 'Baccalaureate origins of recent natural science doctorates.' *Journal of Higher Education 57,* 606.

Tobin, K. (1988) 'Differential engagement of males and females in high school science.' *International Journal of Science Education 10,* 3, 239–252.

Tocci, C.M. and Engelhard, G. (1991) 'Achievement, parental support, and gender differences in attitudes toward mathematics.' *The Journal of Educational Research 84,* 5, 280–286.

Treisman, P.U. (1992) 'Studying students studying calculus: A look at the lives of minority mathematics students in college.' *College Mathematics Journal 23,* 5, 362–372.

U.S. Department of Labor. (June 1987) *Workforce 2000.* Washington, DC: U.S. Government Printing Office.

Valabrègue, C. (ed) (1985) *Fille ou Garçons, Education sans Préjugés.* Paris: Magnard.

Vetter, B.M. (ed) (1994) *Professional Women and Minorities: A Human Resource Data Compendium.* Washington, DC: Commission on Professionals in Science and Technology.

Vetter, B.M. (In press) 'Women in science, mathematics and engineering: Myths and realities.' Cross university research in engineering and science.

Wahl, E. (1993) 'Getting messy.' *Science 260*, 412–413.

Walden, R. and Walkerdine, V. (1986) *Girls and Mathematics, from Primary to Secondary Schooling*. London: Bedfordway Papers, Institute of Education, University of London.

Walker, S. and Barton, L. (ed) (1983) *Gender, Class and Education*. London: The Falmer Press.

Walkerdine, V. (1989) *Counting Girls Out*. London: Virago Press.

Weiner, G. and Aront, M. (ed) (1987) *Gender Under Scruting. News Inquiries in Education*. London: The Open University, Unwin Hyman Ltd.

Whyte, J. (1984) 'Observing sex steretypes and interactions in the School lab and workshop.' *Educational Review 36, 1*, 75–84.

Wilinson, L.C and Marrett, C.B. (1985) *Gender Influences in Classroom Interaction*. Orlando: Academic Press Inc.

Wollstonecraft, M. (1975) *A Vindication of the Rights of Woman.'* In C.H. Poston (ed). New York: W.W. Norton.